Not Enough

Not Enough

Human Rights in an Unequal World

SAMUEL MOYN

THE BELKNAP PRESS OF
HARVARD UNIVERSITY PRESS

Cambridge, Massachusetts
London, England
2018

Library of Congress Cataloging-in-Publication Data

Names: Moyn, Samuel, author.
Title: Not enough : human rights in an unequal world / Samuel Moyn.
Description: Cambridge, Massachusetts : The Belknap Press of Harvard
University Press, 2018. | Includes bibliographical references and index.
Identifiers: LCCN 2017041518 | ISBN 9780674737563 (alk. paper)
Subjects: LCSH: Human rights—History. | Equality—History. |
Welfare economics—History. | Neoliberalism—History.
Classification: LCC JC571 .M8635 2018 | DDC 323.09—dc23
LC record available at https://lccn.loc.gov/2017041518

For Joe

Contents

Preface

History can never remain the same, because every era must rethink its past. Our perspective on our origins changes, and for that reason—not simply because new facts have been found—no account of how the present emerged is definitive for long. Since histories of human rights began to be written, however, I have often felt that the enterprise faces an especially challenging obligation not to lose track of how fast our present is transforming. Human rights are some of our highest ideals, and they have become so in an age when lived history can seem to be accelerating so quickly that written history cannot match the pace of change.

Historians had never written about the origins and path of human rights before the principles ascended to the status of a moral lingua franca in global affairs mere decades ago. Soon after the search for their background began, no earlier than the 1990s, scholars began to dispute how to conduct their inquiries: the uplifting liberal internationalism of the initial post–Cold War moment suddenly looked very different after the Iraq War and the disturbing chaos it unleashed. Having first been tasked with celebrating how the invention of human rights marked the beginning of the end of history, scholarship now became a forum in which to debate the propriety of liberal interventionism abroad, the progressive credentials of nongovernmental advocacy, and the outstanding visibility given to the spectacle of mass atrocity. After their romantic veneration, human rights now courted rude vilification for their entanglements with power: they were steps not from the dark plains of Cold War political compromise into the sunlit uplands of moral purity, but from a bipolar world to one of unilateral American hegemony, with all its benefits and costs.

I participated in such debates a few years ago, though I worried that they were belated, especially after the full consequences of the 2008 financial crisis became clearer. History may be condemned to lag behind the present, but it also has to try to catch up. And there is no doubt that the transition from an era of liberal ascendancy to one of liberal crisis demands an attempt to rethink where our highest ideals of human rights come from. The passages from state citizenship to global cosmopolitanism and from Cold War politics to millennial ethics matter. But the transformation from the era of the welfare state to that of neoliberal economics now appears the most important setting for recounting the vicissitudes that "human rights," along with so many of our other concepts and practices, experienced in the later twentieth century.

After my first book on the topic, *The Last Utopia,* much discussion took place about whether the contemporary idealism of human rights was really as contingent in its formation and shallow in its roots as I had tried to suggest, and whether the actors and locales I singled out in placing stress on a North Atlantic revolution in moral sensibility, political rhetoric, and nongovernmental advocacy in the 1970s—chiefly in response to authoritarianism in Latin America and totalitarianism in Eastern Europe—were the right ones. Unrepentant as I remain about my emphases, I was nevertheless humbled by two lines of criticism. For one thing, I ended my history on the brink of 1980, precisely when it began to seem interesting and an unprecedented density of human rights politics truly began. The centuries before the appearance of human rights, no less than the historic 1970s moment of their emergence, were undoubtedly fascinating. But the complex decades of the ascendancy of human rights, especially after the Cold War ended, are even more so. For another, I identified a chronology that matched that of the shift in political economy from the welfare state to the neoliberal era without mentioning the relation of the human rights revolution to that shift, or indeed the relation of human rights to distributive outcomes and political economy before or after it. In particular, some Marxists asked, was not the story of the rise of human rights yet another example of a shift in "superstructure" that made sense only when taken as an occasion for attention to the base of "capitalism" that is supposed to determine everything built on its foundation?

This rewrite of the history of human rights offers another look for a new era in which, for all the current endurance of liberal political hegemony in the face of strong ideological opposition, its self-imposed crises seem more evident than before, and the relevance of distributive fairness to the survival of liberalism is impossible to avoid. What can make the study of history exciting is that its infinity of sources and our change in perspective can allow two books on the same topic by the same person to bear almost no resemblance to each other—even if the intellectual challenges and opportunities of writing history pale beside the importance of the public and political uses it should serve. On both counts, this book places the trajectory of economic and social rights—entitlements to work, education, social assistance, health, housing, food, and water—center stage. Summing up what is known so far about how such norms have figured in morality, politics, and law across time, it narrates their ascendancy in relation to broader contests over distributional fairness.

This book still locates a pivot in the middle of the postwar age, as anticolonial nationalism saw its plans to globalize justice foiled, as redistributive socialism began to enter crisis, and as the twin alternatives to those prior endeavors of human rights and neoliberal economics began to define our present. But against complacent apologetics and corrosive attack alike, my goal is to stake out a moderate position between those who claim that human rights are unrelated to political economy and distributive injustice (except of course to provide the essential tools for reining them in) and those who think the human rights revolution has been a mere sham masking inhumane domination.

It is very revealing that the prestige of human rights politics and law, from the late Cold War into our time, has shared the same lifespan as their neoliberal *Doppelgänger.* Yet this is not because they abet its victories directly. Instead, it is because the human rights revolution went along with a crisis of ambition in the face of an increasingly neoliberal political economy and the distributive injustice it wrought, which determined the guise of reform and how far it went. Human rights politics and law have both enjoyed successes and suffered limitations alike as a result of their prominence in a neoliberal age. Human rights politics and law went some way to sensitizing humanity to the misery of visible indigence alongside the horrific repression of authoritarian and totalitarian states—but not to the crisis of national welfare, the stagnation of middle classes, and the endurance of global hierarchy. Focusing on sufficient protections, human rights norms and politics have selectively emphasized one aspect of social justice, scanting in particular the distributional victory of the rich. It is as if in our highest ethics, material gains for the poor were all that could matter, either morally or strategically, when human rights placed any stress on material injustice at all.

For this very reason, human rights movements have coexisted side by side with the truly ambitious and successful moral program of our time, a free market "last utopia"—indeed, one in which marketization under Chinese auspices fulfilled far more aspirations to basic social protection from the most abject misery than any legal regime or political movement expressly devoted to them has ever achieved. The selective attention of human rights politics toward a minimum provision of the good things in life has made them unthreatening to a neoliberal movement that, sometimes achieving or tolerating that goal, has devoted itself most unerringly to the intensification of material hierarchy. In the era of human rights, many (though by no means all) have become less poor, but the rich have been even more decisive victors. It follows that human rights must be kept in proper perspective, neither idolized nor smashed, to recognize the true scope of our moral crisis today and the melancholy truth of our failure to invent other ideals and movements to confront it. Human rights, focused on securing enough for everyone, are essential—but they are not enough.

Not Enough

Introduction

In 1981, the playwright Zdena Tominová, on an extended visit to the West from her home in communist Czechoslovakia, came to Dublin for a lecture. A critic of her country's political regime, she was the spokesperson for Charter 77, one of the first prominent dissident organizations to make international human rights activism exciting. In the prior few years, it had drawn many Westerners toward the whole notion of basic personal entitlements under global law on which that pioneering activism was based. The United Nations had issued the Universal Declaration of Human Rights (1948) decades before; now, it became famous and reoriented moral consciousness and practice. But Tominová explained that, as a beneficiary of her communist state's policies, she was still grateful for the ideals of her youth and its politics of material equality. "All of a sudden," she remembered of the leveling of classes she lived through as a child, "I was not underprivileged and could do everything."[1]

Since then, Tominová reported, and especially after the suppression of the Prague spring reforms in 1968, the scales had fallen from her eyes, and she had learned to denounce her state's oppression. For her membership in Charter 77, she had been beaten on the street and her head was pounded into the pavement. But even when her government suggested she leave for a while to avoid imprisonment, Tominová did not renounce her citizenship (although it was revoked soon after her talk). She even remained true to the socialism that had meant so much to her generation. "I think that if this world has a future," she explained to her Irish audience, "it is as a Socialist society, which I understand to mean a society where nobody has priorities just because he happens to come from a rich family." And this socialism was not just a local ideal. "The world of social justice for all people has to come about," she added.[2]

Tominová was clear that socialism could not provide an alibi for the deprivation of human rights. But by the same token, for her nation or for the world, the newer interest in human rights could not serve as an excuse to abandon material equality. Decades later, Tominová's speech looks ironic. Data show that until the late twentieth century, people were overwhelmingly more likely to utter the word *socialism* than the phrase *human rights* in every language until the one began to decrease and the other to spike precisely when Charter 77 was founded. The lines of the terms' relative popularity crossed precisely when the Cold War ended in 1989. Notwithstanding Bernie Sanders's recent candidacy for the American presidency under a socialist banner, our era of market fundamentalism continues almost as if socialism had never been—and as if, in the realm of ideals, human rights alone comprise the highest standards of a just society and world.[3]

The effect is hardly a matter of the history of language. In different ways in different places, not least in Tominová's Eastern Europe, human rights surged as a new political economy triumphed. To the extent that human rights morality and law decree economic and social protections, locally or globally, it is as a guarantee of sufficient provision, not a constraint on inequality. After a long period of negligence, attention to inequality spiked after 2008, and outrageous statistics marred the front pages as newspapers reported often accelerating and always wide inequality in every nation. Stories ricocheted around the internet noting that, even in the midst of less penury than ever in world history, a mere eight men controlled more wealth than half the inhabitants of the planet—several billion people.

The age of human rights has not been kind to full-fledged distributive justice, because it is also an age of the victory of the rich. The free market in its most unfettered form has its staunch defenders, but even those who hope to chasten and guide it have generally dropped material equality as a goal, prioritizing more basic and minimal aspirations to save the poor. It was a sharp break from the highest ideals of our immediate ancestors, who passionately invested in distributive equality, sometimes on pain of apologizing for vast historical wrongs to achieve it. Today, in contrast, people invest their hopes (and money) in human rights, looking the other way when vast inequality soars. Tominová's dream of avoiding a forced choice between indispensable human rights and broader distributive fairness has been shattered—but there is no reason to accept the outcome.

NO ONE OUGHT to be treated differently because of the kind of person they are—on the basis of gender or race, for example. This status equality, however honored in the breach, is more accepted than ever before and thankfully so. It is also a matter of greater consensus than ever that the high and equal status of human beings entitles them to some basic political freedoms, such as the rights to speak and to be free from torture. When it comes to what share people ought to get of the good things in life, however, consensus is much harder to achieve.[4]

Compared to how status equality or political rights became imaginable, the history of economic and social rights (often simply called social rights) has been neglected by historians. But there is no way to study them apart from what one might call the distributional imagination and political economy of human rights. Social rights were part of the canon of ideals consecrated in the Universal Declaration, and for a while they have been central to organized rights activism. But strictly speaking, human rights do not necessarily call for a modicum of distributive equality. And a concern for human rights, including economic and social rights, has risen as moral commitments to distributive equality fell.

It is therefore a fundamental task to chart not merely the history of economic and social rights but also how they fit in the broader struggle, across modern history, to argue and make room for two different imperatives of distribution—*sufficiency* and *equality.* Even when social rights have been given their due, the ideal of material equality has lost out in our time. Before the age of human rights came, dreams of equality were taken quite seriously, both nationally and globally. In the age of human rights, the pertinence of fairness beyond sufficiency has been forgotten.

Sufficiency and equality originally came together and contended with each other as distinctive ideals of the first national welfare state during the French Revolution. And it is critical to notice that they are different. Sufficiency concerns how far an individual is *from having nothing* and how well she is doing *in relation to some minimum of provision* of the good things in life. Equality concerns how far individuals are *from one another* in the portion of those good things they get. The ideal of sufficiency commands that, whether as an operating principle of how things are allocated or after the fact of their initial distribution, it is critical to define a bottom line of goods and services (or money, as in proposals of a universal basic income) beneath which no individual ought to sink. It singles out whether individuals, in relation to complete penury, have reached a defined line of adequate provision. If sufficiency is all that matters, then hierarchy is not immoral. "I care not how affluent some may be, so long as none be miserable in consequence of it," Thomas Paine wrote as early as 1796, expressing this exclusionary commitment to sufficiency. Enough, in this view, is enough.[5]

From the perspective of the ideal of equality, however, it does not matter only that everyone gets enough and the worst off avoid indigence (not to mention homelessness, starvation, and illness). For the egalitarian, morality rules out a society in which, even if the most basic needs are met, enormous hierarchy can still exist. According to this stance, at least a modicum of equality in the distribution of the good things in life is necessary. Otherwise it might turn out that two societies emerge: different ways of life, the wealthy towering over their economic inferiors, with morality satisfied so long as basic needs are fulfilled. Not merely a floor of protection against insufficiency is required, but also a ceiling on inequality, or even a commitment to a universal middle class. No commitment to absolute equality of material outcomes is involved necessarily, but you cross the border from advocacy of sufficiency to advocacy of equality if, beyond some minimum, you insist that it matters ethically how far the rich tower over the rest, even if the rest escape from indecency, however defined. Enough, in this view, is not enough.

The distinction is essential. The imperatives of sufficiency and equality, of course, are not necessarily in stark competition, even in theory. Except for many premodern religious and modern revolutionary ascetics, almost all egalitarians in history have shown great regard for the value of sufficient provision too. But like Paine in the eighteenth century or the philosopher Harry Frankfurt today, a great many more supporters of sufficiency adopt their ideal exclusively, compared to egalitarians who do not generally reject a standard of minimum distribution. In fact, even if it is entirely possible for those who care about sufficiency simply to prioritize it, insisting that they value equality as a postponed next step, it is far more common to believe that the goal of achieving sufficiency depends on embracing *more* inequality.[6]

It is also frequently believed that sufficiency and equality are interdependent, as moral ideals to be judged right or wrong not solely in theory but also in their real life interaction. If it turns out to be true that those who have their most basic needs met through sufficient provision are likelier to achieve equal amounts of the good things in life under their own power, then a difficult choice in theory evaporates in practice. Or else, if you adjust upward what counts as a sufficient amount of the things that matter most, you may come nearer and nearer to indirectly becoming an egalitarian. In effect, somebody has to pay for the high levels of need you have defined upward, and the likelihood is that the rich will inevitably have to be made to descend closer to the level of the ascending poor to do so.

But before concluding too quickly that there is no practical loss in emphasizing sufficiency alone or first, it is critical to remember how easy it is to argue for the opposite conclusions—especially today. Though one might hope that sufficiency (especially if defined upward) might lead to equality, it is equally possible that the poor will come closer to sufficient provision as the rich reap ever greater gains for themselves. In practice, sufficiency may get along better with hierarchy than with equality. It is also increasingly credible that a concern with equality is a better way to achieve sufficiency in practice—or at least that our desire to provide a sufficient minimum to the worst off is under threat to the extent that a frontally egalitarian politics is dropped. What if there is no way to win political support for sufficient goods for the destitute in society, or around the world, unless more equal circumstances are achieved for its members, especially if people feel too different from their fellows to institute guarantees even for a basic minimum? Donald Trump was elected president of the United States, according to such a story, when the right to the most basic health care for those without means became hostage to a broader sense of unfairness among the working and middle classes. Europeans have widely opted for populist leaders, with potentially widespread consequences for basic rights, not out of penury but because they stagnate even as the wealthy soar ever higher. It might be that you have to strive at more equal society even to get the most vital needs met.

The distinction between sufficiency and equality allows us to see how profoundly the age of human rights, while a good one for some of the worst off, has mainly been a golden age for the rich. The meaning of human rights has slowly transformed as egalitarian aspiration has fallen. For a long period, such aspiration had not only remained strong but spread from local communities to the entirety of the world. The French Revolution's dream of a welfare state offering sufficient provision as well as egalitarian citizenship returned—at least in some places—when the Great Depression and

World War II ushered in new kinds of national communities. In that era, human rights partook of the ideal of distributive equality within nations. In our day, human rights have instead become associated (along with the excesses of terrible leaders and the horrors of heartrending atrocity) with global sufficiency alone. Expanded in coverage, human rights have become a worldwide slogan in a time of downsized ambition. Across time, in other words, the spirit of human rights and the political enterprise with which people associate them has shifted from nationally framed egalitarian citizenship to a globally scaled subsistence minimum. Human rights have become our language for indicating that our cosmopolitan aspirations are strong, not stopping at the borders of our particular nation. They have been a banner for campaigns against discriminatory treatment on the basis of gender, race, and sexual orientation. But they have also become our language for indicating that it is enough, at least to start, for our solidarity with our fellow human beings to remain weak and cheap. To a startling extent, human rights have become prisoners of the contemporary age of inequality. The primary goal of what follows is to chart the evolution of human rights to illustrate how—inadvertently and unnecessarily for most of their advocates, I believe—they reached this state of imprisonment.

THE IDEALS of sufficiency and equality coexisted and clashed long before the twentieth century. At least as far back as the French Revolution, it had been possible to formulate socioeconomic rights for individuals as an obligation of sufficient provision. But just as far back, sufficiency came linked to equality. And after the intervening libertarian century between the French events and the rise of the national welfare state, their relationship was cemented. For all the interest of the two ideals' prehistory, from classical antiquity to the nineteenth century, the welfare state's appearance in the middle of the twentieth century was the pivotal event in their careers.

The notion of human rights was nowhere near as prominent in the ascendancy of national welfare as in our own neoliberal age. But for those who championed them, human rights were redefined in the ecology of the new welfare states of the era that compromised between sufficiency and equality, resolving to pursue both at the same time. Just as the notion of individual rights had often conformed to the classical liberal political economy of the nineteenth century, protecting the freedom of contract and person and the sanctity of property and transaction, so now they were reimagined for a new age of national welfare, characteristically in the Universal Declaration of 1948. Even as skeptics worried in the 1940s that rights could not do the job of making people more equal than before, others insisted that they bolstered that very mission.

The Universal Declaration, cited today to justify identification with egregious suffering at the hands of states abroad, is best understood as canonizing political and social rights as part of a consensus that citizens required new and powerful states at home. Those welfare states would provide the new citizenship that survivors of the Great Depression and World War II believed they deserved, and the Universal Declaration would canonize that mode of citizenship. Social rights, in short, emerged as part of a larger egalitarian package. That sufficiency and equality were so often understood to be different emphases in a unified project is the main reason to look back at what the welfare states attempted and achieved. After all, their work not only made progress in helping the indigent, for all their compromises and limitations; they were also the sole political enterprises that, to date, have ever secured a modicum of distributional equality, in particular constraining the dominance of the wealthiest.[7]

Yet they were achieved in only a few places, and in tarnished form, because they subordinated so many on grounds of gender, race, or other privilege. Most of the world's peoples did not have welfare states of any kind, because they lived under empires. The golden age of the welfare state in the developed world did not forbid the global empires of the European states and the global hegemony of the United States at the apex of its power—and neither did the Universal Declaration. As decolonization proceeded all the same, the bulk of humankind dreamed of the social citizenship that the richest countries had now begun to establish. The new states born of the struggle against empire tended to dream bigger when it came to their own national welfare, invoking egalitarian ideals (and adopting socialist programs) much more readily. More radically, their leaders concluded that it would not be possible to achieve a forum of distributive justice at home so long as an exploding hierarchy of growth and wealth remained on the world stage. The idea of "global justice" was born.

After World War II, the Swedish economist Gunnar Myrdal called for a "welfare world" to be built on top of the welfare states. The era of decolonization made this an exciting prospect. For anticolonial icons, egalitarian aspiration had even greater purchase than it had in the original welfare states and greater purchase than concern for a sufficient minimum did. And they advanced a pioneering vision of globally egalitarian distribution.

But in the decolonizing states, unlike most places in the economically developed world—where after World War II, sufficiency and equality were both advanced in circumstances of material abundance—the record was far worse, and their demand for a welfare world was certainly never granted by the powerful and wealthy. Out of the wreckage, sufficiency was hived off, and a new and unprecedented ethic of global antipoverty beckoned for our time. Philosophers thinking about the ethics of world distribution offer a valuable aperture on how this happened: The human rights revolution of our time is bound up with a global concern for the "wretched of the earth," but not in the egalitarian sense that the socialist and postcolonial promoters of that phrase originally meant.

Instead of global justice, market fundamentalism triumphed starting in the 1970s, alongside the new visibility of a more cosmopolitan and transnational understanding of human rights. And once again, human rights conformed to the political economy of the age, not defining it but reflecting it. At different times and in different ways in different places, this dependent relationship was reestablished as the dream of global welfare was spurned and as national welfare states increasingly came under attack. With precedents in the 1970s and after, the first decade after 1989 stands out as the one in which human rights politics surged even as market fundamentalism was consolidated worldwide. Communism died in its original home, and the Chinese state itself marketized. In doing so, it came to fit a global pattern, tolerating greater inequality even as it rescued more human beings from poverty—thereby raising them to the floor of sufficiency protection to which their social rights entitled them—than have ever been helped this way by any other agent in world history.

The companionship between human rights and market fundamentalism was not inevitable. All the same, many factors conspired to bring it to pass. Human rights were cut off from the dream of globally fair distribution that the global south itself advocated during the 1970s. On this ruins of earlier ambition, a neoliberal campaign against welfare at every scale made human rights its hostages. It was not so much that both human rights and market fundamentalism were established on ethically individualist grounds and took the state (and especially the postcolonial state) not as a setting for a collectivist ethics but as a technical intermediary for achieving a global but individualist project. Rather, it was that human rights were extricated from their welfare state crucible and redefined. The attempt to mobilize economic and social rights has remained unimpressive since the end of the Cold War allowed such mobilization to begin, especially when constitutional judges and international nongovernmental pressure groups strove to enforce these rights. Worse, human rights lost their original connection with a larger egalitarian aspiration, focusing on sufficient provision instead.

It mattered greatly that the human rights of women and other especially oppressed groups were taken more seriously than ever before, overcoming the biases of the postwar welfare states and those of postcolonial nationalism and internationalism too. But even as aspirations to status equality advanced, distributive equality usually suffered. Despite ascending to geopolitical primacy in the middle of the twentieth century, America had bucked the dominant trend by failing to move to a welfare state. But its example—and its power—shaped the aspirations of a subsequent neoliberal age much more visibly. It was easier for market fundamentalists in America and elsewhere to obliterate whatever ceiling on inequality national welfare states had imposed and to vault the global rich higher over their inferiors than they had ever been. Meanwhile, the most visible ethical movement was struggling merely to build a global floor of protection for the worst off. As egalitarian ideals and practices died, the idea of human rights accommodated itself to the reigning political economy, which it could humanize but not overthrow.

IN THIS story of how human rights came to the world amid the ruins of equality, the main characters are those who were the most articulate, especially politicians and philosophers. They sometimes voiced popular ideals and practical commitment with clarity and depth. Philosophy in particular is indispensable, because it provides a proxy for understanding wider developments—which is not to say that intellectuals are commonly responsible for change, let alone that they succeed in playing the role of vanguards of the future. In their very attempt to raise existing causes from the earthbound terrain of struggle into the empyrean of moral principle, thinkers often lose touch with the agents and movements that have done most to make the aspirations of social justice current. Intellectuals helped imagine credible ethical standards while also living a broader history that has seen the adoption of some ideals alongside the abandonment of others. As an intellectual and ideological history written out of dissatisfaction with mere sufficiency and committed to a more ambitious equality, what follows therefore pursues a dual agenda: It detects the ethical principle embedded in political action and the social imaginary, which thinkers often voice, and it also brings our ethics down to earth, showing how they exist in proximity to the politics that have inspired and obstructed them. There is no place to take sides about right and wrong except within history, as it rapidly changes from one day to the next. For the moment, at least, human rights history is worth telling because it reveals how partial our activism has become, choosing sufficiency alone as intractable crises in politics and economics continue to mount.

The outcomes pose a stark challenge to our highest ideals, which demand readjustment today. The human rights revolution certainly deserves credit for saving the ideal of social justice from the highly exclusionary form in which it emerged. Today few would countenance authoritarian welfare—even though authoritarians helped birth welfare states. And even democratic welfare states suffered manifold exclusions at the start, based on gender, race, and other factors. Even if they integrated distributive equality better than any political enterprise before or since, no nostalgia for the authoritarian or democratic welfare state is compelling if it means sacrificing one moral ideal to an equally important one. Status equality matters fully as much as distributive equality.[8]

But the reverse is also true, and recalling the distributive commitments of the welfare state therefore raises a series of questions to those who might otherwise celebrate their pluralism and tolerance in the age of human rights. Is the attention human rights allow on global sufficiency at fault for the explosion of inequality in many nations and (by some measures) globally too? Were there alternatives to the redefinition of human rights and their rise in our age as a global political language for long-distance but hollowed-out solidarity? Is there any way for human rights to return to their original relationship with distributive equality, or even—as Tominová wanted, echoing many postcolonial voices—to scale it up to the world stage?

There is no reason for human rights ideals to continue the accommodating relationship they have had with market fundamentalism and unequal outcomes. Human rights may well serve to indirectly indict the consequences of inequality when it threatens the minimum standards of liberty, security, and provision that human rights protect. This does not mean, however, that either human rights norms or the kinds of movements we have learned to associate with those norms—engaging in an informational politics of "naming and shaming," operating in the professional mode, and prizing judges as ideal enforcers of basic norms—are up to the challenge of supplementing sufficiency with equality in theory or practice. I myself suspect that, since the preeminence of human rights ideals has occurred in a neoliberal age, it is exceedingly unlikely that their usual representatives can find the portal to exit it on their own. Human rights advocates can work to extricate themselves from their neoliberal companionship, even as others mark their limitations, in order to restore the dream of equality to its importance in both theory and practice. If both groups are successful, they can save the ideal of human rights from an unacceptable fate: it has left the globe more humane but enduringly unequal.

1

Jacobin Legacy:
The Origins of Social Justice

In 1941, the British people were at war alone against Axis powers, poised on the brink of creating a popular welfare state. The pain and sacrifice their beleaguered and solitary plight required made a new kind of social citizenship necessary. In that year, William Temple, the archbishop of York (and soon after, of Canterbury), coined the phrase "the welfare state." It would differ from the mere "power state" that the German National Socialists had brought about, achieving redistributive policy and social security without destroying personal freedoms. Despite the indispensable alliance with the Soviet Union to put Adolf Hitler down, the welfare state emerged as the sole alternative "the West" had to offer to the totalitarian state, in its various guises to the east. Eventually, the welfare state would appeal the world over.[1]

The truth was, however, that it was still unclear whether liberal democracy could host the kind of welfare state modern economic circumstances seemed to require and that so-called totalitarian states had moved to achieve too. In the United States—which had some New Deal experiments behind it but was still debating whether to enter the fray not only of the war but also of the age of social citizenship—a professor named R. R. Palmer reflected on the beginnings of this new state and the origins of the debate about how precisely to organize it. He traced both back to the Jacobin state of 1793–4 during the French Revolution. The Jacobin state verged toward dictatorship in emergency circumstances, Palmer allowed, as some twentieth-century states did and as his own great Democratic president Franklin Roosevelt had even been accused of doing. Poised between democracy and dictatorship themselves, the Jacobins had pioneered a state that would be "interventionist, offering social services; it was to plan and guide the institutions of the country, using legislation to lift up the common man." Already the French Revolution had not merely introduced human rights as a *lingua franca* of politics for modern states—it had also initiated the contentious struggle for social welfare.[2]

The history of economic and social rights, which has almost never been written, depends on a framework that captures the full aspirations of the political enterprises of which those rights have been a part. It is important to track the annunciation of each of the now-canonical social rights—first, rights to education and public relief; later, rights to work and to workplace protections; and ultimately, a panoply of other entitlements. But followed one by one or even together, the emergence of such rights makes no sense. Rather, a history of these rights requires an account of the main ideological origins of the welfare state and also, therefore, an account of contending responses to what the nineteenth century dubbed "the social question." That account, in turn, shows that reducing the origins of the welfare state and the resolution of the social question to the narrower prehistory of economic and social rights would be a serious mistake, in part because of longstanding uncertainty about whether rights were a viable language for pursuing social justice. Indeed, until the end of World War II, it remained quite unclear what kind of political regime could provide adequate minimal protections. It would have to make the modern workplace more humane. It would need to erect shelters, like unemployment insurance, against the buffeting winds of the modern economy. Finally, it would require basic provision in domains like health and housing for those whose work did not afford them enough means or those who were too young, ill-equipped, or old to work in the first place. But even more important, the emergence of social rights took place in relation to the trajectory of other ideals, especially the distributive ideal of material equality. From the Jacobin state to the twentieth-century welfare state in its dictatorial and democratic guises, the ideal of sufficient distribution, which economic and social rights provide one way to capture, had to be squared with a variety of alternative hopes. These hopes included the aspiration to create a modicum of distributive equality among citizens—not merely a floor of protection against the worst outcomes by affording basic provision, but a ceiling on wealth and a constraint on material hierarchy.[3]

When the United Nations canonized economic and social rights in the Universal Declaration of Human Rights of 1948, it consecrated the democratic welfare state that had emerged victorious from World War II. It thereby did more than simply enshrine the ideal of distributive sufficiency that the declaration explicitly defined in its series of basic entitlements; it also reflected the ambitious political enterprise of distributive equality. The genocidal project of the Nazi welfare state was abandoned, but the democratic welfare states that triumphed were also designed for only some beneficiaries in national communities. The very West European states that went furthest toward welfare were also the larger imperial states that excluded from their generosity the vast bulk of humanity in the empire's territories. The new welfare states also set up hierarchies of privilege at home, especially on grounds of race and gender. Long after Hitler, the very states that, through the 1940s, achieved democratic welfare for their full-fledged citizens continued to rule much of the globe's territories and peoples, a fact the Universal Declaration did nothing to change. The welfare state shouldered the burden of provision for males above all, and ethnic and racial insiders among them. Women and children certainly mattered, but the welfare state's schemes treated their plight as derivative, and its very generosity entrenched their subordination to the destiny of the male working nation, especially when welfare states took up natalist policies—a fact that the Universal Declaration's prohibition of discrimination did shockingly little to affect for a long time. In short, the story of the rise of social rights in the welfare state is unintelligible when separated from that state's equalizations as well as its discriminations.

The Jacobin state did the most in both theory and practice to set off a permanent debate about fair distribution in modern history and especially about the quandary of fulfilling sufficient provision of the good things in life without neglecting the establishment of a rough material equality of citizens. Assessing the contributions of socialist thought and the new parties and trade unions that advanced its ideals from the later nineteenth century opens a path to the twentieth-century welfare states' more important ideological origins in class compromise and their incorporation of egalitarian aims alongside the goal of sufficient provision for the needy. After the Jacobin welfare state, the attempt to balance and combine sufficiency and equality—and therefore master the tension between them—began in earnest once coalitions of social masters and inferiors began to explore whether and how they could compromise between the extremes of doing nothing and changing everything. This new political form achieved unprecedented socioeconomic equality in modern circumstances of abundance compared to the liberal atmosphere of the nineteenth century and the neo-liberal one of the twenty-first. It came bound up with glaring exclusions in its socialization of citizenship—exclusions not just of imperial subjects but also of women and non-whites alongside other unprivileged groups. Yet its modicum of egalitarian inclusion was to travel to the ends of the earth before neoliberalism came in our time, along with a storied human rights movement that remedied the historic exclusions of welfare states even as the material equality they had engineered was undone.

DEFINING and pursuing social justice changed decisively between ancient and modern times. The prospect of growth appeared, and God-given or socially necessary constraints were slowly eroded. Despite longstanding moral ideals both to serve the poor and to arrange distribution equally, to eradicate poverty or strive for a fair society did not seem feasible. "The poor shall never cease out of the land," Deuteronomy explains (15:11). And while Plato entertained "communism" for the guardians of his ideal city, neither he nor Aristotle was in a position to advance a theory of distributive justice from first premises, in part because it was unimaginable that any polity could ever strive to arrange who got what.

As a moral and religious matter, it was long conceivable that provision of a sufficient amount of the good things in life counted among the most essential moral desiderata. Out of humane solidarity, the different mono-theisms have all decreed charity (often through religious organizations) for the most downtrodden and certainly allowed moralizing: "He that with-holdeth Corn, the People shall curse him" (Prov. 9:26). Religious communities could even institutionalize provisions to combat insufficiency. Yet gross hierarchy prevailed with little opposition. In Leviticus 25, God announced ordinances (probably never enacted anywhere) that, every fiftieth year, put all Israelites back at an equal starting point, to correct periodically for mal-distribution. Jesus Christ did not have a soft spot for the wealthy, clearly, but for all his significance as a zealous religious firebrand preaching the end of days, neither did he prompt norms of economic or even political equality—at least not for centuries. In the Sermon on the Mount, he preached to his followers not to worry about the vital needs of food, drink, or clothing, but to seek the kingdom of righteousness in order to be provided them (Matt. 6:25–33; Luke 12:22–31). Jesus's evangelizing disciple Paul arrogated the Greek concept of political equality for an ideal of famine relief through mutual aid: "For I mean not that other men be eased, and ye burdened. But by an equality, that now at this time your abundance may be a supply for their want, that their abundance also may be a supply for your want: that there may be equality" (2 Cor. 8:13–14). Otherwise, the risks of wealth were to one's chances of salvation, rather than an affront to justice in this world. What did emerge with Christianity as it moved from rural Palestine into its first urban settings around the Mediterranean world was a much more powerful norm of solidarity with the poor. The practice in the Roman world of public benefaction for the sake of civic pride—the culture of bread and circuses—gave way to the virtue of poverty relief, including for those outside the faith community.[4]

The very notion of "sufficiency" (*sufficientia*), absent from classical languages before the reception of monotheism, originally (mis)translated the allusion in Proverbs (30:8) to the bread that God was entreated to provide everyone. In the Hebrew, God is implored to provide an amount "allotted" under custom or law, with no implication that this amount would match vital needs. But by the time of some translations—into Greek in the Septuagint, and then in some Latin and later vernacular renderings—the term sometimes was taken to imply a satisfactory amount. Jesus's chroniclers Matthew (6:11) and Luke (11:3) replace "allotted" with "daily." And since early interpretations of these passages, God's largesse has been associated with subsistence. A radical fifth-century Pelagian treatise, *On Riches*, condemning wealth and decrying poverty alike, opined that it would be best if everyone received that adequate amount and no more from divine or human powers, in effect equating a minimum floor with a maximum ceiling in distribution. It even supposed that were wealth to disappear, penury would no longer exist, so that equality and sufficiency were identical in practice. But no one argued that this standard had to be achieved through political authority. Humanity lacked not only modern states to enforce and institutionalize distributive justice but even the belief that it ought to be enforced and institutionalized, except through communal norms. Various communistic schemes over the centuries emphasizing egalitarian distribution amidst plenty or on a higher standard than sufficiency remained millennial and utopian.[5]

Treating a world beyond the antagonism and hierarchy of rich and poor as a pipedream, ancient, medieval, and early modern texts went far further for this reason in anticipating the necessity of some kind of adequate minimum, even if it was rarely framed as an individual right or, rarer still, a political obligation. Almsgiving at various levels of organization, nearly all local, remained as old as the world. Medieval thought even outlined a necessity claim for some cases of thievery in the face of desperate need. Thomas Aquinas believed unavailability of a bare minimum to survive made property "common" for the taking, while Franciscan spirituals in the centuries that followed explained that followers of Jesus who could not own property at all could still use that of others to survive. By Europe's early modern period, even as natural rights of the poor were less and less common to assert, there were ramshackle attempts to reinforce charity for mendicants with policy, essentially as insurance against social breakdown. Primarily, this was a matter of widespread custom and patchwork ordinances, notably in the Poor Law (1601) in Elizabethan England. As late as the Leveller and Digger agitation in the 1640s English Revolution, equality in distribution seemed, for those marginal prophets who imagined it, like a biblical promise reserved for the end of days or a local experiment for the frequently bizarre if morally just. In secular political thought, there had long been claims that the maintenance of republics required bars against disproportionate wealth, out of the prudential concern that doom would certainly follow from excessive inequality, and the early modern period saw these claims revived. From the Greeks to James Harrington in the seventeenth century (not to mention for his followers among American revolutionaries), extremes of riches and poverty were opposed, but as a matter of the stability of the commonwealth, not as a matter of justice, and not in the name of material equality. It was essentially not until the eighteenth century in Europe that anything like distributive justice within political order, whether aiming at sufficiency or equality, became widely conceivable.[6]

When this finally occurred, the credibility of a politics of obligatory sufficiency competed with the credibility of a politics of obligatory equality almost from the first. What followed in the invention of ideals of modern distributive justice was one of the fundamental shifts in our understanding of how human beings ought to live among one other at any scale. Like so many other discontinuities in the eighteenth century, this one took place as the social realm became something distinct. Before, the notion of "society" had been precluded by visions that prioritized God or nature as suprahuman authorities to which humans must conform, and political regimes were defined according to their relation to divine plan or natural law. The Enlightenment inventors of a new understanding of humanity insisted, by contrast, that the structure of social institutions does most to determine a people's way of life, including what they believe about the divine and what sort of political authority they embrace. There was "a fundamental transformation in what might be called the vocabulary of human relations during the period." The newly coined notion of "society" described "an entity which did not owe its existence to any religious or political authority or indeed to any principle external to itself." It signified a profound transformation in how Europeans "imagined the world around them: from a perspective in which the human terrestrial order was seen as subordinated to exterior (particularly divine) determinations, to one in which it was seen as autonomous and self-regulating." And before "society," there was no possibility of "social justice."[7]

This development is essential to understanding of the rise of the modern controversy over distribution. In an influential but misleading argument, political scientist James Scott claimed in the 1970s that rural societies through recorded history as well as in the contemporary world have been organized around the embrace of a moral expectation of subsistence and even an implicit political commitment to "social rights." Peasants adopted various strategies for ensuring their own survival in a world of uncertainty, and they expected local political authorities to play a role when their own dogged strategies of sufficient provision failed. "The right to subsistence is a fundamental social norm in the village," Scott explained, struggling to understand the wave of peasant unrest in his time. Uprisings were a time-honored possibility touched off when governance failed to help peasants secure their basic minimum. For Scott, it was quite important to name the expectation of subsistence as a "social right," though when their own provision failed, peasants had no remedy besides anger and revolt and none ever enunciated a politically significant entitlement. "In all but the most coercive systems of rural class relationships," Scott nonetheless explained, "there is some pattern of . . . *rights.* . . . [This] order was based on the guarantee of *minimal social rights* in the absence of political and civil rights." More than this, Scott went so far as to claim that the peasant actually desires the fulfillment of an expectation of sufficiency *rather than equality*: "that all should have a place, a living, not that all should be equal."[8]

Aside from the hazards of generalizing across time and space, however, it is not so easy to leap from a search for material subsistence to a belief in social rights that impose political duties as a matter of obligatory justice. If it were, such rights would hardly have become so pertinent in modern politics alone. It is even more dubious to suppose that such commitments are somehow more basic or primeval than ones to distributive equality. It is one thing to observe some peasant communities taking care of their own, especially when they are on the brink of starvation, and quite another to posit an immemorial norm of social rights independent of the rise of states and in the absence of an equally new imperative of material equality. In reality, both sufficiency and equality as obligations of social justice only came into view in the eighteenth century, when society itself became newly visible to its members and just social relations became something to bring about through politics and markets. Dismay at the hardships of indigence is no more absent from the annals of moral opinion than fanciful intimations of equality are. But the premodern imagination could not rank sufficiency over equality as goals of social justice, for the simple reason that it had not yet understood that human beings live in a society created and changeable by none other than human beings themselves.

Scott was inspired by the recovery of a widespread set of new popular expectations around survival and subsistence that rose to importance late in the emerging market societies of the eighteenth century. The earliest responses to commercialization struggled to make ethical concern for indigence, which religious imaginaries had made more hortatory and voluntary, the substance of political thought and action. The British Marxist historian E. P. Thompson, writing about peasants in England, showed that a "moral economy" focusing on a sufficient minimum existed; Scott later generalized and globalized Thompson's theory of it. When that minimum failed to be available, especially as a new political economy that insisted on the virtues of free trade displaced the moral economy, sometimes furious revolt could ensue. Thompson did not go so far as to suppose that a full-fledged sense of social rights was implicit in the moral economy; instead, he documented the widespread belief in a "just price" that limited the expense of basic products, such as bread, and that occupied the very center of ordinary people's sense of right and wrong. What Thompson did not see is that the rise of market ideology, which counseled the repeal of the patchwork custom and law that formalized makeshift, stopgap charity, derived from a new sense of the social order as something made by human beings and thus subject to reform, which counted more. Social justice could now transcend the moral economy as propounding ethical principles of distribution became possible.[9]

It is thus no surprise that both sufficiency (including arguments for social rights) and equality surged as expectations of justice were placed on the social order in the late eighteenth century. It was the age in which the notion of specifically economic sociability arose, and more and more surmised that the new commercial processes ushering in modern times would likely lead to fairness on their own. Increasingly, people were willing to believe that, after some time, a new culture of what came to be called "capitalism" would make the poor better off than they were under the old moral economy. Critics such as Jean-Jacques Rousseau doubted it, complaining that the rise of commerce expanded hierarchies of wealth that both morally enervated the rich and fed disorder, even if they left the poor better off. Rousseau's contribution was pivotal in giving rise to a reformist counterblast, mainly because in his early critical screed *On the Origin of Inequality* (1755), he made class distinctions seem so sickeningly entrenched and morally unwholesome. He did propound a right of each man "to everything he needs," but without arguing for a direct obligation (separate from its indirect consequences) for the state to afford a social minimum. Nor was Rousseau committed to a modern sense of material equality as a requirement of justice. In *The Social Contract* (1762), writing in a republican vein, Rousseau recommended that "no citizen be so very rich that he can buy another, and none so poor that he is compelled to sell himself." Extremes of wealth were self-defeating because they would lead the rich to opt out of necessary political equality and the poor to follow suit to survive; a just society would therefore "allow neither very rich people nor beggars," Rousseau explained. This neo-republican call for moderating extremes to the extent necessary to avoid disorder soon ripened into a direct argument for equality's intrinsic moral importance.[10]

Theory evolved in tandem with practice, but rapidly enough that the tension between sufficiency and equality that would reappear in the era of the twentieth-century welfare states was enduringly set by the time of Jacobin rule in 1793–94. The American Revolution, despite its importance for the spread of human rights language generally, did not bear much on "the social question," as its idolizers through Hannah Arendt (and more infrequent critics) always claimed. It may not have been libertarian in spirit, even promoting the cause of activist government for the sake of economic development, but this did not mean it bore on fair distribution of wealth and income for the sake of either entitled relief or fair outcomes. In contrast, the French Revolution from the first set off "the promise of a world beyond want" and an egalitarian community. Occurring in a new era of commercial modernity and indeed globalization, the French Revolution has never been possible to interpret apart from the emergence of the social question, if only because of the comparative prominence of republican commitments and the cult of Rousseau that left luxurious opulence stigmatized throughout. Into the twentieth century, its legacy made separating political feudalism from economic feudalism difficult; both were so closely related in the revolution that few of its heirs could disentangle them. If the social order now seemed under human control, it was corrigible not simply in its political leadership (the early years involving a move to constitutional monarchy) but even in its material outcomes.[11]

The novelty of the French Revolution and its initial contributions is reflected in the spectacular trajectory of the English radical Thomas Paine, who ignited the American Revolution in the 1770s without engaging material obligation before becoming the chief propagandist of its sister revolt fifteen years later with a new distributive consciousness. During his expatriate years, when he did so much to set off the American Revolution, Paine had been a firm proponent of an unregulated economy—Philadelphia's crowds demanding their own social minimum rooted in the moral economy tradition notwithstanding. But already in *The Rights of Man*, his 1791–92 defense of the initial French events, Paine spent much time laying out the first vision of a social insurance policy to end poverty. He did so in parallel with the French Marquis de Condorcet, who was in hiding from the Terror and would soon be arrested and die by presumptive suicide. Condorcet laid out his own scheme directed at achieving sufficiency for all French citizens. Both Condorcet and Paine built on the model of earlier English poor laws that were part of the moral economy, but they went far beyond this model in the extent of the provision they envisioned. Both emphasized not simply poor relief but the central importance of public education. Not coincidentally, these two norms, already figuring as policies in the pre-Jacobin Constitution of 1791, became the first two social rights in world history with the Jacobin Declaration of the Rights of Man and Citizen of 1793.[12]

But the Jacobins in 1793–94 did not stop with novel rights to sufficient provision or with Condorcet's or Paine's impulses. The first years of the French Revolution, before the Jacobins rose to power, were not propitious for distributive entitlements to rise high on the agenda, even if the monarchy's betrayal of social justice counted against its popularity and helped doom it. Now, driven by pressure from insurgents—dubbed *sans-culottes* because of their characteristic short breeches—and contrary to their own relatively libertarian economic starting point, the Jacobins in power instituted commodity price controls, in effect to provide a guarantee against starvation. Throughout the period, both during Jacobin rule and after their fall, meeting a subsistence minimum occupied the center of political debate and popular engagement across the country. People spoke widely of *les subsistances*, which meant "in the last resort, the right to live" and, outside famine conditions, implied "good, varied, and plentiful food," so that poor men and their families would not have to stoop to eat the potato or survive on "roots, berries, nettles, and dandelion leaves." It was never simply the case, however, that the people's precarious state exempted wealth from egalitarian concern so long as adequate social policy existed. Whether driven by envy in view of the privileges even revolutionary leaders claimed for themselves or by inchoate commitments to a form of social justice beyond sufficiency, support for the ultimately terrorist government depended on political claims not just in the face of abject need but also of a rank hierarchy of means. The "right of existence" escalated among the *sans culottes* into a claim for "equal incomes."[13]

Real government policy certainly never matched the high ideals of sufficient and egalitarian provision, but these ideals were institutionalized in combination as never before in history. Still, if this was the first welfare state, it was more in aspiration than execution. Starvation occurred despite price controls, and the larger right to relief and to public education were aspirational. All the same, Jacobin policy hardly stuck to a sufficient minimum, struggling to meet it in the midst of the war the Old Regime powers declared on the revolutionary project. Instead, it promised "fair shares" for all, vacillating between and attempting to harmonize the claims of sufficiency and equality. No wonder Palmer, in 1941, could baptize it the first popular welfare state in world history, requiring "a planned economy more thoroughgoing than anything seen in Europe until the twentieth century." However easily forgotten, the revolutionary origins of the initial impulse to a welfare state remain the principal legacy to recover, both for background to mid-twentieth century social justice and for interrogating the explosion of material inequality in our time.[14]

The Jacobin vision of material equality was, like most such visions, nowhere near absolute. But its policy offered a full-spectrum attempt to reduce the material hierarchy that the Old Regime had left behind and that the early phase of the French Revolution had done little to disturb. "Fair shares" went beyond sufficiency. The Declaration of the Rights of Man and Citizen of 1793 moved to a vision of basic sufficiency, over Maximilien Robespierre's objections that it needed to go even further. As Jacobin rule continued, a concern for fair distribution entered the mix. Fears of agrarian land reform for the sake of equalization were rife back to the history of Rome, and the Jacobins even imposed the death penalty on any who dared propose such a thing. But they proceeded all the same to reform inheritance law for the sake of equalizing redistribution and, even further, allowed division of common spaces and parceling out of seized feudal estates. In part to compensate for their still protective views of private property, the Jacobin convention moved most directly and enthusiastically to institute strongly progressive taxation in order to, as one legislator explained, "destroy inequalities, those monstrous distortions of the body politic, which devour all that surrounds them."[15]

It was a vision of what would come to be called "property-owning democracy," which hoped to guarantee the ownership of some land and the participation in the economy of every man, with fair wages or, for those who could not work, backup support, in order to establish fair shares in the common good. Like later welfare states, the Jacobin one by no means treated all humans—especially women—equally. But while most of the state's programs, including ones in the domain of health and education, remained notional or scattered, they were the means to an end of an egalitarian scheme that proved ahead of its time. As twentieth-century socialist Harold Laski was to put it, "the Jacobins . . . schooled the masses to the understanding that distinctions of wealth are legislative creations, and that, where crisis demands it, egalitarian innovation may be deliberately attempted."[16]

The short-lived Jacobin state left a profound legacy, equally as much as the Haitian Revolution of the same period raised the difficulty of how the empires of the day, including the French Empire, could accommodate new claims of liberty and equality on a global scale. But while a truly worldwide vision of distributive justice awaited a later era, French radicals acted immediately to save the materially egalitarian element of the Jacobin national welfare state from the ruins of its defeat—and indeed to extend it. The notary and self-taught thinker François-Noël "Gracchus" Babeuf, the first modern absolute egalitarian, insisted on going all the way instead of merely constraining inequality. Released from jail just as Robespierre fell, Babeuf understood that the principles of the Jacobin Declaration of the Rights of Man and Citizen and the social policy that followed it had a last chance at realization after a difficult year of wartime dictatorship. He demanded equal outcomes as a matter of principle, hauling full-blown equality from the primitive state of humankind, from which Rousseau believed it irretrievable, to the status of a modern project that Rousseau had never believed either possible or desirable.[17]

In his short time on the historical stage, Babeuf was not above favorably citing the *sans-culotte* ideal of sufficiency, writing in his "Manifesto of the Plebeians" (1796) for instance that the goal had to be "to assure to each person and to his progeny, however numerous, sufficiency, and nothing but." Yet from that last clause equality also peeks out, because it mattered not so much that the indigent get bread and other good things in life but that no one have better and more than others. Babeuf took his Roman name in allegiance to the most famous proponent of equalizing land reform. But in a sense, Babeuf came close to reviving the ideal of the late antique *On Riches:* making people equal involved satisfying their basic needs, but no more. He did not connect the egalitarian aim with a dream of general abundance, and he believed that abolition of property—"simple administration of distribution" of the good things in life to the people—rather than some more detailed institutional scheme would do the trick. Founding a "conspiracy of equals," and executed for his radicalism, Babeuf left a mark thanks to friends and disciples who struggled to keep his message alive as an era of backlash set in. Like his confederate Sylvain Maréchal who penned a "Manifesto of Equals," Babeuf deserves more credit as a founder of absolute egalitarianism than as a founder of the welfare state. Their extremism indicates, rather, that in the revolutionary era and especially during Jacobin rule, it became more and more the common sense that some sort of "reasonable" equality in the distribution of the good things in life was both feasible and necessary.[18]

It was a critical addition to modern social justice, because it made proposals merely to provide sufficient amounts or necessities to the people seem themselves insufficient to a more and more mainstream audience. Babeuf hated Condorcet, who had spoken more plangently about the possibility that equality might materialize without going beyond proposals for a basic minimum. The latter did not survive the Terror. When Paine redoubled his commitment to minimum sufficiency, precisely in response to Babeuf's "conspiracy of equals," he rejected a more robust equality. The two ideals had been implicitly present but in confusing relation, both in popular consciousness as well as in proposed and enacted policy. Before Paine drew the line by endorsing the one and repudiating the other, no one had really ever specifically defended sufficiency *against* equality. "I care not how affluent some may be, so long as none be miserable in consequence of it," Paine wrote graphically in his *Agrarian Justice* (1796). (He was thus the first one clearly to reach the position that Scott later attributed to peasant morality beyond space and time.) Arguing for a rights-based social minimum, Paine extended his earlier claims in favor of the specific social rights that Jacobins had since propounded, such as public relief. The Bible had taught, and no one had ever forgotten, that God gave earth to humanity and in common; while it had later been parceled out, Paine argued, it was in exchange for an enduring guarantee against poverty insofar as property and commerce allowed growth and wealth. On this basis, he innovatively argued not simply for a universal basic income through taxation but also for the state's role in protecting the needy, the young, the elderly, and the disabled as a matter of right. However innovative, the rearguard elements of Paine's scheme need also to be kept in mind. His intent was only to insist no one fall below a threshold standard, not that any kind of distributive equality prevail, and even this generosity would never have been so great without Jacobin experiments outflanking him.[19]

ONE HUNDRED years later, in 1886, Austrian socialist law professor Anton Menger reflected on the contest of socialist ideas as they had developed since the French Revolutionary experience. The place of socialism in the history of social rights is most often badly understood. No one provides a better perspective than Menger does on distributional ideals in socialism between the origins of modernity and our times. Socialists, more than any other force in history, were committed to adequate provision for the needy, but they were divided on whether to propound social rights. For a long time, a commitment to egalitarian distribution beyond sufficiency, which the Jacobin welfare state pioneered, was not prominent among socialist aims. The search for subsistence or a sufficient minimum mattered, but only in relation to competing ideals. Not only did socialists hesitate to formulate the insistence on adequate provision in terms of rights, but they supplemented that aspiration with a different one than material equality until they backed the welfare-state class compromise of the twentieth century.[20]

To the extent that a moral economy existed in early modern history, it had clearly broken down in the century of the "social question," as customs and laws to meet basic needs proved as much a source of outrage for their limitations as a source of praise for the succor they provided. Rampant and rapid urbanization created communities of strangers, not to mention vast slums where no local caretaking spirit prevailed. The new science of

political economy originally voiced moral concern for sufficient provision—
"they who feed, clothe and lodge the whole body of the people," Adam Smith
wrote, "should have such a share of the produce of their own labour as to
be themselves tolerably well fed, clothed, and lodged." But it did this while
accepting that the increasing wealth of nations would drive inequality within
and among them. As political economy came into its own, it developed
the heartless attitude toward subsistence that sparked both humanitarian
and radical responses to the attendant miseries of modern economic life.
"If [a man] cannot get subsistence from his parents on whom he has a just
demand, and if the society do not want his labour," famed political economist Thomas Malthus wrote in 1803 (in a passage he later dropped because
it proved so scandalous), "[he] has no claim of *right* to the smallest portion
of food. . . . At Nature's mighty feast there is no vacant cover for him. She
tells him to be gone, and will quickly execute her own orders."[21]

In reaction to such heartlessness, socialists everywhere rallied behind the
ideal of a sufficient minimum as fundamental to their cause. The renowned
principle that called for distributing "from each according to his ability to
each according to his need" had proven strikingly powerful, from French
utopian socialist Etienne Cabet (if not further back) to Louis Blanc to Karl
Marx himself in his *Critique of the Gotha Program* (1875). Sometimes the
commitment to basic provision was expressed in terms of rights. Even if an
entitlement to minimum sufficiency or an enumerated list of the basic
human needs went back to the 1790s—Menger himself cited English radical William Godwin as the first to propound it in the French Revolution's
aftermath—it was in permanent competition with other priorities for socialists. Indeed, the very social rights that socialists sometimes prioritized
indicated their broader ends.

After the French Revolution, the first right in importance was the right
to work: an obligation on government and society to provide gainful employment if none was available. Despite a mention in the 1793 French
Declaration—with its right to public relief from society—of the means of
procuring work to achieve "maintenance" for "unfortunate" citizens, an individual entitlement to a remunerative job had not figured substantially in
the revolutionary politics. Thinking through the aims of the Jacobin state
and its aftermath, German philosopher J. G. Fichte first propounded a right
to work. Later and independently, early French socialist Charles Fourier both
named it and launched it on its spectacular modern career. Politician and
creative Fourierist Victor Considérant made the right famous in the years

before the 1848 revolution in France, where it played a pivotal role both in advocacy and legislation. "We will do much more for the happiness of the lower classes," Considérant wrote, "for their real emancipation and true progress, in guaranteeing these classes well-remunerated work, than in winning political rights and a meaningless sovereignty for them. The most important of the people's rights is the *right to work*." In the 1848 revolution in France, organizing government to provide useful activity, as in Louis Blanc's famous national workshops, was a major goal.

While socialists then and afterward understood the great potential of demanding guaranteed employment from the state, Menger recognized the right to work as an "offshoot" of the ideal of sufficiency, because a job and therefore a state jobs program functioned as a means toward that ideal, not toward affording more than minimal compensation. Indeed, the rhetoric of the right to work could also serve conservatives, notably when Chancellor Otto von Bismarck, after uniting Germany, set up the first real welfare state since the Jacobin experiment. "Give the laborer the right to work so long as he is healthy," Bismarck said in a much-noted 1884 parliamentary speech—although he did little to institutionalize employment, even when creating the earliest broad-scale state apparatus for the ill and elderly.[22]

If the right to work had been for socialists the only competing priority to the right of subsistence, their early programs would have been unified, directly or indirectly, around the search for a sufficient minimum. Instead, they certainly aimed higher—yet the aim, Menger contended, was not really at the achievement of equal distribution of the good things in life. Early socialists had gone beyond subsistence for the sake of the other new right, from which Menger took the title of his famous book: the right to the whole product of labor. Instead of a system of production in which owners of capital enjoyed rents without themselves laboring (what Marx called surplus value), socialists had striven for workers taking every bit of the value of their work—an ethical principle Menger also traced to Godwin. (He therefore impishly denied credit to Marx, provoking furious howls of protest.) For Menger, the right to all the fruits of one's work was "the fundamental revolutionary conception of our time, playing the same dominant part as the idea of political equality in the French Revolution and its offshoots." In other words, for socialists, the sequel to political equality was not typically distributive equality. Subsistence was not egalitarian because needs were different, depending on one's makeup and situation. "When so many communists speak of an *equal* distribution of wealth in a communistic state," Menger wrote, "it is . . . distribution in proportion to wants and existing means of satisfaction to which they refer. For no one could seriously strive for a really equal distribution in the face of the enormous differences in wants due to age, sex, and individual character." And the right to the whole produce of one's labor was not egalitarian either: it depended on how much one worked.[23]

It would be false to suggest that material egalitarianism found no place whatsoever in socialism at the start. But to the extent it percolated as a barely sketched ideal, it prevailed among those utopians and revolutionaries who designed blueprints for an ideal society and who, either for this reason or out of the priority of moral outrage about existing injustice, simply did not think very carefully about permanent institutionalization of moral principles in a future social venture. Once again, France remained the homeland of such figures through the nineteenth century, especially those who set out to guard the flame of Babeuf's memory. Cherishing not the 1789 but the 1793 declaration for moving toward welfare, a short-lived Société des droits de l'homme (Human Rights Club) took up the revolutionary cause in the 1830s under King Louis-Philippe's "bourgeois monarchy." Babouvist agitators such as Jean-Jacques Pillot preserved his idol's commitment to egalitarian distribution, now adjusted upward so that the good things in life, not simply the necessary ones, would be fairly divided. "Society's goal," he explained, "is to give to each of its members the greatest amount of well-being possible, by assuring him the satisfaction of his true needs . . . while the useful and agreeable will be distributed in the same proportions as the necessary."[24]

As for Marx, while he certainly made room for needs-based subsistence and supported some pragmatic campaigns for reforms, there is *no evidence*—for all his association with the currency of egalitarian justice since—that he envisioned material fairness in a communist state. Marx wanted to bring about a post-market society, eliminating domination and classes. He did not embrace distributional equality before the revolution, because it was hostage to class rule, or after the revolution (to the extent it is clear what he envisioned besides an abolition of private property), because different people may have vastly different needs and work more than each other. Just as important, Marx and especially "scientific" Marxists not only rejected the search for ethical principles like distributional ideals as bourgeois, they rejected the very idea of human rights. They operated on the premise that the essential task was to overthrow "capitalism." In their judgment, as Marx's chief associate Friedrich Engels demonstrated in his vituperative response to Menger, not even conceptualizing a right to the whole product of labor beyond subsistence really made a difference to the campaign of revolutionizing a system of production that needed to be overthrown for domination and exploitation to end.[25]

THIS LEAVES the mystery of how the return of the Jacobin synthesis of distributive sufficiency and equality occurred—as well as how rights to sufficient provision came to be nestled within a materially egalitarian project in the twentieth century. It was, in a word, as part of the class compromise in the origins of the welfare state, which socialists helped bring about even as it transformed their horizons. Even then, it left reformers of all stripes unsure whether to pursue sufficiency within the framework of rights protection, as they embraced equality more and more enthusiastically as a demanding imperative.

On both sides of the Atlantic, the first apex of economic liberalism in the late nineteenth century and early twentieth century led to the largest gulf between the richest and the poorest any society has ever created. As socialists debated their aims and tactics, and in large part because they were doing so with such visibility, a "century of redistribution" began, starting with a more tenacious insistence than ever before on a floor of socioeconomic protection in market economies based on libertarian contract and property rules. The essential alternative posed to it at the time was not distributive equality but political revolution. But an ethics of egalitarian redistribution made slow inroads in compromise projects between classes, the rich buying off their enemies and the rest exerting pressure to sweeten the deal.[26]

The deals were first designed to ensure sufficiency, even as inequality expanded. Social rights, one analyst put it in retrospect, "can boast no lofty pedigree. They crept piecemeal into apologetic existence, as low-grade palliatives designed at once to relieve and conceal the realities of poverty." It is this combination that makes the great era of the expansion of social rights, particularly the late nineteenth century, so reminiscent of a later neoliberal time, when sufficiency gains could sometimes coexist with greater and greater material differences between the most wealthy and the rest of humanity, from the local to the global. The originally socialist discourse of basic needs became the stock-in-trade of early struggles for state-directed welfare, with more and more people calling for the state to be responsive to a poverty that charity could never remediate, given "the human needs of labor." At the same time, that quest for sufficiency sparked debates in natural science and early "social science" about what goods and services (including, for example, how many calories) humans absolutely need to survive or flourish, as well as whether standards should change with collective wealth.[27]

The easiest to agree about was free and compulsory primary education, institutionalized first and most broadly among entitlements in emerging welfare states. It served multiple agendas. The Enlightenment belief in pedagogy, reflected in Jacobin promises; the later need, in an increasingly industrial society, for parents to leave home and have the children occupied during the day, at least until teenage years; and the social value of a minimally literate workforce—all contributed to the early rise of a right to education. In his classic essay on the origins of the welfare state, English sociologist T. H. Marshall could look back and call widespread elementary education "the first decisive step on the road" to "social rights of citizenship." It was a bumpy road, however, precisely because each social right depended on a new configuration of interests to institutionalize it, and no other convergence was as straightforward as the first around education.[28]

For broader entitlements, Bismarck set the tone, giving the socialist right to work rhetorical credence but going further and, in transatlantic context, moving first to institutionalize minimal state protections for the ill, the sick, and the elderly. The foundations for his policies were laid in the 1870s by the pioneering Association for Social Policy, which would soon be matched intellectually in other nations even as its leading figures, such as Lujo Brentano, were denounced as "pulpit socialists" by those who felt humane compromise with hierarchy was a terrible mistake compared to the agenda of seeking fuller-fledged power. Now Bismarck drew on its policy suggestions while banning socialist organizations, and the first national welfare state since the short-lived Jacobin experiment was born.[29]

Elsewhere on the European continent, social reform projects mushroomed in these years, finding early if modest uptake. With their more enduring allergies to the state, and always weighing the risk of creating vicious indolence in the name of providing succor, the United Kingdom—notably in its updated Poor Law of 1834—and especially the United States lagged behind, both in the production of policy expertise and its institutionalization. While conservative Germany took the lead in social insurance, however, reformist England did slowly establish preeminence in workplace standards and rudimentary workmen's compensation. As with the origins of distributive ethics in the eighteenth century, both kinds of program to advance social justice depended on a further rise of the social, now modified from its more familiar guise as the contractual relations (economic or political) of pre-existing individuals. Now "society" increasingly implied a collective unity or even organic body in relation to which individuals were never separate, let alone prior.

This was the most important reason, however far in the background it may have remained for many, why the political language of rights remained permanently controversial in the quest for sufficiency (and never seemed plausible in the search for class equality). But several other reasons also prevailed among reformers. In practice, the individual's rights to sacrosanct private property and "free" market relations were the dominant ones, and even to reformers who did not set themselves on the overthrow of capitalism, extending the list of rights to counteract those two dominant entitlements did not seem helpful. Rather, the whole metaphysics of antecedent individuals with natural rights had to be challenged. In this classical liberal era of modern political economy, as in the two ages of national welfare and neoliberal inequality to come, rights conformed with the spirit of the age. If the rights of man were primarily those of free enterprise and sacrosanct property, many thought it best to oppose the whole notion of rights rather than supplement the list. Accordingly, the broad notion of social rights would not really come into fashion until the mid-twentieth century.

Menger angled for a different outcome. "An exaggerated importance has been attached to the recognition of political rights, which is in striking disproportion to their scanty practical effect," he acknowledged. "Nevertheless, the formulation of such rights is not without value, as they crystallise into a password the chief aims of political and social movements." But he lost the argument for a long time. The socialization of thought that made rights debatable as progressive tools, including in the United Kingdom and the United States, was profound. And where Marx had early mounted the challenge to rights on behalf of revolution, it was equally if not more important that early proponents of the welfare state mounted it in the course of offering *an alternative to* revolution. Reformers had different idioms, whether "idealist" or sociological, in different intellectual cultures. Altogether, the critique of rights in the name of social reform went so far (Menger's friendliness toward the concept notwithstanding) that by 1901, the so-called "new liberal" J. A. Hobson could complain that exploration of the progressive use of rights to advance social justice had been rendered close to unimaginable. "Among modern social reformers," he observed, "there is a tendency to carry the revolt against the theory of natural and inalienable rights of individuals, upon which the eighteenth-century political philosophy was built, so far as to deny the utility of recognizing any rights of the individual as a basis for social reform."[30]

But a last and interlocking reason for the marginality of individual rights in the origins of the welfare state is that not only sufficiency beckoned: equality inspired as well, accompanied by more collectivist languages for it and, above all, ideologies of class compromise, normally described in terms of collective need or greatest benefit. In the Roman Catholic version, as expressed in Pope Leo XIII's classic social encyclical *On New Things* (1890), the rights that mattered beyond the individual right to property were not those of individuals but of "capital" and "labor" to reconcile their interests in view of the common good. This was representative of the collectivist spirit of reconciliation at the heart of the welfare state, where individual rights had an uncertain place, to the extent they were not starkly demoted. And no one ever formulated an individual right to the egalitarian distribution of the good things in life.

Unions, of course, always prioritized the rights to associate, strike, and bargain collectively, and not merely because it served their specific purposes. The importance of the right to strike for unions was as ambiguous as it was telling. Insofar as rights mattered at all in working class movements, the collective right to strike—broadly illegal at the start—drew by far the most attention in every country from the middle of the nineteenth century until the middle of the twentieth. It was far more than just another item on a list of entitlements; rather, its function was to empower unions to exact outcomes both of sufficient provision and beyond, although whether in service to building toward fairer class reconciliation or outright revolution was left open. Unlike the right to work, the right to strike was not just a claim to basic provision by another name. It portended more, but precisely what remained unclear. The right to strike remained so controversial that it would not make it into the canonical text of the Universal Declaration of Human Rights (1948).[31]

Despite some radical versions of trade unionism, labor movements ultimately trod a path toward the reconciliationist welfare state. It was not an inevitability, certainly, and it was achieved best where some unions and parties worked for gains in bargaining and representational power in the shadow of others insisting on violent revolution. Trade unions and socialist parties became the central agents—and the male working class they represented became the main beneficiary—of welfare state legislation that aimed at sufficiency and equality alike. There were places (notably the United States) where socialist parties did not survive or unions rarely feinted in the direction of revolution, just as after 1917 there came to be places where revolution succeeded. Some parties and unions remained officially revolutionary in their aims; having been burned by Bismarck's maneuvers, when it became legal again, the eventually massive German Social Democratic Party adopted Marxism in theory in its Erfurt program (1891), while vacillating in practice as activists such as Eduard Bernstein and Rosa Luxemburg vied to define socialist aims. In France, some "anarcho-syndicalists" held out for a *grand soir* of a general strike supposed to bring the system to its knees with one massive blow, and the main organization of trade unions, the Confédération générale du travail, opposed social reform legislation as a bourgeois sham as late as 1928. Yet in the shadow of workingmen and their representatives debating tactics, and perhaps because they were doing so, norms of sufficiency began to crystallize, legislation on the workplace and initial social security regimes were institutionalized, and equality dawned on the horizon as part of the believable agenda of a new form of state.

Notwithstanding the permanence of the debate on the left about whether to argue in terms of rights and what more ambitious ideals to pursue alongside the fulfillment of basic needs, the welfare state became the ultimate prize. The originally Jacobin ideals of sufficient provision and egalitarian distribution finally revived in the cross-class ratification of progressive welfare after Bismarck, notably as socialists and trade unionists embraced equalization of outcomes as a fundamental ideal and were transformed into willing participants by welfare states. The rise of welfare states did as much to saddle forces that had flirted with other outcomes with more egalitarian purposes as vice versa. Compromise between capital and labor as a middle path between libertarianism and revolution formed the aspiration to material equality that welfare states struggled to fulfill alongside a sufficient provision of the good things in life.

Social rights were one version, for those willing to talk about rights at all, of a welfare compromise. In 1982, the great English Marxist social historian Eric Hobsbawm was summoned to Emory University, in the midst of the greatest spike in history of rhetoric about human rights, to explain what labor had contributed. Hobsbawm reminded his audience of the many reasons why workingmen's movements had steered clear of rights in order to focus on power, whether through collective bargaining, democratic representation, or (if they were Marxist revolutionaries) state capture. Hence "the paradox," he concluded. "More than any other force, the labour movement helped to unlock the politico-legal, individualist straitjacket which confined human rights. . . . If the UN Declaration includes economic, social, and educational rights . . . it is primarily due to the historical intervention of labour movements. At the same time labour movements demonstrate the limitations of a 'human rights' approach to politics."[32]

THE COMMUNIST state that grew up on the territory of the old Russian Empire after World War I certainly claimed the Jacobin legacy for itself, but it was in Western welfare states through the 1960s and 1970s that the actual Jacobin legacy was strongest in socioeconomic affairs. Its project, in the tracks of the Jacobin experiment, was to go beyond a sufficient minimum for all citizens in order to achieve some modicum of egalitarian citizenship. However pursued, egalitarian aims were especially prominent in Continental Europe due to traditions of so-called "national economics," the strength of domestic socialism, and the proximity of the new Soviet experiment. Even in England, however, ethical socialists such as the "new liberals," who were acutely sensitive to the value of freedom amid the goals of social reform, moved to argue for egalitarian outcomes. In a famous minority report to a late-Victorian Poor Law reform project, Fabian Beatrice Webb issued a radical call for "a national minimum of civilised life." By twenty years later, as the Great Depression ushered in an egalitarian moment, Christian socialist R. H. Tawney could explain its necessity in the most laudatory terms. "The reason for equalizing, as means and opportunity allow, the externals of life is not that the scaffolding of life is more important than the shrine, or that economic interests, for all their clamour and insistence, possess . . . unique and portentous significance. [It is] to free the spirit of all [and achieve] a much needed improvement in human relations."[33]

The chronology and mechanisms of the birth of the welfare state differed profoundly across space and time. Leading with sufficiency, the different welfare states ended up constraining inequality more and more, ultimately as an end in its own right. It is certainly true that, even in its glory years after World War II in selected West European states, the welfare state has never been "*very* egalitarian—and it does not even really try to be." The often modest extent to which its redistributive effects, even at their most thoroughgoing, have in fact gone beyond achievement of sufficiency to egalitarian outcomes was once, indeed, the source of widespread derision. At the same time, however, it was the welfare state's very embarkation on a project of equality beyond sufficiency that once drew its fiercest criticism for falling short. And it is now confirmed that, through a suite of approaches, the mature national welfare state, shot through with exclusion though it always was, constrained material inequality more than any other political arrangements that modern humanity has learned to bring about. The bar of expectations needs to be set correctly to perceive how fundamentally egalitarian its purposes and many of its tools for achieving those purposes were—as the fullest realization so far of the Jacobin project of policies that pay due attention to sufficient provision without neglecting equality of outcomes.[34]

Before the Great Depression and after experimental responses to it, the social insurance schemes Bismarck introduced in the 1880s were always the dominant form of meeting needs and, later, of furthering equality, since programs could vary tremendously in how redistributive the pooling of collective risk became in practice. Bismarck's constrained and ungenerous version was soon transformed, and not merely by recognition of manifold forms of vulnerability. Elevating French constitutional provisions from 1793 and 1848 into a radiating ideal, the pioneering 1917 Mexican Constitution kicked off a global moment of the ascendancy of social rights in constitutions. The trendsetting constitution of the Weimar Republic (1919) propounded a number of social rights. With a nod to the once-famed internationalism of the left-wing parties, which had suffered so grievous a blow when workers of all countries engaged to the hilt in World War I, it even referred to "an international regulation of the rights of the workers, which strives to safeguard a minimum of social rights for humanity's working class." The canonization of rights for the sake of regulating work became popular in interwar constitutions, perhaps most generously in the 1921 Yugoslav constitution, and did not change much after World War II. As founder of the discipline of comparative constitutional law, Boris Mirkine-Guetzévitch, recorded in 1928, one of the most characteristic "new tendencies" of constitution-making was not just consecrating political and civil rights across Europe after World War I but also augmenting old lists with newfangled economic and social rights. And there was pressure to do so in places without new constitutions: "In the twentieth century, the social meaning of law is no longer a doctrine or a slogan of a clique but life itself,"

Mirkine-Guetzévitch explained. "Nor is it possible to distinguish between the political and social individual, so we witness a transformation not merely of the general theory of the state but of the doctrine of individual rights."[35]

But it took the greatest crisis of capitalism for more than piecemeal reform to take hold, always in connection with egalitarian pressure and whether in the name of social rights or not—most of all in the famously isolated "Nordic model"—before World War II drove the rest of states much further than they had ever gone before. There is no doubt that the constant social pressure of labor activism, whatever its intended ends, contributed strongly to the relatively more egalitarian results than before (or since), most of all when social democratic parties could take control of policies of taxation and redistribution. All along, the possibility—however exaggerated—of working class revolution and its new symbol in the Soviet Union drove egalitarian generosity in response to a mixture of inspiration and fear. No event more than the Russian Revolution and the Soviet experimentation that followed brought a materially egalitarian dream home to so many people. In 1918–19, V. I. Lenin issued (and Nikolai Bukharin and Josef Stalin edited) a "Declaration of the Rights of Toiling and Exploited People," which asserted the prerogatives of workers against capitalists. Two decades later, the Soviet Union's new "Stalin" constitution (1936) laid out the most full-fledged catalog of rights ever propounded, with its most unique attention given to a long catalogue of social rights. But precisely because it stood for the proposition that social justice required political revolution, no one thought the Soviet Union stood for the ascendancy of basic economic entitlements, certainly not alone.[36]

Now claiming to institutionalize socialism, the new state struggled with many problems Marx had not and, like socialists elsewhere, embraced ideals of equality as governing philosophy. The equality that began as class compromise in "bourgeois" states became a distributive ideal in the first worker's state. There were two periods of powerful social leveling: just after 1917, in the experience of the abolition of private property and forced collectivization, and in the 1930s, with the war against "kulaks" or wealthy peasants that turned genocidal. Lenin had anticipated the need in "the first phase" for continued differentiation of income and wealth after exploitation had been abolished. As a new Soviet class structure arose as that phase continued indefinitely, his successor Stalin gave a much-noted speech in 1931 criticizing "equality mongering." But because equality was the "central element" in the utopian thinking the revolution had inspired, the new Soviet state managing its divisions bred outsized dreams of even more equality, just as the Jacobin state had in its time.[37]

More than most have been willing to acknowledge, however, it was rightwing regimes, breaking with parliamentary government, that created their own welfare states focused on sufficiency and equality. Indeed, they were far more directly influential models on Western countries than the Soviet Union was before World War II led to reversals for fascist welfare (outside the Iberian peninsula and, later, in Latin America). All advocates of social justice in the 1930s were aware that welfare and even social rights had become more associated with illiberal states, which were quickest out of the gate in redistributive policy after the Great Depression, not just on the left but also and even preeminently on the right. Under fascist auspices before the stock market crash, the Labor Charter of Italy (1927)—like the Portuguese Constitution (1933), the Labor Charter of Spain (1938), the Brazilian constitutional reforms under dictator Getulio Vargas (1943) after the crash—showed that not merely constitutions but social rights very specifically were part of the agenda of reactionary states. Equality was too, leading far-right regimes to siphon support from previously progressive sources. It is no accident that the inventor of the still most widely used measure of national inequality, Italian statistician Corrado Gini, was a Fascist.[38]

True, National Socialists had condemned the very idea of individual rights—"the year 1789 is hereby eradicated from history," Nazi propagandist Joseph Goebbels crowed shortly after the Nazi seizure of power in 1933—and took the racialized structure of social policy that characterized all welfare states to a genocidal extreme. But the regime made shockingly impressive egalitarian strides for the *Volksgemeinschaft* even as it moved to exclude so many—eventually fatally. After painful memories of the starvation of World War I, during which hundreds of thousands died as a result of blockade, and the hyperinflation soon after, the depression saw Germans looking for policy-enforced subsistence minima that their former monarchist and democratic governments could not provide. And with the commitment to socialism and workers that other right-wing populisms shared, and taking economic nationalism to the point of autarky, the state Adolf Hitler founded became the clearest example not merely on the right but across the political spectrum of how far welfare states could go to create intentionally egalitarian outcomes. Hitler called for "the highest degree of social solidarity . . . for every member of the German race," while pitilessly decreeing it would become the "absolute master" of other races. "The National Socialist German Workers Party was founded on a doctrine of inequality between races," one historian comments, "but it also promised Germans greater equality among themselves than they had enjoyed during either the Wilhelmine empire or the Weimar Republic." And through devices like quadrupled corporate taxation, in the midst of state-funded military buildup (without much thought for who would take care of the debt), the redistributive effects were a great cause of the regime's popular support.[39]

For all its extremism, Hitler's welfare state shared a disturbing amount with other states on the common road to constraining inequality to a historically unprecedented extent. The restriction of the redistributive community to national borders in an age of continuing global empire reflected far more than a reluctant logistical confinement of generosity. In the communist East, Josef Stalin announced a policy of "socialism in one country," and the struggle for welfare, too, occurred country by country. Democratic though they usually were, new states after World War II, starting with India and Israel, were often founded by national socialist worker's parties. And within the borders of each twentieth-century national welfare state, patterns of exclusion privileged male whites (notably in Jim Crow America), conditioning distributive equality on discriminatory exclusion. It was not accidental that the famed Swedish welfare state grew up in close connection with long-lasting eugenic policies, ones that even a future proponent of the expansion of the welfare concept to the world stage, Gunnar Myrdal, originally supported. Even among white males, the roles of socialist parties and trade unions in paving the road toward welfare often meant that the welfare states that emerged favored industrial workers first and foremost, not the categories of people Marx himself had originally disdained so much, the urban *Lumpenproletariat* and the rural peasantry, both often the most destitute. In the case of the female half of the population, the most numerically glaring case, no welfare state designed policies that treated them equally; most often, they took the benefit of wage-earning husbands as proxies for that of their wives. The excluded and marginalized suffered even more.

Sufficiency and equality had come together, the Jacobin ideals revived, but as a model of social justice the national welfare state of the mid-twentieth century left much to be desired. It consecrated a high set of aspirations attempting to balance and resolve sufficiency and equality, but sharing much of the exclusionary spirit of Hitler's welfare state. In the long run, the ideal of human rights would forbid such compromises in the democratic countries where it could become the watchword not simply for foreign victims but also for those domestically subjugated on the grounds of gender, race, disability, or sexual orientation. Yet for all these flaws, the ideology of national welfare included more people in a community of distributive justice than ever before. The ideal of distributive sufficiency that remains powerful today had been consecrated. But achieving unprecedented consensus around a modicum of material equality had also been embraced—a commitment since lost.[40]

THIRTY YEARS after Palmer set off in search of the Jacobin origins of the egalitarian welfare state, a young student at his university at the same time, John Rawls, published his epoch-making *A Theory of Justice* (1971). After an age of national welfare states, Rawls had set out to justify the welfare state's egalitarianism in a new way, formalizing as an ethical theory of distribution what activists and statesmen had begun to bring about in practice. Reviving the early-modern theory of the social contract, Rawls contended that fair distribution must obey his famous "difference principle," which forbade material inequality unless it improved lot of the worst off and not simply the better off. Drawing on and transforming a phrase from British argument, Rawls later insisted he was speaking out in favor of "property-owning democracy." But there is no doubt that his thought reflects the achievements of welfare states stretching back to the Jacobin example.[41]

After World War II and especially after the American Civil Rights Movement, the community of distribution was fully inclusionary for Rawls. As a liberal he ranked personal freedom as the most important value, with fair distribution coming second—though he did signal that it might be acceptable to relax liberal priorities when it came to the developmentalist agenda of the still-new postcolonial states. Still, what is remarkable in retrospect is how Rawls captured a once-dominant egalitarianism that placed limits on hierarchy in the distribution of the good things in life. Ironically, he let loose the owl of Minerva on the achievements of the best liberal welfare states: the difference principle that Rawls championed may never have come closer to fulfillment—especially in his own country—than the day his book was published. His thought sparked a massive philosophical debate about the nature and scope of distributive justice, but it was in a neoliberal age, when national inequality in transatlantic states generally expanded and sometimes exploded. Some even worried that his own commitments to implicitly neoliberal premises about how to justify an egalitarianism of fair shares ruined his last-ditch attempt to save it.[42]

In the long view, however, it was perhaps most revealing that sufficiency went missing in Rawls's thought. Fair distribution was organized around how well the worst off did. But fair distribution was not concerned, either at the initial stage of moral principles or at the later stage of political institutions, with the pressing moral importance of a sufficient minimum of the distribution of the good things in life, even as a first step on the egalitarian journey. It permitted departure from perfect equality only for the sake of the worst off, but it did not concern itself with whether they transcended a line of minimal provision. As one Rawls's most brilliant early critics, legal scholar and fellow Harvard professor Frank Michelman, noticed, in formulating his principle of just distribution, Rawls remained ambivalent about a basic minimum of provision. "A precept for the distribution of material social goods which ignores claims regarding basic needs as such . . . will for many of us seem incomplete," Michelman observed, as part of his own plea to constitutional judges to safeguard minimum standards as entitlements of citizenship.[43]

As judges helping the poor replaced workers transforming society at the center of the imaginary of reform, the goal of sufficiency would loom ever larger in the global political imagination. It never progressed far in the United States, where Michelman hoped to see the Supreme Court act, but it has in the end become vital for the global human rights movement today. Yet that happened as a demand for sufficiency came not to balance and supplement but to displace and leave behind an emphasis on equality. Rawls did not use the phrase *human rights* and in 1971 likely did not know of the Universal Declaration of Human Rights, with its specific social rights— it was not yet famous. In the years after his book, the national welfare state that Rawls theorized faced the objection that it had no implications for global fairness, except that the peoples of the world could strive on their own for their own national welfare states. But in the age of human rights, as the social rights of the global indigent have come into sharper focus, the egalitarian dimension or even preference Rawls still retained—even if for local rather than global purposes—has been abandoned. In the history of distributive theory, John Rawls was the last Jacobin.

2

National Welfare and
the Universal Declaration

In 1949, the English sociologist T. H. Marshall delivered some classic lectures on the welfare state at the University of Cambridge. Marshall offered his thoughts when the extraordinary accomplishments of the Labour Party, in power since 1945, were certain, but the strict limits of those advances— let alone their future reversals—were not yet apparent. Unsurprisingly, therefore, Marshall's triumphalist narrative could end in a climax because of the arrival of the welfare state he and his listeners were experiencing. It is both of great interest and potentially misleading that Marshall famously characterized that climax as the coming of economic and social rights. He was interested as much in the equal relations of British citizens as in sufficient provision for them. And though he rose to the lectern to collect his vastly influential thoughts mere weeks after the General Assembly of the United Nations passed the Universal Declaration of Human Rights on December 10, 1948, he did not mention it—even though the document incorporated the very social rights that Marshall himself put center stage.

A genteel but large-minded heir of English ethical socialism, Marshall was hired after World War II to teach social workers at the London School of Economics by the politician and reformer William Beveridge, who was famed for his World War II report calling for the welfare state. Marshall was fundamentally interested in how social citizenship had been achieved as an overlay on the civil and political citizenship that the centuries prior to the twentieth had birthed. And Marshall's account is entirely about *one nation's* citizenship and its evolution. Indeed, his lecture turns out not so much to vindicate the importance of the category of social rights in the

1940s as to confirm the ambivalence of a fully nationalist welfare aspiration toward the goals of sufficiency and equality, at a moment when Marshall fondly hoped they would harmonize. He was wrong, but his beliefs are essential to understanding the original ambiance of the Universal Declaration—and why so many could afford to ignore it at the time.

Marshall made clear that what truly interested him was the rise of materially egalitarian citizenship under the auspices of the welfare state, not the pursuit of basic provision alone. The essence of social citizenship was not rights. Marshall specifically distinguished the significance of social citizenship in the twentieth century from the earlier view that, so long as indigence were remedied, inequality was allowable or even indispensable. "Citizenship, even in its early forms, was a principle of equality," Marshall insisted. For a long time, however, commitment to equality in the civil and political spheres had had spectacular ramifications for the production of material inequality. Stratification had gone so far that early attempts to set minimum standards in distribution in response to it had to be interpreted as indirect attempts to establish social equality and engage in "class-abatement." As for the turn to the welfare state, it involved even more grandiose aims. As Marshall explained in a critical passage, there was "no longer merely an attempt to abate the obvious nuisance of destitution in the lowest ranks of society." The welfare state, rather, "assumed the guise of action modifying the whole pattern of social inequality. It is no longer content to raise the floor-level in the basement of the social edifice, leaving the superstructure as it was. It has begun to remodel the whole building, and it might even end by converting a skyscraper into a bungalow." What he meant is that it was bringing up how the poor lived so that they were no longer indigent, but not while ignoring how far the rich still towered over them or how much they might even increase their gains.[1]

Stated more clearly by Marshall than by other analysts of the national welfare state in the 1940s, the egalitarian ambiance of social rights is critical to understanding the character of the era and what has changed since. Marshall admitted that, as they had come to work by 1949, the indirect effects of social minimum policies in the various fields of medical care, public housing, and unemployment relief were spotty and had more immediate implications for equality of status than of distribution. Recognized as fellow citizens and afforded a floor of protection, so far people felt more equal in their standing without yet enjoying corresponding material equality with limits to hierarchy. In fact, Marshall acknowledged, sometimes social rights functioned to entrench or even expand distributive inequality: "citizenship is itself becoming the architect of social inequality," he recorded glumly. Ultimately, however, Marshall felt he could place faith in the fact of the evident compression of the income scale and above all the "enrichment of the universal status of citizenship," which allowed significant inequality to persist but within a new conception of national community that moderated the gap between the rich and the rest. Its destiny was to subordinate not just old aristocratic privileges but the new non-egalitarian action of the market to its norms. An ideal of sufficiency was not separate in practice from a principle of distributive equality; the welfare state had fused them in one package.

Remarkably, Marshall's vision, like that of the larger welfare state, was inclusionary and egalitarian for some while exclusionary in the extreme or at least patronizing and subordinating for others. The passage of the British Nationality Act the year before he spoke had formally included hundreds of millions of former imperial subjects as imperial citizens, in tune with the attempt to preserve European empire through reform across the continent. Yet Marshall gloried in the long- and short-term achievements of the British welfare state without ever mentioning the British Empire. He did not mention women, either, who were generally the beneficiaries of social rights in his model only through male family wage and their husband's prerogatives as a default, and at a cost to earlier proposals for welfare more sensitive to the insecurity of women. And Marshall understood social rights to be broad ideals of state reform, not much concerning himself with what would happen if majorities excluded minorities, or for that matter if majorities did not want social provision anymore. But then, no one considered social rights in the ascendant as apt for judicial enforcement like other liberties in the common law or in constitutions elsewhere. For all these shortcomings, however, social rights did breathe the materially egalitarian spirit of their moment, and they struggled to include more people in social justice than ever before.[2]

Investigating what social rights meant within the larger ecology of the egalitarian national welfare state in its era of triumph is not only crucial for charting the later trajectory of human rights; it is a valuable exercise for its own sake. The association of rights with the libertarian political economy of their time had occurred in the century before, and this had led many reformers to doubt their viability as progressive tools. Now, in the 1940s, the category of "social rights" received a new level of promotion. Above all, social rights gained currency at the climax of distributive equality in global history and in a founding relation with it. In this ambiance, the category of social rights had various functions, but the most important were signaling agreement about unprecedented intervention by the state in economic affairs and distinguishing liberal democracy from rival visions for the welfare state (even though authoritarian states both left and right trafficked in the principles). Agreement was, however, far from universal: a great many intellectuals were still not altogether convinced that the language and politics of rights could ever serve the ideal of sufficiency, let alone equality, in practice.[3]

The rise of the welfare state during World War II across the North Atlantic was the most important and is, in turn, the most neglected context for the Universal Declaration of Human Rights (1948). It is the most decisive explanation for both its own marginality and that of the larger political language of rights that it attempted to consecrate. The fact that the Universal Declaration was rediscovered in recent decades, as commitments to national welfare waned, made it close to unintelligible as a product of its time, but it fit snugly in its era as a charter or template for national welfare states and a canonization of some premises of twentieth-century citizenship. It was centrally about distributive justice, not merely the liberties of mind, speech, and person that made "human rights" so prominent decades later. It was about national communities and their redemption, not primarily a warrant for supranational concern. It envisioned the welfare state at home as a talisman against the geopolitics of war, not some supranational authority for a politics of atrocity prevention abroad. It is perhaps above all this fact that makes newcomers to the document in a neoliberal age surprised to find it focused on the modular reproduction of the welfare state, not the founding of the global project of monitoring despots for the worst abuses and genocidal violence before all else.

And the Universal Declaration was connected with the believable empowerment and intervention of the state, not the prestige of non-governmental action or the cautious reform of judges with which social rights became bound up in a neoliberal age. For all these reasons, the Universal Declaration has to be reread. Most historians of the document, celebrating it for an internationalization of rights politics that occurred decades later, have omitted the welfare state that it canonized. The Universal Declaration has to be seen circling around the project of national welfare. It was the satellite, not the sun. But if it orbited the welfare state, vigorous debates about what sort of welfare state to build, not to mention uncertainty over whether rights were the proper language for imagining the equalization of classes, left it in the shadows for a very long time.[4]

FOR ALL the prehistory of rights naming citizen entitlements to sufficiency, it was during the course of World War II that specific events set the stage for the full-throated promotion of social rights in subsequent global politics. The setting for this moment was geopolitical and philosophical alike. It reflected years during which, as the war continued, reformers wrestled with American president Franklin Delano Roosevelt's 1941 State of the Union promise of "freedom from want," struggling to give it meaning as vital to a fair world—especially after the United States was goaded into military alliance against the Axis later that year. Above all, it demonstrated the growing strength into the 1940s of an egalitarian impulse beyond the terms of sufficient provision.

Not that social rights principles were new. Against the background of French social rights, stretching back via 1848 to 1793, and the Mexican and Weimar constitutions at the close of World War I that kicked off interwar trends, the rights provisions of the Soviet "Stalin" constitution of 1936 stood out. Among many other promises, it offered the first right to leisure ever constitutionalized, which the Universal Declaration later included. But by the time of World War II, not only did communists have no particular lock on announcing social rights; they also continued to symbolize the ideology of revolution, balancing their promotion of sufficient protections and equal stature of workers with a critique of bourgeois democracy and its rights and liberties. As a result, even more socialists across the world were compelled to debate whether to prioritize the search for power over other ends. They had to decide whether to champion any rights, and whether the right of each worker to the whole product of his labor counted for most—especially since unlike early-modern lists of basic entitlements, the Universal Declaration no longer featured a human right to revolution. Everywhere, "social" states were the vanguard of history. Needless to say, all the East European countries conquered for communism after World War II advertised their social goals. But in West Germany, the new constitution (called the Basic Law, 1949) likewise named the country a "democratic and social union"—though without enacting social rights. The postcolonial Indian Constitution (1950) named "justice, social, economic, and political" (the order of the terms is revealing) its highest end. Similarly, the Israeli state, founded by socialists, mentioned social before political rights in its Declaration of Independence of the same moment. Spain and Portugal, unique states under the rule of right-wing authoritarians that survived World War II, paid much attention to social provision too.[5]

In short, entitlements to sufficient provision had already become almost a constitutional orthodoxy under both capitalism and communism—in the new fundamental law of nearly all Continental European states, in the French and Italian constitutions in 1946, as they already were on the Latin American scene, and in East European states before and after communist takeovers. It was true that, in 1941, Roosevelt had both given that State of the Union address promising "four freedoms"—including freedom from want—and incorporated its rhetoric in the Atlantic Charter, which formalized principles of American alliance with Winston Churchill while the United States was still hamstrung from entering the war in earnest, as it did late that year. But it was stating an increasingly conventional, though not universal, wisdom, and late in the day. Some new constitutions, like Ireland's shortly before World War II and that of India itself shortly after, were not ready to name such entitlements as matters of rights, choosing instead the concept of "directive principles" for state policy for the same precepts. Whatever the difference in nomenclature, by the late 1940s such themes were undeniably a necessary responsibility of a modern state and therefore of the citizenry to one another.[6]

As one might expect, given the long association of the very idea of *les droits de l'homme* with French politics, social rights were most vigorously announced during wartime itself in France during the Resistance rather than in Great Britain (where national welfare was never strongly associated with individual rights) or America (where social rights had their own idiosyncratic trajectory). "All the constitutional projects presented by members of the European Resistance," recalled Mirkine-Guetzévitch (a Russian Jew who rose far as a French professor before fleeing to New York during wartime), "insisted resolutely on the defense of social rights." Common ground in social rights was easy to find among socialists, communists, and social Catholics, whether they wrote from overseas or in clandestine networks under German occupation and Vichy rule. Each tradition found its own way to this conclusion. The Catholic philosopher Jacques Maritain explained in books parachuted into and messages radioed home to France during the war how religious natural law justified certain modern social rights within a communitarian framework. Famed leftwing Catholic

Emmanuel Mounier, though he had flirted with the Vichy government and would later turn angrily on such things, endorsed a "Declaration of the Rights of Persons and Communities." For secular socialists it was the same. Léon Blum, former Popular Front prime minister, explained in his best-selling work, published on his release from Buchenwald, that "socialism will bring the glorious slogans of the French Revolution to their complete satisfaction and true justification." Or, as Mirkine-Guetzévitch commented on this passage, "By proclaiming the subordination of social reformism to the rights of man, Blum decisively ended the old quarrel of individualists and collectivists."[7]

But while social rights became popular in constitutions West and East from this moment, outside the Austrian and West German cases, they did not become a slogan for popular mobilization. Next to no one considered them standards for judicial enforcement either; instead, they marked the ascendancy of class compromise and the fact that labor power deserved a seat at the table of government, even outside of regimes that ruled in its name. In the West, the trade unions that were so pivotal to the origins of social rights reached the zenith of their power upon entering bargains with employers under the supervision of states in hopes of securing a better share of industrial power and improved class outcomes. Wherever socialism or communism were strong, it went almost without saying that some form of social minimum would be included among the highest priorities.

And there were still many frameworks for a social minimum other than that of social rights—which in any case tended to be described in expansive terms. As for equality, social protection was popularly understood to be about the moderation of class privilege—if it did not require outright revolution. In Marshall's Great Britain, for example, there was next to no usage of the concept of social rights in the glory years of the welfare state's creation. In his celebrated 1942 report, Beveridge had not described minimum standards provided by "cradle to grave" social protections in terms of individual rights. That Marshall in 1949 chose to work with the notion of social rights may indeed have been largely accidental; he gives no impression of having been influenced by any of the wartime or immediate postwar social rights talk elsewhere. And as for so many of his contemporaries, not to mention ancestors in the renovation of citizenship back to William Godwin, for Marshall, talk of social rights really prompted more attention to welfarist duties. "If citizenship is invoked in the defence of rights," he observed, "the corresponding duties of citizenship cannot be ignored, [requiring that one's] acts should be inspired by a lively sense of responsibility towards the welfare of the community."[8]

As before in its prehistory, in the 1940s, the national welfare state was the essential setting for those who did choose to frame their commitment to sufficiency in terms of rights, and either way the stakes were always to connect that commitment to an egalitarian project. That is why the very meaning of social rights in the 1940s depended on the parallel and more powerful breakthrough of the dream of egalitarian welfare. Outside Iberia and, later, Latin America, the fascist welfare state now seemed outmoded because of the military collapse of the countries that had opted for it. But its onetime popularity suggested that the future would be controlled by a move far in the direction of solidarity and social redistribution. Compounding the upheavals of the Great Depression, the war itself had gone far to create lived solidarity and augment pressure for social redistribution. It also empowered the working class to make gains it could not have achieved before. Socialism looked to be on the march, and its visions of postwar welfare in its various guises were asserted most optimistically and competitively, in the shadow of the Soviet ally's appeal, to its own people and many others. And because the working class had been swept so deeply into the war, equality's prominence as the conflict wound down—with the promise of social rights trailing it by a good measure—made clear that the bill was due.

Unlike the fascists, the Soviets had actually based their assertions about the importance of sufficiency on claims of universal rights. But they were more renowned, of course, for calling for a classless society (though it was unclear how unequal it would allow citizens to remain). By 1945, the U.S.S.R. had gone through one incredibly successful five-year plan to achieve both ends and had since kicked off two others. Among those who cared about sufficiency and equality under the auspices of a strong and interventionist state, it was impossible to look away. Much as in the West, the "great patriotic war" of 1939–1945 required a Soviet return to more generous policies of distributive equalization at home. A more universalistic egalitarianism than fascists could countenance surged in global consciousness as the Soviets fought back from Moscow to approach the gates of Berlin; American dithering on social policy had far less impact. It thus mattered more to the postwar enactment of egalitarian policies than did any other factor that the Soviet Union emerged as a decisive victor over the Nazis—not the cordoned off and weak pariah it had been after World War I but a geopolitical force and a moral exemplar for all its faults.[9]

Similar intermittent equalizing drives would occur with the Sovietization of the rest of Eastern Europe from 1944, as well as in China after its 1949 communist transition, albeit with much less impressive results. On the Soviet model, all of the regimes presented themselves to their populations and the world as worker's states, the fulfillment of socialist party and trade union activism that now refused to work within the limits of private property. To state the obvious, equality did not simply materialize; even under communism, it required policy and faced strict limits. But it was socialism in power that taught everyone, East and West, that distributive justice would depend on what kind of distributive programs industrial states enacted—even or especially when socialism was in power. Nowhere was absolute distributive equality seriously envisioned, let alone pursued, but the structure of society was transformed and hierarchy was drastically reduced. It would have been anathema on the two sides of what emerged as the Cold War split to describe both as engaged in a similar sort of welfare state creation—a once scandalous thesis of a Cold War theory of "convergence." But there was a kernel of truth to it, with capitalists and communists differing more over whether to find room for democratic governance in a planned economy than on whether to balance sufficiency and equality under its auspices.[10]

In the West, as fascism died, the suite of state tools to plan the egalitarian welfare state was enormous and certainly did not track the fulfillment of individual social rights precisely, even if the latter emerged as one rhetoric justifying policy. These tools took different forms in different places. After years of conservative rule, the British Labour Party's superintendence of extraordinary transformations over a few short years after 1945 stood out to all observers, as had the Nordic model before it, because they were achieved in a free society. There and elsewhere, the newly invented science of macroeconomics had now grown up as an adjunct to the duty to continue full employment after the wartime state. In continental European economies, nationalization of industry was rife. At a lower but still historically radical level of ambition were much copied policies that intruded deep into the "free" market, especially through antitrust laws, or allowed for vast redistribution thanks to higher taxation than before or since. Empowerment of the working class to enter social compromise, with a turn away from violent strikebreaking practices and historically extraordinary generosity in unionization and bargaining rules, was also critical.

In this reformist mix, proposals for economic and social rights for individuals were included, but were merely some policies among others as welfare states came about, designed to cushion shocks for those for whom sufficiency still needed to be achieved, and galvanizing those over that threshold to undertake social mobility under their own power. Labor rights made sense, not solely for their own sake, but for empowering a class to enter fairer compromise. The huge prestige of the Beveridge plan, coming after the Allied victory at El Alamein, portended an end to very dark years and gave Britons—not to mention a broader transatlantic audience—cause for hope for a future social improvement that bordered on the euphoric. Without an interventionist state and egalitarian ends, social entitlements on their own would have been a very different enterprise. "Fair shares for all," a phrase which originated in early wartime rationing policy, slowly expanded into a peacetime ideal in the Labour Party's 1945 election declaration and beyond. In the single best stocktaking of welfarist ambition—aside from Marshall's lectures—influential University College London professor of public administration William Robson insisted that the goal had become not merely "to level up" but also "to level down"—"to establish a ceiling as well as a floor" and "to impose a national maximum of individual wealth as well as a national minimum." Aged English ethical socialist R. H. Tawney, revising his *Equality* in order to take stock on the quarter-century since the Great Depression, rightly acknowledged that "a somewhat more equalitarian social order is in the process of emerging."[11]

The imperatives of sufficiency and equality meant, in a sense, that not human rights so much as a vision of distributive national socialism still set the bar of achievement for states and citizens, even when and where socialism did not take command or, as in the unique case of the United States, even exist. Communist regimes set up national welfare states, accounting for their widespread appeal at home and abroad despite their terroristic shortcomings. Another model was explicitly social democratic, with that movement capitalizing on its 1930s Nordic success to achieve breakthrough in Great Britain. Where such social democracy did not win—in part because of the strength of communism in places such as France and Italy, forcing socialist parties into two-front wars—a new ideology of Christian Democracy came to the fore and built welfare states according to ideologies of religious care. Typically though not always conservative, this way of thinking about social order answered social democracy from the right, and with slightly less enthusiasm for the state, with a kindred set of proposals about the necessity of redistributive provision. Influenced on the social question since the late-nineteenth-century days of Pope Leo XIII by the explosion of socialist parties and trade unions, Catholic social thought now survived interwar uncertainty about whether a democratic regime could host just accommodations among professions (which it preferred to the notion of classes) and sponsor the Church's reconciliation of the interests of capital and labor. Updating these earlier teachings for a confusing world in which communism and fascism proved popular alternatives to liberalism, the interwar pope Pius XI had first invoked "social justice" as a Catholic notion too. "To each," he wrote in the encyclical Quadragesimo Anno (1931), "must be given his own share of goods, and the distribution of created goods, which, as every discerning person knows, is laboring today under the gravest evils due to the huge disparity between the few exceedingly rich and the unnumbered propertyless, [and] must be effectively called back to and brought into conformity with the norms of the common good, that is, social justice." The resolution of World War II opened new pathways for a socialized liberal democracy under Christian auspices. New Christian Democratic parties took command across Continental Western Europe. All of them were equally parties of "the social" and built their own versions of an egalitarian welfare state with their own suite of tools.[12]

THE DREAM of the new egalitarian welfare state was fundamental to ideological debates about social rights at the end of World War II, which evolved from promotion during the conflict itself, when ideal commitments could remain vague, to being hashed out in real policies in the postwar period. In 1943, Julius Stone, an English-born international lawyer writing from Australia about the meaning of the Atlantic Charter, argued that there was a plurality of approaches to what Roosevelt had memorably dubbed "freedom from want." All agreed it implied new imperatives for the state, but on a spectrum of intervention. The two main plans in contention were "social and economic betterment without radical change in the economic structure," which Stone then associated with Roosevelt, and a more thoroughgoing socialist transformation of the economy advocated by London School of Economics socialist and occasional Labour Party consultant Harold Laski as well as other Marxist theorists. In between, Stone linked the "remarkable revival of the popularity of Declarations of the Rights of Man" with an "eclectic" approach that involved "a searching out of evils and the framing of proposals to meet each particular evil without much reference to economic causation." The fact that social rights took the form of a *list* allowed the notion to be associated with targeted interventions in the economy, doing neither nothing nor too much. It was a highly penetrating comment about the wartime excitement around social rights, mistaken only in that it did not anticipate how, as the din of battle subsided, many people—including Roosevelt himself—shifted toward eclectic rhetoric in the face of the even greater popularity of socialism.[13]

Even more important, intellectuals fanned out to capture the slogan of social rights for democratic rather than totalitarian countries, even though it was the latter that had an impressive claim on the rhetoric's origins. The ascendancy of this invidious argument was intended to make clear that the liberal democratic countries could achieve social justice too—not just freer but fairer societies. Karl Polanyi, a refugee from Austria who spent the war in London and the best remembered thinker about the relationship between rights, justice, and the economics of this moment, put it well in his 1944 classic *The Great Transformation.* Founding a tradition later pursued by Edward Thompson, James Scott, and others, he looked back to the long ago premodern or away to the still-feudal peasant world for a society in which the "economy" was subordinate to communal social norms. The crux of politicizing distribution now that the modern economy had become "disembedded" and subordinated everything to it, Polanyi explained, was to do so without loss to the personal freedoms—freedoms that a depoliticized economy had successfully achieved in the nineteenth century for the wealthy alone. "The institutional separation of politics and economics, which proved a deadly danger to the substance of society," he observed, "almost automatically produced freedom at the cost of justice." Only a blind enthusiast for restoring the balance would deny that it risked personal liberty; but fortunately the risk that had to be courted did not have to be incurred. As Polanyi explained, "Every move towards integration in society should be accompanied by an increase in freedom; moves toward planning should comprise the strengthening of the rights of the individual in society. . . . Such a society can afford to be both just and free." At least some of the work of social justice, Polanyi added, was to be achieved by expanding the list of rights into the economic domain. "Rights of the citizen hitherto unacknowledged must be added to the Bill of Rights." Even so, Polanyi warned, "No mere declaration can suffice: institutions are required to make rights effective."[14]

Polanyi touched on the need to establish a free and fair society through rights only in passing. The same year, sociologist Georges Gurvitch spent part of his time in exile in New York during the war writing the first overall book on social rights ever published, which made the same point at greater length. Entitled *The Declaration of Social Rights*, Gurvitch's book appeared in French in 1944 and English in 1946 and established him as the chief intellectual promoter of the concept for decades. Gurvitch emphasized the congenital linkage of social rights not simply to democracy but also to the democratic planning state. Social rights were part of a liberal drive to "economic democracy" that required a massive turn toward state planning, even as Gurvitch and others were quite intent to insist that the birth of the new planned economy and the annunciation of social rights by no means meant the death of personal freedom.[15]

For those seeking a middle path between communism and fascism for the sake of a reformed democracy, the very idea of a "social right" signaled a move toward the socialization of governance that the individual freedom implied by rights had once forbidden. What if securing the first required the constraint of the second? What if, indeed, political freedom demanded more state, not less, and constraint of economic freedom rather than its protection? In this view, the notion of "social" in "social rights" referred not solely to a specific domain of governance like economic relations; instead, it also captured a new collectivist mentality in all spheres and rudely hauled the older concept of rights into a new era. The phrase "social rights" fit the bill because it alchemically combined long opposing elements and harmonized the claims of society and the claims of the individual. (For others, the phrase was a sleight of hand or a play on words for all the same reasons.)

Gurvitch's own evolving thinking to the point of advocating "social rights" in the mid-1940s concisely illustrated how social rights emerged through the embrace of collective interdependence without prejudice to adequate personal freedom. His beginnings as a Russian liberal before his flight to France had involved a great interest in rights in the history of what became his adoptive country—but not yet an interest in social rights. As a professor in Strasbourg before World War II, Gurvitch had become well-known in jurisprudence and sociology for offering an account of "social law." As Gurvitch elaborated it over a decade, his sociology was "pluralist" and saw the purpose of the state not as absorbing or bringing about so much as making possible the interdependence of social relations. At stake now, he explained in introducing his thought, in 1941, on his arrival in the United States (where he taught at the New School for Social Research, alongside many fellow emigres), was whether democracy could refine its own interdependence in the face of the social "fusion" that totalitarian states presented. Introducing social rights was a modest revision to but also a subtle departure from this framework: without reneging on his commitment to the need for social interdependence, rights clarified the democratic carapace under which it takes place. It was convenient for Gurvitch that in French, to make the move from social law to social rights, he merely needed to shift from the singular to the plural: *droit social* became *droits sociaux*.[16]

Like Mirkine-Guetzévitch, an émigré in flight from the revolution in his home country before World War II, Gurvitch supposed that the Soviet Union had fulfilled a vast range of social rights through top-down imposition, and the critical step to take now was to preserve the virtues of "bourgeois" freedom without the vices the communists had more clearly committed to overcoming. "It is indisputable that the inspirations and intentions of this [Soviet] State are incomparably better than those of its predecessor, because its main effort is directed toward the liberation of man's labor from the domination of money." Such examples of wartime admiration for what the Soviet Union had done under the regrettable auspices of absolute power were not hard to find. Hersch Lauterpacht, a Galician-born English international lawyer whose proposals to transcend the national forum for rights protection were generally spurned in the 1940s, nevertheless thought a great deal about the content of rights schemes at every scale when writing his wartime study issued by the American Jewish Committee in 1945. Revealingly, Lauterpacht took the radical step of concluding that it was time to exclude any right to private property from lists of entitlements, certainly if the right was considered absolute. "That character of sanctity and inviolability has now departed from the right of property," he observed. The Soviet Union had disrupted a millennium of expectations by abolishing it, but even absent this radical step, Lauterpacht argued, "private property has tended increasingly to be regarded not only as a right but also as a social function and duty. In States in which private property is the basis of the economic structure, it has become the object of State interference through taxation, death duties, and regulation in pursuance of general welfare, on a scale so wide as to render its inclusion in a fundamental Bill of Rights somewhat artificial."[17]

Social rights thus held out the prospect of transforming a language forged in one age for the sake of another. Its genius as a language was that, in the face of totalitarian experiences, the notion maintained individual freedom by converting the social justice proposed outside liberalism by full-blown collectivists into matters of personal entitlement. Enthusiasm for planning gave many supporters of social rights reason to analogize their cause to the liberal revolutions that originally gave political rights their importance. The old challenge had been political feudalism and tyranny, which required rights to limit the state. The new and supplementary menace since industrialization was "economic feudalism" and the expansion of tyrannical power beyond the state proper into the non-state territory where private entities, especially large corporations, exerted unconscionable sway over individuals. At times, the analogy was taken so far that the spirit of social rights as individual privileges was interpreted in a profoundly anti-hierarchical way to imply the end of economic "aristocracy." The goal, Gurvitch explained, had to be "escaping at the same time from the totalitarian danger and from the individualistic anarchy which leads to industrial feudalism." Wartime taught him that social rights were the true essence of the revolution that now must function to harmonize and socialize rather than merely liberate individuals.[18]

As Gurvitch more than Marshall most clearly recognized, however, the Soviets exemplified a broader difficulty of state-accorded social protections for the new era. If rights could name those protections, the new entitlements were nonetheless in tension with the stereotype that the whole purpose of rights is to limit the power of the state and to allow aggrieved parties to hold it accountable. Accorded by states as wise policies from above, social rights in between and after the world wars were not intended to provide a basis for ongoing agitation from below, and certainly not a basis for demands for enforcement (including judicial enforcement). One of the most striking facts about social rights, even in the age of their twentieth-century constitutionalization, especially compared to the last few decades, is that there was almost no debate about how they were to be enforced, and judicial enforcement was far from anyone's mind. Social rights in the 1940s had not even come to be regarded as categorical "trumps" in policy formulation; instead, they were regulatory guidelines for states struggling to provide citizen welfare. In that spirit, they were linked to the idealization of high-capacity states and their empowerment to save the public realm from private interests, rather than to force public power to vindicate fully "private" rights.[19]

Social rights were so top-down in this era that many of their own supporters worried that they still sat uncomfortably with the background value of personal autonomy that the idea of rights consecrated. Across the Atlantic, social rights in the era of the welfare state's birth were a "language of the state." The fact that, outside the United States, many new constitutions went so far as to honor historic trade union activism by naming social protections as individual rights did not mean the principles were possible to assert against state power, in order to constrain or direct it. In fact, nearly the reverse, as Gurvitch observed: "the Bourgeois States and the Social [i.e., communist] States appear here as the only real subjects of the new rights, which they affirm in their capacity as servant, protector, benefactor, and master." A state that updated the terms of citizenship, whether communist or "democratic," threatened to become excessively managerial rather than genuinely participatory, as in fact occurred whether to the east of the Iron Curtain or to the west. Gurvitch's warning was in this sense prescient of a long age of bureaucratic welfare to come, whether under communist or capitalist auspices: "If the problem of Social Law and rights could be reduced to the State's regimentation of relief, rehabilitation, and distribution of material satisfactions, the authoritarian and totalitarian regimes could, perhaps, be considered in principle as well fitted for the realization of 'social rights' as the democracies."[20]

Given such anxieties, Gurvitch's own proposals for a bill of social rights—he presented both a draft and an article-by-article commentary—were less oriented to achieving some ethical standard of distributive justice than to what he saw as a deeper goal of social integration with assistance from the state, but not wholly defined by it. "The Social Law being a law of integration," he insisted, "the *Social Rights* proclaimed by the new bills must be *rights of participation by groups and individuals* in the autonomous and self-governing wholes in which they are integrated, rights guaranteeing the democratic character of these latter: rights of worker, consumer, and common man to participate in the national community and to co-operate within it on equal footing with the citizen." Most of Gurvitch's draft articles insisted on a generous package of entitlements to work and, for those who could not, to subsist, thanks to the welfare state. The consumption right was one to "maintenance in conditions worthy of human rights, e.g., guaranteeing him sufficient assistance for minimal comfort." But Gurvitch also accorded a more egalitarian (if vague) "right to share in the distribution of the fruits and benefits of the national economy." And he was quite clear on the principle, however instrumental, that property and the economy generally would need to serve social integration. "All the country's wealth, whoever may be its owner," Gurvitch explained, "is subordinated to the Right of the Nation."[21]

For spokesmen such as Gurvitch, social rights expressed a new mode of socialized citizenship in which a set of minimum entitlements meant far more generosity than sufficient provision for basic needs. Authorizing unprecedented state intrusion in economic affairs and even the necessity of state planning, the highest goals were to fend off the threat of a new depression and to create and maintain conditions for egalitarian growth and prosperity. "The *social control of liberty* has thus introduced itself in every domain of life. But to what extent? The whole problem of democracy lies in that question," Mirkine-Guetzévitch wrote, aware the agreement easily broke down within the new consensus. One thing was sure: "Social control must serve the collective without erasing the individual."[22]

THE UNITED NATIONS General Assembly voted the Universal Declaration through as a template for national welfare states in December 1948. That this occurred was not terribly important at the time, in view of the campaign long since embraced to set up welfare states from place to place. In fact, the path from 1944 through the following four years looks different when social rights come to the fore and when they are put in context. Given the canonization of social rights in new constitutions since 1917, it was entirely unsurprising that they accompanied political and civil rights in their transit into the international sphere. As John Somerville, an expert in Soviet philosophy at Hunter College, commented, now that fascism had been put down, neither the capitalists nor the communists were opposed in principle to anything on the standard list of rights. Almost no one in the negotiations disputed the inclusion of social rights, although everyone knew that the ideals that were going to be canonized in the Universal Declaration were far from universally supported back home, especially in the United States.[23]

Soon after the United Nations Charter of summer 1945, which alluded to human rights without specifying what they were, efforts toward a Universal Declaration began, under the authority of the Economic and Social Council (human rights having figured in the preamble of the Charter and then as part of the humanitarian rather than the security purposes of the organization). There was never any serious doubt that social rights would figure in the document, as they did in every single draft statement and most of the prior constitutions the various United Nations bodies considered during the two-year process.[24]

From the first negotiations over the Universal Declaration, representatives of the Soviet Union and other communist states were proud of their commitment to the various rights of workers (they were less enthusiastic about housing and food as rights), but it is false to say that their primary emphasis fell on economic and social rights. Their dominant position in foreign affairs at the time, born of a perception of geopolitical weakness, was the defense of national sovereignty. That those who wanted any rights should select socialism as their economic philosophy was otherwise the main Soviet message, not the preeminence of specifically economic rights. In the early days of the negotiations, a "right to equality" was mooted. The American Federation of Labor, for example, called for "a constantly more equitable distribution of the national income and wealth" in its submission, and the Soviet representative (who bickered with the AFL as representative of "bourgeois" labor) proposed going beyond equality of individual status to reach the equality of social conditions. Neither version of distributive egalitarianism, however, made it further in the discussion. Thereafter, when it came to the substance of the declaration, the Soviets and their allies dedicated their main energies to agitating for the prohibition of discrimination rather than for economic and social rights. The Soviets also rallied around the self-determination of peoples.[25]

The unanimity as to the inclusion of economic and social rights in the Universal Declaration is completely unsurprising. After its preamble's allusion to the Four Freedoms, several such provisions figured uncontroversially across the negotiations and in the final document: the right to work, and the right to various forms of social provision for those who could not. Even the sometimes ridiculed right to rest and leisure entered the Universal Declaration drafts from the first. A matter of slower consensus—though they were still inserted in an early stage, after trade union pressure in the Economic and Social Council—were rights involving trade union membership. The Universal Declaration, thanks to several constitutional precedents, in the end guaranteed the right to form trade unions. No right to strike, however, made it in; it was still too controversial. How to include property, given the states that had abolished it in private form and the commitment of all supporters of national welfare to yoking it to social purposes, proved more contentious, but the problem was solved by omitting the word "private" from the Universal Declaration's provision on the topic.[26]

Even social rights with relatively newer credentials, such as the right to health, invited no fundamental skepticism. While it was once again Latin American states that contributed the most before World War II to the notion that modern citizens were entitled to some modicum of medical care, the notion took a quantum leap when the World Health Organization (WHO) announced in its 1946 constitution a commitment to "the highest attainable level" of health as a right. This extraordinarily generous commitment was notable in several respects. It went far beyond the characteristic of social rights that promised a minimum of entitlements to a good or service of which wealthier individuals and families could justifiably buy more. It was so radical a promise that the Universal Declaration itself bypassed it, speaking more weakly of "the right to a standard of living adequate for the health and well-being of himself and of his family, including food, clothing, housing and medical care and necessary social services." (The more florid language would return in later international law.) Finally, with the brief exception of the International Labour Organization, no other entity in the alphabet soup of emerging specialized agencies the United Nations formulated its agenda around human rights in the 1940s. And despite the WHO's own constitution, health care did not come to be broadly conceptualized and pursued as a human right until decades later. Yet the very fact that the unusual moral ideal was possible to outline in 1946 reflected the conventional opinion that one of the greatest tasks of the new welfare states was to achieve some standard of medical care, along with public health management and disease control measures.[27]

Of course, by 1946–48, there was much more abstraction about the setting of the entitlements and much less acknowledgment of how the rights depended on the planning state. But there is something ironic about the Universal Declaration when it is restored to its proper historical status of a charter for national welfare states rather than narrated melodramatically on its own. For a long time, the world did not seem to need such a thing. That the Universal Declaration was so ignored for so long in largest part depended on how late it came. No one has found examples of national settings where, at the late date of 1948, the Universal Declaration proved relevant to determining what sort of welfare state to frame or how to combat enemies who disagreed. Its low visibility may have been due to the fact that it came so long after the high tide of welfarist aspiration, when battle lines were already drawn and repetitious wars of position about how far to go and through which institutions were already underway. The compelling truth, in short, is how belated and uninfluential international norms were on the ongoing welfare experimentation in its various guises, as states each embarked on a national economic project. International in source and form, the Universal Declaration does not appear to have added much to the pre-existing ideology of national welfare in providing a template for what already existed.

As for the rest of the world, the document's uses in envisioning welfare were scant. Colonial powers in Western Europe arranged for the document itself to be studiously neutral as to whether nation-states would provide the sole site for welfare, or whether empires engaging in reform—notably when it came to labor standards—could make the same claim. By the same token, the Universal Declaration was mostly irrelevant to anticolonial ideology, except perhaps within the remnant, mostly African trusteeship program the United Nations resurrected after World War II from the earlier League of Nations mandates system of colonial guardianship. It is even an open question whether, given that it largely reflected constitutional orthodoxy, the Universal Declaration served its core purpose as a template once anticolonial movements won sovereignty. Global constitutions framed during the high era of the welfare state around the world relied mainly on prior national constitutions, including the Weimar or Soviet when it came to social rights, and consulted but did not privilege the Universal Declaration among a mix of sources. All the new states reproduced the tension between sufficiency and equality in aspiring to national welfare, but they did not require a formal charter for national welfare to do so.

Then there was the crucial ambiguity about how precisely the Universal Declaration related to the deepest aspirations of the welfare state. Registering the state of constitutional orthodoxy when it came to political economy, the Universal Declaration, as its preamble says, declared social rights as "a high standard of achievement for peoples and nations." In the thinking of the period, the demand for a floor of sufficiency harmonized with a desire for a ceiling on inequality—or the floor was placed so high that any contrast between the one and the other made little sense. The very strength of egalitarianism at the time, as a more demanding imperative of socialist parties, trade unions, and others concerned with the gap between the wealthy and the middling classes, affected the articulation of social rights. Yet in its text, the Universal Declaration made no explicit reference and paid no mind to distributive equality. Perhaps the fact that the document failed to capture a strong contemporary impulse to social equality well enough, and not merely a social minimum, is the critical one to account for why it was so ignored in its time—and why it could later become retroactively so idealized in a neoliberal age.

And the Universal Declaration left as very speculative how the annunciation of social rights would ever be internationalized beyond setting up a template for nations, as if the richer and poorer alike could establish social justice with equal ease, and as if the international economy were not relevant to doing so. Through the war, however, welfare was everywhere established as national welfare, and the same fate awaited the idea of social rights. "We have founded [the United Nations] upon a principle of national sovereignty," Harold Laski bitterly observed in 1947, "that is on any rational showing wholly incompatible with the fulfillment of its purposes." Not only was it belated and uninfluential, but the Universal Declaration also did very little to portend a post-national solution to either immiseration or inequality. True, its preamble referred to "progressive measures, national and international," while a late article referred to "national effort and international co-operation," but practically no one seriously envisioned a cross-border politics of social rights, let alone a global program of equality.[28]

DESPITE the promotion and theorizing of social rights, and despite their ratification as norms in a new international template for national welfare, the long progressive skepticism toward rights as tools of social reform did not simply disappear in the 1940s—especially not when so many intellectuals were still unsure that sufficiency or equality were achievable within the capitalist welfare state. When UNESCO, the United Nations' education arm, organized an inquiry of intellectual opinion in 1946–47 in parallel with the processes that led to the Universal Declaration, the caution before any proposed rights revival—including the now ascendant notion of social rights—was exceptionally plain. Worry, in fact, came predominantly from socialist and social democratic partisans of the consensus around national welfare, who dwelled on the great uncertainties of the consecration of social rights.[29]

Strangely, for all the attention the processes surrounding the Universal Declaration have received, and even the UNESCO survey, the contents of the book that resulted from the survey have rarely been seriously read. The symposium is most famous for Jacques Maritain's lapidary assurance that everyone involved agreed on the substance of human rights on the condition that nobody asked how they could agree given their divergent metaphysics. The text shows, however, that it remained the vocation of intellectuals to keep posing questions and, when it came to social rights, they could not muster enthusiastic answers. The focus of UNESCO's own memorandum on the topic, as the great Lithuanian-French philosopher Emmanuel Levinas observed at the time, was whether the notion of individual rights could survive the enormous contemporary emphasis on social reconstruction. "Personal freedom is inconceivable without economic liberation," as he put it, "while the organization of economic freedom is not possible without an enslavement for the moral person—temporary but for an indeterminate duration." Nobody could deny the paradox. And within the symposium itself, many people expressed the anxiety that social rights could not overcome it.[30]

Many agreed that the threshold question was whether rights could be saved from their libertarian associations of the nineteenth century to serve a process of social reconstruction in the twentieth—and it was an open question. It is critical to recall that progressives across the Atlantic had generally been wary of or downright hostile toward individual rights for the prior half century, given their most common nineteenth-century deployment as bars to state intervention in the ostensibly private domains of contract and property. This was especially true of transatlantic and Latin American socialists as a whole and, notably, the Marxists among them, who held out for full-blown revolutionary justice and frequently suspected (if they had read Karl Marx's youthful denunciation of rights) that an "egoistic" rhetoric of individual entitlements simply could not serve their purposes. But it was also true of those who simply prioritized the provision of minimal amounts of the good things in life together with some modicum of egalitarian distribution. For them, too, the fear was that economic liberalism regularly won out when rights claims were made, and if so, then the best strategy called for the pursuit of other moral and political frameworks.

There were few grounds for thinking an individualist philosophy deployed so long in defense against the poor and working class would easily avoid that gravitational pull now, Laski insisted. Early in his career, Laski had been associated with "pluralist" trends that identified equality with a struggle against the power of the state; for this reason, he had been much closer to propounding social rights as a younger thinker than as the grizzled veteran he now was after the war. His egalitarianism was strong throughout his career, but he vacillated about whether to prioritize a social minimum or overall equality, or even whether there was a difference. In wartime, it became self-evident to him that "there is no effective freedom in a society if there are wide differences between citizens in their access to the good things of life." Now strongly affected by Marxism's traditional skepticism of rights, Laski insisted that people recognize that "though their expression is universal in its form, the attempts at realisation [of human rights] have too rarely reached below the level of the middle class."[31]

Already before the war ended, Laski had correctly identified what the true bone of contention between capitalists and communists would be: not whether but to what extent personal freedom survived the unanimous move to a planned society. And he waxed lyrical about the Soviet experiment, which he saw as the natural successor to Christianity and the French Revolution in its promise of equality and renovation. "The small, wealthy class had made the morals of our civilization no more than an argument for the defence of its own claims," he inveighed sternly. After the war ended, it was not at all obvious that social rights without revolution would bring sufficient change. It was fair to be anxious about the fate of liberty, he acknowledged, but not if it meant forgetting that it is under permanent threat—not merely from the Soviets—insofar as inequality reigned. "Any society, in fact, the fruits of whose economic operations are unequally distributed," Laski warned in 1947, "will be compelled to deny freedom as the law of its being."[32]

Laski concluded in his contribution to the UNESCO survey that human rights were possible to recuperate only insofar as they were made compatible with planning. "One of the main emphases which have underlain past declarations of rights," he wrote, "has been the presumed antagonism between the freedom of the individual citizen and the authority of the government in the political community [as a result of] the unconscious, or half conscious, assumption of those who wrote the great documents of the past that every addition to governmental power is a subtraction from individual freedom." An even more devoted English Marxist, John Lewis, penned an acerbic chapter for the symposium that began with the forthright observation that history had shown that rights, understood as "absolute, inherent, and imprescriptible" checks on government, were now dead—though reclaiming them as a statement of the current needs of important groups remained plausible. Lewis admitted that economic libertarianism "has given a permanent cast to the idea of human rights, which persists, although we have long ago entered a new period in which the rights of property are not the most important, and in which new functions are found for government every year." That "new period" would continue now, but there was little likelihood it would ever fully convert human rights away from their role as a universal language for the victory of the rich over the rest.[33]

Added to the fact that declarations of rights hardly operated on their own to secure the values they announced, even for hallowed civil liberties, a new approach would have to verify whether rights could help capacitate government for the sake of all rather than constrain it for the sake of a privileged few. And social and economic rights faced this test most burningly. "Any attempt to formulate a Declaration of Rights in individualist terms would quite inevitably fail," Laski concluded. "It would have little authority in those political societies which are increasingly, both in number and in range of effort, assuming the need to plan their social and economic life. It is, indeed, legitimate to go further and say that if the assumptions behind such a declaration were individualistic, the document would be regarded as a threat to a new way of life by the defenders of historic principles which are now subject to profound challenge." Such hard-hitting skepticism within the group of UNESCO respondents only hinted at the extraordinary general unpopularity of individualism and rights—and therefore individual rights—in view of decades of thinking undermining both. And this was not even to mention the new movement known as existentialism that dismissed the very notion of "humanity" as a basis for ethics and politics, and whose main representatives—Jean-Paul Sartre leading them—were too bored with an antediluvian notion such as human rights to bother with it.[34]

E. H. Carr, the English historian, political scientist, and founder of international relations theory, made up for their absence from the UNESCO deliberations by taking the trouble to contribute an essay of his own and then review the entire book that resulted in the *Times Literary Supplement.* It was the genius of the symposium, unlike the drafting committee of the Universal Declaration, Carr mordantly observed, to include a wide spectrum of philosophical opinion about "the classic issue of the relation of man to society." Unlike the concurrent Universal Declaration project, Carr remarked, the symposium was "immune from political preoccupations and inhibitions." The idea that the symposium proved agreement would have surprised him, since its main virtue compared to the work of diplomats was its dogged honesty about the dubious credentials of human (including social) rights at a dramatic moment in history.[35]

For Carr, economic and social rights were the most remarkable things about the entire project of reconsecrating rights, but their breakthrough only exacerbated doubts about the viability of rights as a language of reform. Social rights were, the volume showed, "the most signal and unmistakable advance in the conception of the rights of man registered in recent times," Carr remarked. Surveying all factions, from Roman Catholics to Marxists and liberals, showed there was at least consensus to make sure the "conception of human rights at the end of the eighteenth century" is "corrected or supplemented," for "the unqualified upholders of the eighteenth-century bill of rights are surprisingly few—perhaps rarer among intellectuals than among the politicians who directed the proceedings of the United Nations." Roosevelt's Four Freedoms implied that the ascendancy of economic and social rights was now as much an orthodoxy for liberals as for their rivals. "The main anxieties of human beings at the present time in almost all countries are clearly quite as much social and economic as political," Carr explained. "No political party would venture to appeal to the electorate of the most orthodox democracy to-day without inscribing in its programme the right to work, the right to a living wage, and the right to care and maintenance in infancy, old age, ill-health, or unemployment. These rights to-day . . . make up the popular conception of the rights of man." Carr also acknowledged, however, that this new consensus only masked persisting dispute.[36]

Were economic and social rights, Carr asked, connected to the widespread campaign of the welfarist era for "economic equality—or at any rate some enforced mitigation of economic inequality"? A social minimum such as the Universal Declaration was to offer might require redistribution, but would it do so for the sake of a broader agenda of material equality? There was reason to doubt it. Worse, it was not obvious that putting rights to social purposes would in fact function as their promoters asserted. Where human rights had first been announced in the French Revolution "against a rigid and cramping social system," the "modern revolution," Carr asserted, "comes at the end of a long period of buoyant and almost unrestrained individual enterprise, when the individual has tended more and more to claim his rights against society and to forget the corresponding weight of his social obligations." How could more rights change the equation, when "the leaders of the liberal democracies, no less than of totalitarian states, are finding it to-day increasingly necessary to dwell on what the citizen owes to the community of which he forms a part"? True, Carr admitted, on its own this perspective was entirely "trite," but then it was routinely overlooked, and the task now was to work out the new welfare commitments in institutional practice. With the Cold War now on, it was a forbidding task—although Carr remained optimistic about moving from the nineteenth-century world of freedom-for-some through planned economy, welfare state, and mass democracy to freedom-for-all.[37]

If an intellectual history of social rights in the UNESCO symposium reveals common ground, it was between enthusiasts and opponents of the individualist principles of rights, who agreed on the imperative to construct welfare states for the sake of "social freedom." The tension between them focused not so much on whether to globalize rights principles beyond national spaces but on whether they aided or threatened the broader consensus around collectivist responsibility and welfarist institution-building. The Universal Declaration, as a list of norms alone, did nothing to help, Carr concluded in closing his assessment of the survey. "Had the promoters of the UNESCO inquiry into human rights desired to provide a justification for their work, they could hardly have done so more eloquently than by printing without comment in an appendix the declaration." After all, "since [the] authors [of the Universal Declaration] were certainly not ignorant of the real issues, it can only be supposed that political expediency made it necessary to keep them decently out of sight."[38]

THINKING through the path to social citizenship exclusively (but unsurprisingly) within the framework of one national welfare state, Marshall believed there was no real choice between sufficiency and equality. To socialize national citizenship by according social rights would automatically translate into rough parity. That belief, however, turns out to be an illusion brought on by its 1940s moment. It now looks like a wildly overoptimistic and temporary scenario, perhaps induced by the fact of Labour's supremacy for the prior years and unaffected by the ideological consequences of the Cold War (which, like the international scene generally, Marshall never mentioned). As W. G. Runciman, one of his Cambridge friends, later wrote, it turned out the specter Marshall could briefly exorcise from social rights has come back as a nightmare. Policies aiming at a social minimum not only began to falter as the postwar era wore on, but have sometimes proven compatible with the expansion rather than the reduction of material inequality.[39]

Across the Atlantic in the 1940s, social rights did the valuable work of defining some moral ideals within a modern economic setting—a list of critical thresholds human dignity demands when it comes to some of the most basic goods, above all remunerative work and relief (housing, clothing, food) should circumstances not provide that work. But the Universal Declaration did not announce, though it depended on, a much larger consensus concerning the purposes of the state and even its role in planning the economy—a critical fact that has generally been omitted from surveys of social rights in the era. No one who endorsed social rights in the 1940s did so on the premise that the unregulated market itself would generally fulfill them. Rather, social rights were an indirect justification for a new kind of state. And it is also true that most endorsed social rights as part and parcel of an egalitarian set of aspirations.

Yet if social rights were one idiom for a massively popular egalitarian national welfare where it was available, few signed on to social rights: defining and pursuing a modicum of basic individual entitlements never came close to entirely or even fundamentally defining the agenda of the welfare state in general or the planned economy in particular. In fact, other ways of formulating welfarist visions generally prevailed in the 1940s, and the more so the further east across the Atlantic one went. One reason was that so many still doubted that they were the best principles for achieving social justice in the welfare state. And never did welfare, whether focusing on social rights or not, transcend the state. By contrast, human rights, and especially international human rights, became famous in the midst of national welfare's crisis—but not before some dreamed of globalizing the welfare state rather than struggling, as people do today, for a global social minimum alone.

3

FDR's Second Bill

In January 1944, over crackling radio, American New Deal president Franklin Delano Roosevelt delivered his penultimate State of the Union address as one of his beloved fireside chats. Roosevelt's vision in this "Second Bill of Rights" speech was undoubtedly inspiring. "We have come to a clear realization of the fact that true individual freedom cannot exist without economic security and independence," he noted. His list of new rights included:

The right to a useful and remunerative job in the industries or shops or farms or mines of the Nation;

The right to earn enough to provide adequate food and clothing and recreation;

The right of every farmer to raise and sell his products at a return which will give him and his family a decent living;

The right of every businessman, large and small, to trade in an atmosphere of freedom from unfair competition and domination by monopolies at home or abroad;

The right of every family to a decent home;

The right to adequate medical care and the opportunity to achieve and enjoy good health;

The right to adequate protection from the economic fears of old age, sickness, accident, and unemployment;

The right to a good education.

All of these rights spell security.

And this list bears a tolerable resemblance to that consecrated several years later in the Universal Declaration of Human Rights (1948) and thus to a now-worldwide set of possible aspirations.[1]

The speech is now best remembered in the spirit of Roosevelt's early wartime promises, but the context was critically different. In 1941's State of the Union, Roosevelt had called for "four freedoms" everywhere in the world, including "freedom from want." In that earlier speech, Roosevelt had thus offered a vision of a fairer globe. In the Atlantic Charter detailing the Allies' plans that followed the same year, however, it was the decolonization of peoples under empire, the British and French alongside the German and Japanese, that achieved the most enthusiastic global notice. Then Winston Churchill had convinced Roosevelt to rescind that global promise, and a consolation rhetoric of "human rights" without self-determination filled the void. Roosevelt's 1944 message was thus distinctive in audience and in time. No longer at the precipice of conflict, before the United States had been pushed into war (which the earlier rhetoric failed to achieve), Americans received the 1944 speech with millions of their fellow citizens already at arms across the globe as their leaders plotted endgames in different theaters of war. Indeed, the tide of the violence had turned at Midway and Stalingrad, and it had become imaginable that it would subside. The new message was not about the world. It explained what Americans deserved for their sacrifices, envisioning basic economic and social entitlements for a country at peace, from guaranteed employment to a humane workplace to social protection for those too young, injured, sick, or old to labor.

The speech poses the conundrum of how the United States fits in the global story of the rise of social rights through the 1940s, and the broader arrival of the dream of the egalitarian welfare state of the period. America was more than just one country among others, for it was embracing its destiny as global leader on the basis of unprecedented wealth and power. It was also, however, distinctive in another way. Its territory among those least touched by fighting among the parties to World War II, the United States also went least far in establishing a welfare state in the period—though what one historian has dubbed a "warfare state" did come about, and mechanisms that constrained material inequality resulted. All the same, Roosevelt's rhetoric has been lionized, not merely for opening the prospect of America's joining or even leading in the global opinion that states must shoulder the burden of social protection as a matter of obligation. It has even been praised for holding fast to the vision of a better America that would bring the globe such protection through international governance, affording minimum standards of provision for every person by virtue of their humanity alone.[2]

For better or worse, Roosevelt's speechmaking cannot bear the weight of such interpretations. Far from being a gift to humanity, it was a failure for Americans. In the 1940s, Americans were global latecomers to economic and social rights, and thanks to history and experience, they diverged at this very moment from the construction of interventionist and protective welfare states that became the dominant norm in comparable locales and the highest aspiration elsewhere. At the epicenter of the Great Depression that dealt a grave blow to liberal regimes across the Atlantic, the United States was spared—except for one terrible day at Pearl Harbor and the fight that followed over the country's Pacific holdings—the dreadful carnage and awesome destruction on its territory that all Europeans saw. The American experience thus differed dramatically from the years of pain that led all of Europe to opt for social welfare states, whether under liberal, social democratic, Christian democratic, or communist auspices. But even considered without that larger context, often missing in parochial accounts of the Second Bill of Rights, the truth about it within a more narrowly American history is a hard one. The annunciation of social rights for Americans in January 1944 was the death knell of the already stripped down New Deal, not its animating spirit at its most robust. It preserved New Deal aspirations to an egalitarian state and economic planning to get there, but only as a last reverie allows for recalling one's dreams when it is too late to live them out.

While the idea of a new charter of economic rights had most prominence in the United States in the 1940s, it turns out that Roosevelt's address itself was not primarily associated with that project for about fifty years. In 2003, the constitutional scholar Cass Sunstein published *The Second Bill of Rights*, which more than any other work of scholarship has drawn attention to Roosevelt's speech, indeed linking it to social rights more than its own contemporaries did. If the Second Bill deserves attention, however, it is for its tragic relationship to the original New Deal commitments, not as a substitute for their ambition. A product of the triumph of the ideology of market freedom in world history, Sunstein's book aimed merely to envision this ideology in humane form. Sunstein put the focus on the possible infiltration of economic and social rights into the American constitutional imaginary. And with one eye on the fate of American progressive causes since the New Deal—especially backlash against the interventionist habits of liberal constitutional judges—Sunstein emphasized that judges must seek a properly modest stance to defend them wisely. The suggestion was that, after the Cold War, Americans might well finally reclaim economic and social rights for themselves. And, just as judges associated with the prominent attempt to turn the international human rights movement to concerns with distribution were doing abroad, American judges could someday join the trend of learning to interpret them without courting disaster.[3]

Yet for the original advocates of such a bill in the 1940s, the goals were entirely different. Their ambition reveals egalitarian hopes and interventionist tools that Sunstein did not care to feature, and their failure illustrates the enduring limits of American reform. The original New Dealers were trying their best to create an egalitarian welfare state, not merely a war economy, as well as to save the latter from impending peacetime "reconversion." Their handiwork, racialized to the core because of their necessary if unholy dependence on Southern Democrats in Congress to pass legislation, shared the exclusionary spirit of kindred welfare projects abroad. But the New Dealers behind the Second Bill also boasted an aspiration, common to democrats across the world, to plan a more egalitarian polity (at least for whites and tailored for men), not merely to compensate for market freedom with a sufficient minimum alone. This grander agenda, in fact, was the barely concealed purpose of the American intersection with the rhetoric of social rights in the period. To a remarkable extent, compared to their European opposite numbers, American reformers massively failed in both their overt plans of institutionalizing a social minimum and their covert mission of endorsing a planned economy for the sake of distributive equality—even if an impressive moderation of income inequality was achieved in other ways in the period and lasted for some time.[4]

What Sunstein envisioned in reviving the Second Bill is far less revealing, from both a moral and an institutional point of view, than what he omitted about the origins of American social rights along the way. Sunstein offered the uplifting promise of norms of basic sufficiency for citizens so as to screen out the distributionally egalitarian ideals of the age he claimed to resurrect in the very different neoliberal era when those ideals were liquidated. He offered a New Deal, in short, for an age of inequality, as if the Second Bill had not been not a remnant of a more ambitious politics that had shipwrecked. And overemphasizing judicial enforcement, which the original New Dealers treated with extreme skepticism—and for good reason— Sunstein entirely scanted the New Deal era's institutionalist approach to political economy, with its brief for a managerial and planning state. During the New Deal in real time, before it encountered stricter limits than social justice faced elsewhere, equality mattered as much as sufficiency, and judges were viewed by reformers as unlikely agents of social change—indeed were frequently regarded as its most threatening enemies for their characteristic interference with reformist politics.

To defend the New Deal against neoliberal reclamation requires dropping the notion that Roosevelt's call concisely summarized its goals. The New Deal had already taken on a number of different incarnations. By 1944, it was on the extreme defensive and in the midst of minimization with the approaching peace and, therefore, the war economy's end. Aside from neglecting its egalitarian and institutional aspirations, Sunstein's rosy account of the Second Bill avoids its most consequential lesson. Even when it came in the exclusionary form common to the origins of the welfare state everywhere, American reform of markets for the sake of the moral ideals of sufficiency and equality alike faced uniquely powerful opposition—especially at the very moment, late in the war, when Roosevelt flirted with social rights. The bill's fate confirmed his country's divergence from the mainstream development of national welfare states and illustrated the endemic power of economic libertarianism in American political ideology. The chronology of the emergence of American social rights *within* the New Deal therefore matters far more than their emergence alone.

THE DISTRIBUTIVE ideals of sufficiency (or the narrower one of subsistence) and equality had been in rivalry as leading principles of social thinking long before and mainly outside the United States, whose anti-statist and libertarian default had been and still remains so comparatively distinctive. Similarly, institutional planning for social justice had been experimented with for decades, with economic rights, when invoked in various places, serving to justify a series of institutional experiments. Many peoples in 1944 had long since reached, or were independently reaching, the basic notion that modern citizenship must incorporate socioeconomic entitlements to a sufficient minimum of the good things in life or even plan for a more generous modicum of egalitarian distribution. To the east of the United States through the Soviet Union and to the south in Latin America, the social welfare state became a much more consensual ideal, even if the means to bring it about were often comparatively weak.

Constitutions, for all their rising talk of social purposes in the middle of the twentieth century, generally focused on basic entitlements and subsistence minima, without prejudice to the larger campaigns for social justice, and especially egalitarian justice, undertaken within the structures they set up. During and after World War I, such charters for new states—typically born after revolution or war, beginning with the pioneering Mexican one in 1917—made large strides in various respects in according socioeconomic rights, whether in Central and Eastern Europe or the rest of Latin America, and as a result global constitutional expectations shifted. And there was the novel model and threat of the Soviet Union, as well as the reactionary welfare state that Benito Mussolini began to erect in Italy before the Depression, and which other fascists built in many other places as the tumultuous 1930s passed. Right-wing states had involved a great deal of talk about distributive fairness, at least for privileged citizens: it was not for nothing that Adolf Hitler had named the party that he promised would bring about a welfare state a national socialist worker's party. While famous as a classless society (even as it set up new hierarchies), the Soviet Union announced in its 1936 "Stalin" constitution more social rights than appear in any national charter so far in history, while a number of authoritarian regimes, such as Portugal's, made social rights equally prominent in their own sham constitutions of the same moment. All of the above states, however, were also interested in talking the talk and sometimes achieving the results of more egalitarian distribution—albeit, in the right-wing cases, for a narrow and often ethnonational community.[5]

America was late to action, neglecting distributive reform based on the ideals of sufficiency or equality. Rather, it was the Great Depression that unleashed the most important conditions for the possibility of the country's flirtation with either and both. One reason Americans were so tardy was that the country's isolation, despite its hemispheric security zone under the Monroe Doctrine and far-flung global holdings beyond it by the time of World War II, allowed it the formal continuity of a constitution that other nations were forced to relinquish earlier, for better and worse. Americans inherited a republican tradition that, back to Rome and in its modern versions, prohibited extremes of wealth and poverty as a risk to stability; but its origins offered no principled rationale for economic equality, especially not in a modern industrial circumstance. Americans had had their own progressive movement; besides their constitution's Sixteenth Amendment allowing federal taxation, it generated a suite of reform proposals overlapping with those Europeans and Latin Americans developed, ranging from minimal revision of nineteenth-century private rights schemes to full-blown socialistic experimentation. Fatefully, however, no one successfully convinced the American people to drop their antediluvian constitution for a new one, despite its flaws; more important, while trade unionism surged, no self-styled socialist party (left or right), of the kind that were to play pivotal roles in the origins of European welfare states, including the canonization of economic rights, gained traction. Starting behind, Americans could only get so far against dogged homegrown opposition.[6]

As far back as 1932, campaigning for his first election in the shadow of the Great Depression, Roosevelt had anticipated the need for a revision to inherited ways of thinking about rights. Claiming the authority of Thomas Jefferson, Roosevelt asserted that in addition to time-honored property rights, the American Revolution had also consecrated rights of "personal competency," protecting gainful laborers in their status as self-starters and saving them from becoming abject paupers. Without competency, a system of private rights did not function, and required "the government [to] intervene, not to destroy individualism but to protect it." The industrial transformation of the United States, Roosevelt continued, changed the substance of this problem but not its form. It implied that America needed a second revolution, like the insurrection its people had once staged in order to found their government, this time to regulate corporations. Just as the first time around rights had provided public safeguards against public abuses, so now rights could counteract ubiquitous private abuses. "The task of government in relation to business," Roosevelt affirmed, "is to assist the development of an economic declaration of rights. . . . It is the minimum requirement of a more permanently safe order of things."[7]

This was a distant anticipation of Roosevelt's now-famed call for a second bill of rights, little more than a year before he died—in fact a far closer approximation of that bill than at any point in his actual presidency, until the end. In his State of the Union address for 1941, Roosevelt did approach announcing a second bill of rights with his rhetoric of "four freedoms," including freedom from want, which then figured in the Atlantic Charter later that same year. But unlike the economic rights rhetoric before and after, the Four Freedoms were widely understood to be a war program, as much a set of aspirations for the world and a justification of fighting as they were a part of the New Deal as a domestic program of political economy. The main thing that intervened in between 1932 and 1944 was the series of experiments at domestic programming in response to the Great Depression, before the war began and brought with it a new political economy of its own. None of the initiatives was justified to Americans in terms of individual rights, and none aimed exclusively at a sufficient minimum of social protection.[8]

The heroic years of the New Deal had instead followed earlier and contemporary European welfare experiments in taking on ambitious structural intervention in agricultural and industrial production rather than aiming solely at providing compensatory redistribution (for example, to fulfill a social minimum) after the fact, for the core white male beneficiaries of the rethought American social compact. Soon after Roosevelt's March 1933 inauguration came the National Industrial Recovery Act (NIRA), with its unprecedented state intervention in economic affairs. "Nothing like this comprehensive restructuring of market capitalism by a national state," one historian goes so far as to write, "had ever been tried before in a constitutional democracy, even in countries governed by social democratic parties." Aside from empowering the federal government to make industrial policy and kick off its own public works, it accorded very different rights of collective labor organization and corporatist power—an agenda close to the heart of socialist and trade unionist aspirations going back decades—than the Second Bill of Rights later consecrated. With longstanding taboos against comparing the New Deal to European fascism recently lifted, it has become much more common to explore parallels active in the consciousness of the mid-1930s about how close the United States might need to come through such programs to the policy toolkit and strong leadership of the European planning states—especially on the right. But in part by paying the price of accommodation to Southern racist sentiments, which privileged white males among the beneficiaries of his innovations, Roosevelt kept the country formally democratic during this pivotal era. Despite its great strides in the face of emergency, civic nationalism could not ever fully disentangle itself from racist nationalism.[9]

Historical debate has swirled around how effective the initial national recovery scheme was before the U.S. Supreme Court struck down the NIRA in 1935. It is clear that, in response, New Dealers attempted to save some elements of the earlier scheme as well as to respond to its demonstrated limitations. The Social Security Act of 1935 furnished basic aspects of social insurance that the federal state had lacked before, but the centerpieces of the New Deal continued to be controversial attempts to regulate the basic functioning and organization of the economy, and not only to guarantee individuals a cushion against remaining shocks. The same year as Social Security came online, the National Labor Relations (or Wagner) Act went even further than the NIRA had to institutionalize and guarantee collective labor rights. It was a step, as contemporaries saw it (whether gleefully or indignantly), towards so-called "industrial democracy." Dispute raged then and has since about how far the checkered prior history of the NIRA meant that the planning impulse was already off the table for the American people, even if Roosevelt's court-packing threat put the Supreme Court in its place for meddling. Whoever was (and is) right about how starkly limits to planning had now been imposed, in function the Wagner Act was nonetheless extraordinarily interventionist in comparison with the origins of Social Security and with the later Fair Labor Standards Act (1938), which provided basic protections to workers in the form of a minimum wage and a safer workplace.[10]

The larger social vision of this era in which the ambition of the New Deal reached its heights was directed not simply at the need for a bare minimum of social protection but also—in the depths of economic crisis—at a vision of a fair society that vividly featured egalitarian critiques of wealth and "oligarchy." Discussing the Second Bill of Rights without this background is like discussing the tearful death scene of a tragedy without the great expectations (or overweening hubris) that make the drama meaningful in the first place. It shows irrefutably that the New Deal was never confined to an ideal of a threshold of individual sufficiency in the distribution of the good things in life and that, indeed, the minimal standards associated with the Social Security Act and the Fair Labor Standards Acts were not standalone ends. This bolder set of aspirations endured into the period after 1937, when reformers struggled for a new opening they were never to find for the egalitarian ideal. Perhaps even by that moment, an ingrained conservatism may already have set limits. It was now self-evident that "any national system designed to create equality would threaten opportunities for those who had enjoyed previous advantages at the same time that it revealed the depths of inequality that remained to be overcome." As for the Second Bill of Rights, nothing like it was in prospect yet; the context for it was very different.[11]

In the decisive experimental years of the mid- to late 1930s, the main proponent of a basic provision scheme on its own was John Winant, a centrist Republican who served as governor of New Hampshire until Roosevelt appointed him the first head of the Social Security Board created under the act and, later, wartime ambassador to Winston Churchill's government. "We have been the last civilized nation of the world to recognize the need of social economic protection," Winant said in 1936, in welcoming the law he supervised. Before the act, he added, it was a scandal that a seventh of Americans relied on "charity" for "subsistence," in the absence of even the outrageously spotty national programs that Europeans had had for decades. By 1941, after a stint leading the International Labour Office before taking his ambassadorship, Winant stood up for American intervention—his predecessor in London, Joseph Kennedy, having been a staunch isolationist— by justifying the war as one "of and for social principles. . . . We must first justify our beliefs by strengthening the fundamental economic, social, and civil rights of all free citizens. . . . Each one of us must keep in mind, now and in future, that social justice is a basic requisite for a united and alert citizenry, for war and for peace."[12]

For Winant, however, the content of social justice moved in a strongly egalitarian direction until 1947, when his thwarted political ambition and a star-crossed affair with Churchill's daughter that ended badly led to his suicide. His experiences abroad taught him (as he put it the year before he shot himself in an upstairs bedroom) that welfare states were not solely about subsistence minima but also about the moderation of "gross economic inequalities. . . . Resentment and fear grow easily into hatred and we have seen how quickly these emotions can be played upon by the unscrupulous to make a people go to war against their fellow man." But in effect, the lesson that Winant personally learned about the need to establish both sufficiency and equality risked being lost as the New Deal headed toward its last days and the Second Bill of Rights attempted a last-ditch effort to save its agenda while the end of the war drew nigh.[13]

EASILY the most significant fact about the Second Bill of Rights package, then, is that it came so late, when the energies of the New Deal were nearly spent and in the very different context of wartime. Now experts looked ahead to the "reconversion" of the war economy that had done so much to institute full employment and temporary planning. The proposal crystallized as politicians prepared Americans for the Normandy invasion that would occur shortly. The proposal's fate as the war rushed toward its end was revealing. Its partisans hoped against hope, and often against their better judgment, that the Second Bill could maintain the move to fair shares for all and the economic planning necessary to accomplish that fairness, which the New Deal had initially proposed. They were to be disappointed.[14]

It is now well-known that the National Resources Planning Board (NRPB) was the central organ for the resumption of ideas about social rights on the American scene a decade after Roosevelt's campaign talk. Founded in 1933, the board stretched back to the New Deal's beginnings and represented a kind of think tank within government under the NIRA's auspices to encourage the habits of planning the economy after gathering information for the sake of coordination. After the Supreme Court invalidated the law that gave the board life, Roosevelt saved it, and it came into its own during the war, when it became the crucible for social-rights talk, American-style.

The vital issues for the NRPB in 1942–43 were how to plan for a continuation, after the war, of the full employment that the war economy itself had provided and how to offer a vision of social citizenship that would begin filling out the vague promises of Roosevelt's rhetorical flights. It was, in fact, the closest thing America ever got to what the illustrious English social planner William Beveridge proposed for the United Kingdom in 1942: the blueprint for the welfare state that the Labour Party enacted when it came to power. This analogy was understood at the time: in the year after Beveridge's report, NRPB staffers invited him to visit the United States, and he obliged in May–June 1943. As Winant had come to understand, the point of a welfare state was not simply to establish a floor of sufficiency but mainly to lay the groundwork for a fair society. As one NRPB staffer put it in placing the Board's work in the context of comparable overseas planning, the United States could join in the consensus that connected full employment and a social minimum with the assumption that "bettering the condition of the people will bring about a greater economic and social equality among all groups and classes." Of course, this referred to equality of means for privileged citizens across classes—the common man, so long as he was white—without taking on the gendered and racialized form in which the New Deal had come. But in the view of its promoters at the time, setting a social minimum was not separate from the achievement of a more materially egalitarian society than ever before (or since, to judge by the portion of the national income the wealthiest have recently captured).[15]

Both the relation of social rights to egalitarian planning and its ethical and institutional dimensions are most easily tracked through the thinking of University of Chicago political scientist Charles Merriam, the NRPB's "most influential figure" all along. More than a deep thinker, Merriam was an academic entrepreneur with a vast following in his time, as well as the premier representative of what he styled a Chicago school—albeit one with commitments very different from those later associated with the place. Merriam brought a political scientist's respect for empirical research with him, but he also insisted on defining ethical ideals for a program of American planning, in order that it might transcend a narrower economist's focus on growth and employment. If it were indeed true that, as of the U.S. Supreme Court's decision in *Schechter Poultry Corp. v. United States* to strike down the NIRA in 1935, the welfare state was a "mirage," Merriam did not realize it. Long into the war, he did not want to see domestic pressure groups and less ambitious reformist visions lead to what one commentator called "a nation more planned against than planning."[16]

Throughout the period, Merriam was an indefatigable votary of "democracy," but what this meant shifted a great deal, much as the animating philosophy of the New Deal did over the course of the 1930s and the war years. As late as 1939, rights did not figure seriously in his thought, because "democracy" seemed to him much more distinguished by its commitment to human perfectibility, the consent of the governed, and—above all—the "consciously directed social change" that went under the heading of planning. The choice, he often put it, was not planning or no planning, but democratic planning or totalitarian planning. While the enemies of democracy were hereditary nobilities, cultural aristocracy, and more recently Friedrich Nietzsche's call for "supermen" (regrettably taken so seriously in Germany under National Socialism), Merriam also inveighed against the "economic inequality" that put democracy at risk from within. "It is . . . a short way from *laissez faire* in economics to elitism in political and social theory," he explained in 1939. "Democracy may be tolerated or welcomed as long as it leaves the domination of industry to a few, but repudiated when it begins a process of social control."[17]

There had been discussion of a new bill of rights even before Roosevelt's Four Freedoms speech—including a memo by Merriam on the topic as an aspect of planning in July 1940, as the NRPB moved in earnest toward finalizing its list of entitlements in 1941. In spring of 1941, Merriam gave the Godkin lectures at Harvard University, championing egalitarian planning as both the past and the future of democracy—"The Constitutional Convention itself was a large-scale planning board," Merriam exclaimed—but now, it identified new content in the democratic pursuit of happiness: social rights. For Merriam, the "freedom from want," which Roosevelt mentioned again in the Atlantic Charter of late summer 1941, had to be made more generous for Americans and would involve equal access to basic security, defined as food, shelter, and clothing "on an American minimum standard," along with a fair wage, unemployment relief, safeguards against accidents and illness, and guaranteed education. Much as Norman Rockwell depicted "freedom from want" in a widely circulated 1943 series of paintings as a well-appointed white family enjoying a roast turkey dinner, Merriam's adjustment of minimum provision to be not bare but "decent" also marked Roosevelt's later speech. And it was not as if this basic provision ruled out other rhetoric concerning the elimination of privilege and fair distribution, alongside a commitment to a constant increase in living standards, which figured frequently in Roosevelt's rhetoric. "Democracy is not merely a mechanism through which personal development might possibly be achieved," Merriam concluded, "but also one for facilitating the fullest development of the personality within the purview of the common good." (Perhaps intuiting the potential difference between an instituted social minimum and broader distributional fairness, Merriam tried to resolve it by suggesting the state-protected minimum would constantly rise, while still allowing "differentials over and above the basic minima.")[18]

The NRPB's mammoth report on security—completed before Pearl Harbor, though Roosevelt then sat on it for a year—actually did not speak in terms of social rights. It made clear, however, that beyond destitution, all Americans deserved that "decent" minimum security if they were unable to work, thrown out of it due to economic dislocation, or too poorly compensated, with relief organized through public insurance with funded backup where needed. Merriam, not directly involved in the details of the lengthy document, took a fateful step when he added a new idiom in annual reports that followed. Behind the new rhetoric of social rights lurked fear of a crash in the difficult transition away from a war economy and anxiety that ideals of national welfare, realized indirectly through wartime measures, needed to be institutionalized in earnest now or never. In early 1942, the NRPB referred to "new freedoms," while by late 1942, it began to emphasize that, in effect, a new bill of social rights was on offer to citizens. Old aspirations were being translated into new rhetoric.[19]

When rolled out, the NRPB's report was certainly received as the American Beveridge plan, except that its fate was the opposite of the original: it was consigned to the dustbin rather than enacted as policy. Whether it was the underlying scheme or the new social rights rhetoric, some Americans were thrilled, but a good number were horrified. *The Nation*, the progressive magazine, garlanded the work with superlatives, calling the report "a dramatic reply to the question: 'What are we fighting for?' . . . This new Bill of American Rights might well serve as a statement of the war aims." It added that, while it was "a natural supplement to the Atlantic Charter, it is far more specific, far more inspiring to the average man, than that document." Among the rights bruited about at this moment, most of which envisioned a decent minimum of labor, food, clothing, shelter, leisure, and medical care, one aimed beyond a threshold at a defeudalized and democratized economy, outlining an entitlement to "live in a system of free enterprise, free from compulsory labor, irresponsible private power, arbitrary public authority and unregulated monopolies." It was a commitment that in effect pursued the then-familiar analogy of state and market as twin sources of despotism that rights had to counteract equally. As the Columbia University political scientist and expert on the New Deal's Work Projects Administration Arthur MacMahon put it, in a special issue of *Frontiers of Democracy* devoted to the NRPB's list of new rights, the point was to stigmatize "a feudalized private economic structure" as the *Doppelgänger* of tyrannical political authority.[20]

The adjustment of the arguments of Merriam and others to the rhetoric of social rights continued his ideology of planning for a fair society while altering their defense of it. Merriam later joked that when the board "put out a bill of economic rights, a very distinguished statesman . . . said, 'This is a mixture of moonshine and socialism.'" But Merriam had long been an inveterate defender of the state's role in achieving the good life against the "Jeremiahs" who "undervalue the capacity of the state for promoting the common weal by the balance and integration of social forces" or who "think of the state in terms of its primitive tools of force and violence." Formulating the expansive agenda through a rhetoric of individual rights made planning for social justice appear compatible with American traditions and especially with culturally inveterate libertarianism. At the same time, as a votary of a state that would synthesize freedom and planning or even redefine the first in terms of the second, Merriam and others still understood social rights to be about reshaping the economy. Neither he nor anyone else involved mentioned judicial enforcement, let alone intended to set off a debate about how passively (or for that matter actively) judges ought to behave.[21]

As a result, few were fooled by Merriam, for good or for ill. The *Wall Street Journal* denounced the NRPB's scheme for the indirect justification as the "government planning" it was, "which means despotism or nothing." (The report was "a perhaps unintended disguise" for "totalitarianism," the newspaper added for good measure.) The rollout, or the substance, of the American Beveridge plan proved disastrous, and within months the NRPB was no more. The report was so controversial that it was decried in the press, and Congress defunded the agency almost as soon as the ink was dry on its proposals for social rights. *Time* called it "the flop of the year." "Seldom has so important a report disappeared from public debate so quickly," *Newsweek* noted. And yet the larger lesson of the barrage of ridicule from the conservative and mainstream press and Congress's blunt rejection has not been drawn. It is certainly true that Roosevelt, announcing a second bill of rights in his now much-celebrated State of the Union address in January 1944, saved not the substance but the new packaging in which planning had been wrapped in 1942–43. But for Americans, social rights were propounded at the "end of reform," when its most egalitarian and institutional versions begun the prior decade were left behind in a series of steps, and even the residual ideal of a social minimum was lost, except for certain state programs.[22]

It would be wrong to say, however, that the Second Bill of Rights fully accomplished the move from an institutional plan to a list of entitlements or entirely converted a call for equality into one for sufficiency alone, decisively opting for one component of national welfare rather than the other. At the same time as institutional scheming died, Roosevelt never fully committed to a vision of the state as providing a social minimum alone for citizens. As there were so often for Merriam, for Roosevelt there were residual egalitarian ideals in the speech, especially his call for an end to "special privileges for a few." With thresholds in the areas of work, housing, food, clothing, medical care, and recreation, Roosevelt's list also preserved the anti-oligarchic principle that was irreducible to social rights.

AT THE SAME time, there were wartime paths not taken thanks to the annunciation of social rights, especially when it came to the notionally global horizons of the Four Freedoms rhetoric. Some have gone so far as to claim that the Second Bill epitomized a "New Deal for the world," but it was never really so. Henry Wallace, vice president from 1940 to 1944 and a divisive but popular mouthpiece for an extended New Deal for after the war, dreamed of economic utopias at home and abroad, crisscrossing the nation evoking considerable enthusiasm while in office. His visions of freedom from want, however, revolved around engineering full employment and were unaffected by the enumeration of social rights. As far back as April 1941, he had proposed not a second bill of rights but a "Bill of Duties." "Under the Bill of Rights and Duties," Wallace explained, "we can have a flexible structure into which each citizen may make his productive contribution to the general welfare." At the highpoint of his popularity, a year later, with his Christian millennialism in full bloom, Wallace responded to the Four Freedoms speech with one of his own. In it, he demanded that Americans choose not an American century (in *Time* magazine publisher Henry Luce's 1941 phrase) but a "century of the common man," adding once again that the main imperative was to declare four duties, not more rights.[23]

But Wallace's hopes for the New Deal in wartime were quickly marginalized. He took seriously the promise in the Four Freedoms address that America stood against penury everywhere in the world. Wallace foolishly reported in his speech a conversation with the wife of former Soviet foreign minister and then U.S. ambassador Maxim Litvinov; the two wondered, Wallace recounted, whether the Allied war would allow every child in the world to have a mere half pint of milk each day or a whole quart. It got him into serious trouble after the president of the National Association of American Manufacturers made hay of it. The apparently frightening notion that the obligation to provide "a quart of milk for every Hottentot" might fall on the American people proved a scurrilous talking point, and the episode contributed to Wallace's cashiering as vice presidential candidate for 1944 in favor of Harry Truman. Given its subsequent consequences for the world, this was perhaps the most fateful event in this period.[24]

As Wallace's example shows, there is no doubt that the Four Freedoms address and the Atlantic Charter had been catalytic contributions to transatlantic and even global discourse, both because they came so early in World War II and because their great indeterminacy left them open to divergent responses. Reflecting some of the same aspirations for postwar order, the American Law Institute issued its own statement of essential human rights in 1944, including by now globally standard social rights. Thanks to its professionalism, the institute's statement would play an especially significant role in the United Nations in the path to the Universal Declaration—though no role in the country's domestic politics. In a broader context, it is not altogether clear how much America's feint toward and move away from social rights mattered, even if the country's extraordinary economic and political ascendancy after World War II gave all its actions (and inactions) more significance than those of other states. The general consensus around social rights in the 1940s meant that they were hardly an export of the United States, which remained most hesitant about them despite joining the consensus when the Universal Declaration was drafted. And it is hard to believe that the flirtation of some American liberal elites with economic and social rights in the mid-1940s affected the crystallizing worldwide consensus (or that its absence would have deterred it). It is, of course, clear that had some American elites not supported economic and social rights in the 1940s, the norms could not have entered the Universal Declaration—but then, the United States was crucial to every aspect of post–World War II order. When, soon after, the "myth" emerged that the United States was genetically opposed to social rights, it was one of those myths to which there was, and is, a kernel of truth.[25]

Though it preserved some modicum of distributive egalitarianism and institutional experimentalism, the story of the origins of the Second Bill of Rights in the United States starkly illustrates the ultimate constraints on any profound socialization of political economy on the American scene. With due allowance made for the inheritance of the earlier New Deal, the Fair Labor Standards Act, and, before it and even more boldly, the Wagner Act, which provided for workingmen's empowerment, the American warfare state did not successfully translate into a welfare state. As his biographer perceptively noted long ago, "Merriam's generation knew the New Deal to be a dramatically unfinished operation . . . but they were not giving up. [Yet] after an initial flurry of debate, the idea [of social rights] died as far as most Americans were concerned." That the NRPB's welfarist reports and social rights rhetoric appeared precisely when opposition to progressive economic planning was spiking appeared courageous, perhaps, but stupid— as one observer put it, like a "Jersey bull charg[ing] the railroad freight engine head on."[26]

If anything, the American version of the move toward an interventionist government—and thus toward economic planning and social rights—stood out for the force with which business interests resisted it and the threat that resistance posed to Roosevelt's experimentation all along; the closure of the NRPB was simply a conclusive and graphic example. In America during the New Deal, as for so long before in modern history, the language of rights typically functioned to defend private transactions from ostensibly grasping

that would ultimately bring low the very dream of national welfare that was canonized everywhere except in the victorious hegemon. Whereas in Europe, both West and East, as well as in Latin America, a stronger commitment to social citizenship crystallized, a proper reconstruction of the Second Bill of Rights emphasizes how gingerly Americans were about entering the consensus around national welfare of the time—with lasting effects. Despite enthusiasm for public spending a few years before and the near passage of an Employment Act in 1946, Americans woke up to a world in which, having begun on a welfare state during the 1930s, they had trouble transcending the warfare state they in fact achieved. By 1947, Dwight Macdonald could liken the Four Freedoms to an "advertising slogan" which was now "as mercifully forgotten as Phoebe Snow and the Sapolio jingles"—referring to Madison Avenue advertising campaigns that had once been all the rage too, but were consigned to oblivion soon after.[30]

The glory years of the New Deal had begun "the great exception" in between one libertarian "age of acquiescence" to economic hierarchy and the neoliberal one of our own time. The tremendous difference is that great strides in adequate or sufficient provision were made since the 1960s "war on poverty," alongside the even more spectacular lifting of the most egregious racial exclusions and the emancipatory integration of women into the formal workforce. Roosevelt's final campaign for president, even after his Second Bill of Rights speech, prioritized full employment, the reigning ideology of late wartime. The Congress of Industrial Organizations, in a "People's Program for 1944," alluded to the need for an economic bill of rights, but likewise put full employment at the top of its agenda. Otherwise, the bill of social rights never reappeared in American politics, though some of its substance was slowly achieved in more limited and piecemeal form. Visionary American liberals retained considerable ambition after the 1940s, but did so by focusing heavily on full employment until the war on poverty, in the midst of the greatest era of prosperity any nation has ever enjoyed, and before the country's policies began their ongoing return to its default.[31]

Thereafter, American liberals aimed not for a modicum of material equality, a dream that new policies smashed, but for sufficient distribution alone—though their more minimal ambitions in this regard hardly spared them a bitter fight, as later wrangling over partial health care provision graphically proved. Even if by the end of World War II, a more libertarian impulse had asserted itself strongly, the true revival of utopias of freedom in markets was reserved for the 1970s and since, with predictable effects in the direction of ultimately massive hierarchy and decisive consequences for the world. It became imaginable to champion the New Deal nostalgically while really only proposing to humanize neoliberalism, even as human rights could become America's bequest to the world, past and future.

4

Globalizing Welfare
after Empire

"In the pre-war world," American Under Secretary of State Sumner Welles noted at Arlington Cemetery, on Memorial Day 1942, "large numbers of people were unemployed; the living standards of millions of people were pitifully low; it was a world in which nations were classified as 'haves' and 'have nots,' with all that these words imply in terms of inequity and hatred." Then Welles, imagining the nature of the world after the embers of war cooled, continued: "When the war ends . . . only the United States will have the strength and the resources to lead the world out of the slough in which it has struggled for so long, to lead the way towards a world order in which there can be freedom from want." But it did not happen, either to interrupt global inequity or even to secure a global social minimum. In fact, like global equality, the internationalization of social rights never had a chance. There was no New Deal for the world.[1]

The signature form of political economy, especially after Welles was marginalized and other Americans took charge of planning, was nationalist. A system of international governance was established, but it aimed to entrench the great power rulership that the Allied governments established, to create fail-safes against another economic catastrophe, and to implement new initiatives for West European and transatlantic interdependence. During and after World War II, welfare was everywhere established as national welfare, and the ideals of sufficiency and equality alike were cabined to extant and new spaces, not raised to the global level. "The Charter of the United Nations was bound to be built upon the preservation of the national sovereign state, and bound, therefore, to be an unsatisfactory compromise disproportionate to the scale of the problem it was intended to meet," Harold Laski observed grimly in 1947. Registering the state of constitutional orthodoxy when it came to political economy, the Universal Declaration of Human Rights (1948) declared social rights; but it did so, as its preamble says, above all to lay down a template for national welfare: "a high standard of achievement for peoples and nations." Even the surviving forms of communist internationalism did not focus on a sufficient minimum, let alone on global equality. Josef Stalin had long since declared the priority of constructing "socialism in one country." While he moved to build a regional empire as World War II ended, it was composed of a series of examples of national welfare states. West and East, a national security internationalism for a bipolar world emerged.[2]

The welfare state boasted increasing social protections and constraints on inequality for its national community, but it often also took the form of an imperial state. With Adolf Hitler's East European empire destroyed and Stalin's taking its place, there was at least formal nationhood and citizenship for everything living from the Iron Curtain east. West European empires, however, established spaces not so much for citizens as for subjects. Following a wave of colonial reform before World War II was a brief experimental phase of reimagining empire, but it was a flash in the pan. As anticolonial agitation spread from the beginning of the twentieth century, empires responded by increasing the promises of civilizing progress they had already been making for decades. It was not enough. Despite the prior achievement of the national welfare state and its occasional promise of increased generosity towards imperial subjects, it took the decolonization of the globe after World War II, as old empires disgorged new states, for the ideals of just distribution of the good things in life to become truly globalized. Decolonization not only brought the ideology of welfare to far more human beings than ever before; at its most ambitious, it broke with the national framework that originally confined its aspirations to a series of boundaried communities.

The specific distributive ideals and policies of postcolonial states, locally and globally, are an almost unstudied topic. Their zeal between World War II and the 1970s, not only to establish their own welfare spaces but also to globalize distributive equality to a greater extent than anyone had previously envisioned, is essential background for the rise of global sufficiency around "human rights" and associated concepts in a neoliberal age. But it is also much more. Like the distributive ambitions of the welfare state, which have since been widely spurned, the fact that, just before neo-liberalism exploded, the dream of a fully global equality was dreamed demands recovery. In the same era, the postcolonial states sponsored the legalization of economic and social rights in an international treaty. Twenty years before, the Universal Declaration with its social rights provisions had been a minor satellite circling around the program of national welfare. Now, rights that aimed at a sufficient minimum in distribution were vaulted into international law, but only in pale comparison to even more ambitious postcolonial hopes for egalitarian global justice.

The dynamics of the rise and fall of great powers had been pondered for a millennium or more, and the wealth and poverty of nations had been contemplated for two centuries. But the distributive justice of world order was a challenge without any precedent. Shouldering the burdens of sufficiency and equality alike for their new citizens, postcolonial states prioritized not the former but the latter when it came to social justice and, especially, to its prospective globalization. Their vision of it remained strikingly nationalist, with equality of states the most frequent goal, even if most understood such equality as merely an acceptable proxy for equality of individuals. As for their unprecedented globalization of social justice, most notably in the New International Economic Order (NIEO) proposals of 1974, it contemplated not the cancellation but the preservation of hard-won sovereign states. It was cosmopolitan, but for the sake of the underprivileged nations.[3]

The era of the French Revolution and its pioneering Jacobin welfare state had seen a renewal and transformation of ancient "cosmopolitanism," but no classical or even modern thinker in the Western canon had ever envisioned expanding our distributive obligations beyond the polis, empire, or state before decolonization. Thomas Paine, the first clear adherent of an obligation of sufficiency without any further commitment to equality, was representative. He consistently viewed ethics as universal across time and space—"the peculiar honor of France," he wrote, "is that she now raises the standard of liberty for all nations; and in fighting her own battles, contends for the rights of all mankind"—but assumed these ethics were to be vindicated in national spaces. He never propounded anything remotely resembling a commitment to cross-border distribution, not even for the sake of sufficiency. It was a far cry from the memorably strange German baron Anacharsis Cloots, elected to the French National Assembly (like Paine) as representative of all humanity. Urging military conquest of the remaining

Old Regime beyond French borders, he promised in one speech that "once delivered, the human race will one day imitate nature itself, which knows no foreigners; and wisdom will reign in the two hemispheres, in the republic of united individuals." But even he never drew implications of this globalism for distribution.[4]

It was two later traditions that made a further flung distributive consciousness more readily available. Easily the most important was the bundle of late-colonial visions that posed the need to shoulder some sense of greater fairness, but always in terms of the persistently hierarchical power relations that empire always maintained. The other was socialist internationalism. As at home, however, the socialist legacy for distributive ideals was complex. Already in the "Communist Manifesto," Karl Marx had referred to the forces of capital as "cosmopolitan" and implied that its overthrow would require global solidarity and response. Marxist calls for worldwide revolution, however, were much more in the tradition of nineteenth-century socialism, demanding not fairer distribution but an end to hierarchical power. No attention to fair distribution, sufficient or equal, on a global scale is to be found in those calls, which stopped at nothing short of abetting or awaiting the self-destruction of capitalism, not least since Marxists in the tradition of V. I. Lenin considered imperialism its "highest" and terminal stage. As for the path socialists found domestically to demand distributive justice—including to press for egalitarian justice—they did not find one to travel at the higher level of global politics before postcolonial activists blazed it. Most important, across the first half of the twentieth century, European and Latin American socialism tended ineluctably toward nationalism, so as to confront the most powerful form of modern internationalism, which revolved around the establishment of market freedoms with minimum interference by states. After World War II, the internationalism of communism transformed from the top-down guidance of the Soviet state over the local initiatives that had characterized the Comintern into a series of locally managed national struggles and parties that presented even less of a global program than it had in earlier days. Meanwhile, non-communist socialist internationalism—of minor importance in any case—did not highlight distribution either, focusing on the modular reproduction of national welfare in social democratic guise.[5]

As a result, the postcolonial states, with a huge range of ideologies, took the lead in pointing out the nationalist restriction of welfare states as they were established during and after World War II. They set out at once to copy and globalize their achievement. Lost in the shuffle was the idea of individual sufficiency, which would conquer the world in a neoliberal era that liquidated egalitarian hopes, especially on the world stage. While there was no international human rights movement or legal protection for three decades after World War II, the globalization of national welfare projects through decolonization and the attempt to raise welfare itself to a global scale attracted extraordinary attention and enthusiasm. Not only the values of civil liberties but even those of material sufficiency took a backseat. Human rights both political and social, like campaigns against global poverty, were missing, waiting for calls for global equality to disappear and for a dramatic neoliberal realignment of the global economy to take their place.

THE ALLIES put international macroeconomic governance in place after a tempestuous summer 1944 conference at the Bretton Woods resort in New Hampshire, where the American and British governments hashed out their differences. With a new trade regime saved for later and the robust governance of which some dreamed never coming to pass, the system concentrated on the transatlantic zone rather than the global scene. The priority was to institutionalize insurance against catastrophe, an all-important if lesser ambition, on the assumption that national policies of full employment might well require a fail-safe. Despite a certain amount of rhetoric about individual social entitlements, such as Welles's and even at the Bretton Woods meetings themselves, before Franklin Roosevelt's death in spring 1945, no provisions for individual social entitlements were built into the scheme. And while Swedish economist Gunnar Myrdal and others worked through the mid-1940s to inject greater ambition into the organization of international political economy, neither he nor others believed social rights were the best way to formulate the goals. In the end, macroeconomic internationalism adapted to serve macroeconomic nationalism.[6]

E. H. Carr, acerbic about the human rights symposium he was asked to organize for UNESCO, explained around the same time that the nationalist premises of the coming of the welfare state simply made social justice at a higher level unlikely anytime soon. In his *Nationalism and After* (1945), Carr suggested that while in the nineteenth century, the middle classes had been nationalized in the pursuit of their class interests, the working classes remained internationalist—because those who claimed to speak for the nation did not take their interests into account. After World War I, what Carr accurately and incisively dubbed "the socialization of nationalism and the nationalization of socialism" set in, with the whole idea of social justice becoming linked to national integration and outsider exclusion, including when it came to economic policy. Decolonization had begun in the multiplication of nations within Europe and now was set to continue at the end of the war. As for a new vision of internationalism that would avoid repeating the errors of the old, it was not impossible, but neither was it likely. Since an international project of equalizing nations in a new age was unfeasible, Carr concluded, it was best to remain on the lookout for individuals not well-served by their nations, rather than to take the latter's interests as an unfailing proxy for the former's defense. With his peculiar blend of idealism and realism, Carr proposed that reform somehow work against the persistence of economic nationalism, without making designs on overthrowing it anytime soon. "The *laissez-faire* individualism which purported to interpose no effective economic unit between the individual at one end of the scale and the whole world at the other is," Carr observed, "gone beyond recall." The nationalism created by "a cumulative process of combination between individuals to protect themselves against the devastating consequences of unfettered economic individualism has become in its turn a threat to the security and well-being of the individual, and is itself subject to a new challenge and a new process of change"—and "the forces which produced the socialized nation are still operative; nor will its demands be abated." Carr hoped one day to see an internationalization of social justice, but it was a distant millennium. "Internationalism, like nationalism, must become social." But it was not going to occur anytime soon.[7]

Roosevelt had certainly spoken of freedom from want "everywhere in the world." And there is no doubt that the 1940s saw an "emergence of globalism" among a crew of intellectuals, peripheral but perhaps less so than before or since, who believed a radical transcendence of national sovereignty was in the offing. On balance, however, policymakers in the 1940s stuck with the conclusion that globalism had conquered the world in libertarian form in the era leading to the Great Depression, and for the foreseeable future, the nation-state served as an indispensable bulwark against the same thing happening again. Both human rights generally and social rights specifically were accommodated to a world in which the economic nationalism that Adolf Hitler had made so central to the rise of the welfare state remained an enduring premise. In wartime and shortly after, several advocates of social rights, recognizing the ultimate conditions of political economy to be unmanageable in exclusively local settings, had indeed insisted that an internationalization of social rights that went far beyond the Universal Declaration's template for national constitutions was necessary. Georges Gurvitch—primarily interested in affecting the constitution of the Fourth Republic—had insisted in his 1944 study of social rights that someday the guarantees must apply at an international level. Charles Merriam, though his mission to institutionalize equality and planning in his country through a second bill of rights had failed, insisted on the same as part of American discussions leading to the Universal Declaration. All, however, had directed their work at their own national settings in the first instance, and their international proposals were non-starters. If egalitarian distribution or a social minimum were to be institutionalized, it was within rather than beyond strengthened borders.[8]

A few reformers had insisted, during wartime and shortly after, that there was a fundamental connection between economic problems at home and rights abroad. It was this that justified, as Australian foreign minister and central negotiator of the United Nations Charter Herbert Evatt put it, embedding full employment as a goal of the organization. "The great threat to human freedoms which we have been combating for five years arose out of and was made possible by an environment dominated by unemployment and lacking freedom from want." Evatt celebrated the fact that, due to various kinds of agitation, not merely human rights (although with no mention of social rights specifically) but also rising standards of living made it into the document. But Henry Wallace's ousting in 1944, after his foolhardy speculation regarding how much milk the century of the common man would allow every human being, provided food for thought. Optimistic visions for the role of the United Nations Economic and Social Council, which tasked it with more ambitious global economic welfare, did not stoke sufficient enthusiasm (or elicit sufficient funds). West Europeans facing their own reconstruction—and the preservation of their own empires through unprecedented adjustments to distribution within them—were not interested in globalizing social justice either. And new schemes of "development," such as Harry S Truman's Point Four program, reflected only slightly more munificence, mainly because the Americans' Soviet ally during World War II was transformed into a Cold War threat.[9]

Before decolonization, the main exception to the exclusively nationalist boundaries of social justice came in the form of sufficiency rather than equality and did not get far. In May 1944, the International Labour Organization (ILO) issued its Declaration of Philadelphia, looking ahead to a postwar era in which it would try again to make labor more humane in the North Atlantic and, soon, around the world. The ILO had originated as part of the settlement after World War I, largely in response to the revolutionary ardor that the Soviet Union seemed to inspire—or that some feared it might. And in its 1944 declaration, the ILO reframed its longstanding mission of formulating standards for a humane workplace in terms of social rights.[10]

The organization's importance was real, but its role in the promotion of social rights was insignificant for decades, especially since it did nothing to change the fundamentally nationalist terms of political economy at the high tide of welfare ideology. After its origins and before World War II, the ILO had acted as a forum for the interests of capital and labor to agree on transnational standards under the directorship of French socialist Albert Thomas. In an age before the notion of internationalizing rights had much traction, the ILO did not propagate a general vision of them. It long focused on the workplace, not a broader vision of social citizenship, as its assigned priority. Progress in the interwar period was meaningful but limited, preserving a double standard for metropolitan and colonial workers, though acting within reason to regularize a revolution in workplace safety for the former and formally banning forced labor for the latter. Its contribution to the coming of welfare provisions in the transatlantic zone was negligible, but more significant in some places, especially Latin America. Its humanization of empire made a more definite if morally fraught contribution.[11]

In 1944, the ILO was afflicted by unappeasable curses. Having taken refuge in Montreal during the war, it was the unique survival of the League of Nations and could not escape the League's bad reputation. In consequence, the ILO was frustrated in its bids to insert itself as a premier entity in the emerging United Nations organization. It was not even mentioned in the Dumbarton Oaks proposals that saw the light of day that summer, providing the first indications of what postwar international order would look like, and it missed any serious role in postwar reconstruction. It would become an auxiliary part of the United Nations machinery on economic and social affairs, one acronym in the international alphabet soup. After a long and tumultuous relationship with the Soviet Union, which was a member for three short years in the mid-1930s, the ILO failed to entice it to rejoin until long after World War II. While the ILO incorporated in its deliberations the International Federation of Trade Unions whose members clustered across the Atlantic, it was not well poised to adjudicate the major dispute between capitalism and communism, in 1944 and after, over what approach to political economy would best serve organized labor. The Philadelphia declaration was primarily a bid to be noticed.[12]

It worked only briefly. Coming three months after Roosevelt's State of the Union referred to a "second bill of rights" for Americans, the ILO's conference promised to reestablish the organization with the mission of spreading social rights, going far beyond the humanization of the workplace and entitlements to bargain for the inclusion of full employment, necessary planning, and public assistance. In a public relations opportunity for the organization, Roosevelt likened its meeting to that in Philadelphia in 1776, where self-evident truths were proclaimed for the world of states—though, after thinking twice about his prepared statement, he immediately clarified that "if these were not the goals of national policy they could never become the goals of international policy." At best, in other words, the ILO could play the role of companion of experiments for national welfare of the past and future. After a minor role in the negotiation of the Universal Declaration, it spread information about labor standards. Beyond Philadelphia, its trajectory towards the global promotion of social rights awaited the explosion of international human rights politics later, something a not-yet postcolonial world could not sustain. It then passed from its florid 1944 rhetoric into a long age of finding its feet in providing technical assistance, under the directorship of American New Dealer David Morse and in the midst of the founding of the United Nations, the beginnings of the Cold War, and during decolonization. In these years, the ILO defined what it came to call "core labor standards" universalistically, but without major impact on broader controversies about planning and development. It made little sense in such circumstances, even outside places where authoritarianism crystallized, to recommend that states bent on national growth pursue social rights for individuals as a first and independent move.[13]

Even more revealing about the nationalistic premises of welfare was the complete exclusion of social rights from the first attempt to vault human rights into international law, in the form of the regional European Convention of Human Rights. Negotiated in parallel with the Universal Declaration and finalized the following year, the European Convention reflected the Cold War's crystallization, foreclosing social justice as a significant goal of international rights protection. Officially, this treaty was focused outward, towards the communist bloc, in order to symbolize the personal freedom for which "the West" now stood. By 1949, when the European Convention was concluded, it was broadly felt that inclusion of social rights would interfere with the main goal of signaling contrast. More disturbingly, and unofficially, its chief advocates—whether Winston Churchill in the United Kingdom or a strange coalition of ex-reactionaries and economic liberals on the Continent—hoped to use the regionalization of Cold War conservatism to interfere with ongoing domestic welfare initiatives from place to place, especially domestic socialism. Opposition to the very planning for which social rights had now become a synonym stood out in much of the rhetoric about the need to defend freedom at home, which victorious welfare projects supposedly trampled. In this regard, too, it was opportune to lop off social rights.[14]

That holdouts from the consensus even in Western Europe fled to the regional level to seek brakes and limits, however, confirms the nationalist premises of the welfare state, most of whose advocates barely paid heed to the new regional language of human rights in this period. The importance of human rights protection and its association with a distinctively European model of welfare awaited future decades, beginning symbolically with the European Social Charter more than a decade later. But critics of European empires overseas were by no means waiting, and they moved to establish their own unique visions of national welfare, as well as to voice expansive and unprecedented calls for global justice.[15]

THE DECOLONIZATION of the world after World War II was easily the most startling event with the widest-ranging implications in the history of distributive justice. It suddenly created whole zones of entitlement and demand that had simply been off the grid and left out of account for too long—most certainly during the making of the post–World War II international economic order. In virtue of the sheer number of new subjects and agents who suddenly had a voice, it created the conditions of possibility for something like the globalization of visions of distributive justice. The leaders of African independence were especially exemplary. Last to achieve freedom, they were first to propose global justice.

As with human rights in the era of the welfare state, it is easy to be distracted by the marginal problem of how far human rights protection developed under the internationalization of governance—most notably, in the new United Nations human rights apparatus or in the organization's Trusteeship Council, its now defunct institution for international supervision of foreign rule. But it is vastly more important how distribution was conceived within late-imperial circumstances and, especially, the postcolonial states, and how once again social rights figured in debate and decision-making. More important than looking at formal international organization is understanding how colonial subjects, giving up on imperial assurances of greater fairness in the future, moved to end empire and found their own welfare states—recognizing soon after that to do so might demand something even more ambitious. In the interwar period, both critics and defenders of empire found reason to consider whether a new organization of empire might achieve these ends itself, but by an early date, territorial nationalism won out as first among all ends, despite the risk that it would leave new states untethered from their wealthy former masters. Self-described welfare empires were almost everywhere, dealing with the full range of education, labor, health, and social services, before the phrase "welfare state" became popular anywhere. Welfare thus began as a colonial promise and was wrested from empire to become the new states' highest aspiration.[16]

Along with novel development schemes, colonial "humanism" and reform had already been the order of the day before World War II. Then old empires were recast, with subjection becoming more like citizenship in the renovated British "Commonwealth of Nations" and the relabeled French Union that dared no longer call themselves empires. Attracted by the possibilities of these innovations, some found common cause in federalist solutions that would retain some bond between metropole and colony without the old subjugation—including for the sake of economic obligation towards imperial subjects turned fellow citizens. Hypothetically, proposals for unity meant avoiding ratification of the division between a rich north and a poor south, thus implying some concern for distributive equality across what became sovereign borders. "Decolonization"—itself a European conception—was not foreordained, nor was its nationalist form. Advocates of national independence such as Frantz Fanon shot back at federalist scheming that it reflected little more than the "desire to maintain colonial structures intact" and was a naïve endorsement of hierarchy that would "guarantee certain forms of exploitation." These arguments, as much as the imperial bait-and-switch preserving old subjection under the mask of new "citizenship," had the effect of spreading the earlier national framework of welfare to the ends of the earth.[17]

Visions of sufficiency had had a better chance of implementation under late-imperial rule than equality within empire did. Throughout the period, furious debates raged about whether colonial workers might enjoy the same entitlements, including social rights, as metropolitan ones, and there were also late-colonial schemes of social security. But on both fronts, promises to achieve better outcomes with something short of full independence looked increasingly hollow, and optimistic assessment that nationalists could provide something better prevailed. It was increasingly orthodox to think that gaining more power at the risk of distributive gains was better than the reverse. "Seek ye first the political kingdom," Kwame Nkrumah, the iconic first president of Ghana after 1957, advised as the flood of African decolonization began, "and all else will be given you." Ahmed Sékou Touré, first president of Guinea as of the next year, protested that nothing but a new state could improve on the raw deal offered by the declining French Empire, even as the "French Union" was rebranded a supposedly post-imperial "French Community." As he put it: "We prefer poverty in liberty to riches in slavery."[18]

Within the new states, prioritization of material equality prevailed, even to the extent that riches were viewed as attainable—and they were desperately wanted. Few postcolonial leaders failed to dream in public of providing the sort of fairness on the basis of economic abundance that extant welfare states increasingly conferred on their metropolitan citizens but denied to their empires, before losing them. The central plank of anticolonial rhetoric was commitment to industrial modernity and national development, which would make it possible for equality and sufficiency both to be pursued—"in short," as one analyst at the time observed, "the modern welfare state." The commitments of the pioneering nationalists in south Asia—despite Mohandas Gandhi's very different vision of village utopias—had already set this pattern, which was transplanted universally after World War II. The contemplated growth would, it was hoped, skip the step of classical liberalism and industrial class politics, now that the end of the road in welfare-state class compromise was known. The challenge was national fairness without the mistakes it had taken elsewhere to get there. "If the distribution of wealth is not done properly," the first president of Zambia, Kenneth Kaunda, worried, "it might lead to the creation of classes in a society, and the much-valued humanist approach that is traditional and inherent in our African society would have suffered a final blow."[19]

Not that anticolonial leaders rejected basic entitlements out of hand. They frequently claimed to reject "growth" in aggregate terms in favor of a more broad-minded "development" that would incorporate the fullest picture of human expectations, though of course policies rarely distracted themselves from the preeminent goal of launching their states, from which all other goods would flow. But officially, at least, nearly every leader insisted that the superiority of African strategies was that they never mistook overall national improvement for broad-based popular welfare. "My first object," Nkrumah explained in one of his legendary Christmas Eve addresses, "is to abolish from Ghana poverty, ignorance and disease. We shall measure our progress by the improvement in the health of our people: by the number of children in school and by the quality of their education; by the availability of water and electricity in our towns and villages; and by the happiness which our people take in being able to manage their own affairs. The welfare of our people is our chief pride, and it is by this that my Government will ask to be judged." Egyptian anticolonial icon Gamal Abdel Nasser noted that he saw "freedom as more than liberty of thought and speech and writing. It is the liberty of a full stomach, a good home, health, education, work, security in old age." Of course, none of that was possible unless massive and rapid transformation into new circumstances occurred. "Given economic self-sufficiency," he explained, "[Egypt] can proceed to equality of opportunity for all citizens and social equity and fundamental human rights." For new Tanzanian president Julius Nyerere, everything must "depend on economic and social development. . . . Freedom from hunger, sickness and poverty depends upon an increase in the wealth and the knowledge available in the community."[20]

Sufficient provision for individuals would depend on growth, and it was inseparable from maintaining domestic equality in the swift modernization of economies to levels resembling those in the developed world. This is perhaps best indicated by the marginality of the Universal Declaration in setting the exact terms of distributive sufficiency, even as the same states proceeded in the United Nations to formulate a new treaty legally protecting their economic and social rights. Rather than invoke those sources, it was more common to offer homespun lists of entitlements. As his list, Nasser outlined:

1. The right of every citizen to receive medical treatment. . . .
2. The right of every person to study. . . .
3. The right of every citizen to work. . . .
4. The scope of old age and sickness insurance must be broadened. . . .

5. Children are the future. . . .

6. Women must be equal to men. . . .

7. The family is the foundation of society. . . .

8. The freedom of faith and religion must be secure.

Kaunda followed suit in his own way: "(a) No person should starve in Zambia because there is no real land hunger as is the case in many other parts of the world. (b) No person should really fail to have a decent two- or three-roomed Kimberley brick house. (c) No person should really ever dress in rags in Zambia nor indeed go barefooted. (d) No person should ever suffer from malnutrition in Zambia." Despite the Indian example, not many post-colonial constitutions listed social rights, except for the several African ones that directly cited the Universal Declaration—and therefore, if implicitly, its social rights—as state-of-the-art. If they aimed at decent minima when it came to the good things in life for their populations, however, sufficiency was always premised on prior national development. And overall, it was rare for postcolonial leaders to rhetorically prioritize sufficiency, as compared to intra-national and international equality, which they never slighted in favor of the provision of the most fundamental goods and the fulfill-ment of the most basic needs.[21]

More often than in Western Europe and (especially) the United States, the creation of economic circumstances of plenty—and the freedom and equality in the global context that went with them—were said to require a much fuller commitment to socialism than other states had made. A number of constitutions from Algeria to India evoked or came to evoke the ideal of socialism in their texts. Not only was socialism more popular in the cam-paign to transplant welfare to postcolonial circumstances, but that campaign bred new versions of socialism that focused on material equalization at a local and later on a global scale. "Socialism [is] the best means of ending the poverty which denies human fulfilment," Nasser explained. It did not so much involve toppling the local rich and powerful as it did mastering the forces of global empire that still thwarted advancement—an agenda that required strengthening the hands of the postcolonial elite to rule for the sake of the nation. It was not uncommon to deny local class divisions and internal conflicts, in order to claim that only national solidarity could lift the oppression of a global class system that tracked a global color line with disturbing proximity. "If the problem of the individual is a central concern in other continents—in countries that are free and independent—the first and the only true problem for the colonial peoples," Touré put it in 1959, even after Guinean independence had been won, "is that of the attainment of independence. It is consequently a collective problem." Senegalese poet and politician Léopold Sédar Senghor agreed, noting that "capitalism works only for the well-being of a minority." The values of sufficiency it had accommodated under pressure were themselves insufficient, "because, whenever state intervention and working-class pressure have forced it to reform itself, it has conceded only the minimum standard of living, when no less than the maximum would do." Throughout Asia and Africa, it was so axiomatic for capitalism to be held responsible for imperialism that postcolonial economics were almost always presented as an alternative to capitalism. "Since nationalism is thus necessarily an enemy of capitalism," summarized Rupert Emerson, premier student of the transition from empire to nation, "the way of economic and political salvation must lie through some alternative to capitalism, such as socialism."[22]

As before in the twentieth century, socialism in Africa and other postcolonial areas came to strongly imply material equality. On occasion, it was even reminiscent of a more austere position that promised to convert mass equality in penury into mass equality at some level of sufficiency, without risking the luxury and opulence that seemed deeply unethical even when economic growth up to a point was acknowledged to be indispensable. "We have to work towards a position where each person realizes that his rights in society—above the basic needs of every human being—must come second to the overriding need of human dignity for all," Nyerere argued in an interesting passage, "and we have to establish the kind of social organization which reduces personal temptations above that level to a minimum." Other times, however, he simply insisted that the masses of people achieve slow improvement before anyone else was allowed to surmount their level, so that "all have a gradually increasing basic level of material welfare before any individual lives in luxury." In practice, Nyerere's experiments, which included constraining the income and wealth of top earners, were tremendously controversial and violent, and how African leaders might have reconceptualized their moral ends if abundance materialized remained speculative. They may not have been sure themselves.[23]

One thing, however, was clear from the start: socialism would have to take the form of a global project, especially to the extent that inequality was globally organized and enforced. It was very plain to observers at the time that, at least initially, state-organized economic nationalism prevailed ideologically in the postcolonial countries, not least because it became so orthodox in the interwar period and remained so strong in the postwar age. But the new states gave rise more or less immediately to a broader if largely idealistic subaltern internationalism, one aiming at material justice of global dimensions. "The consciousness of economic inequality," the first Senegalese premier Mamadou Dia wrote in *The African Nations and World Solidarity* (1960), "align[s] the nations of Africa and Asia on the same battlefront against the West. With the consciousness of underdevelopment, a new idea appears, that of proletarian nations . . . confronting rich nations with a geographical unity that widens the gap between them." Senghor agreed: "The social problem today is less a class struggle within a nation than a global struggle between the 'have' nations (including the Soviet Union) and the proletarian nations (including the Chinese People's Republic), and we are one of these 'have-not' nations." What such welfare on the world scale would mean, however, awaited further precision in the 1960s and 1970s.[24]

Such endorsements of welfare at every scale, at times rescuing socialism from its earlier nationalization, left the whole idea of rights—including social rights—distinctly in second place rhetorically. Rather, both intranational and international equality as aims of a new political economy were preeminent. "A national policy that speaks of a people solely in terms of its rights is a mystification, a mythology," Dia commented. No other leaders volunteered to lead with such an international policy either, particularly when it came to economic and social rights. Trade unions aside, it was several decades before there were serious non-governmental movements in the global south agitating for social rights. That left the ILO as the main entity attempting to globalize a rights-based vision of social citizenship. Having been born to make work more humane in intra-European and colonial circumstances after World War I, the ILO reformulated that project for the new postcolonial setting after World War II, but its standard-setting and technical assistance offered little ideological excitement and uncertain impact.[25]

UNLIKE Carr, who barely thought beyond Europe when pining at the close of World War II for the social question to move from nationalization to internationalization, one prestigious analyst in the 1950s discerned the need for distributive justice to be globalized as a result of decolonization. The Swede Gunnar Myrdal pioneered a truly global economics. He was inspired by his country's creation, before World War II, of a renowned welfare state; in spite of his support of eugenics then, he became best-known after the conflict for his vastly influential thinking about improving American race relations. October 1955 found Myrdal, who had recently served the United Nations in European affairs, on the road to Egypt, where he lectured at the National Bank. Later, these lectures became *Rich Lands and Poor: The Road to World Prosperity* (1958). The same year as that book appeared, Myrdal gave the Storrs lectures at Yale Law School, which took up what he cast as the defining challenge of the age: scaling up the welfare state to the world stage.[26]

Myrdal's impression by the late 1950s that the construction of the national welfare state in the global north was for all intents and purposes complete is itself revealing, given how discriminatory it had often been in favoring white male citizens and how it was soon to be targeted for attack and "reform." In Myrdal's view, the welfare state already provided the revolutionary departure for an even more revolutionary welfare world to be constructed. "We see no limit to the further perfection of our national communities," he wrote, with steady growth locked in, political democracy effective, and equality of opportunity achieved (more or less). The sheer fact that previously divisive and unbelievable visions of national welfare had already come true allowed hope to conquer skepticism: "In their lifetime the proponents of what is now almost unanimously acclaimed were obnoxious to many—sometimes to most—of their compatriots, but some of them now have statues erected to their memory by grateful nations." Why not the world?[27]

There were, of course, significant geopolitical, structural, and technical difficulties to contend with in envisioning welfare's leap from nation to globe. For Myrdal, the preponderant truth was that bringing the welfare state to the world now had a precedent in the erection of the welfare state itself. This fact might counterbalance the obvious and hardly minor quandary that he dwelled on specifically in his Yale lectures: that *precisely the nationalist policies that had made the welfare state possible at home* now impeded its institutionalization globally. This, not the Cold War, is the problem that would have to be solved for a welfare world to take root, Myrdal assured his readers. Touchingly, he considered such obstacles almost secondary in importance if an ideological chasm were leapt—and now it was narrowing. In these years, Myrdal liked to cite his economist forebear from the turn of the twentieth century, Englishman Alfred Marshall, anticipating that "a time may come" when distribution would "be treated as of cosmopolitan rather than national aspiration," though it was "not yet in sight." Now, Myrdal said, it was.

"Solidarity between the various members of a nation [in] every . . . Western country can now afford to make increased sacrifices of material wealth for the purpose of raising the quality of life throughout their whole population," Marshall had written. "Not merely to save the world, but primarily to save their own souls, there should again be dreamers, planners, and fighters, in the midst of our nations, . . . [who] enlarge the scope of their interests to encompass the world scene," Myrdal added.[28]

As so often in his career, Myrdal's partner Alva was a full participant in his imagining welfare world. At this point the social science director of UNESCO, Alva did not use that phrase, but in her own lengthy 1953 contribution to the Florina Lasker lectures at Columbia University on the theme of "international social welfare," she understood it as a high task that "no generation before ours has had to face." It was "the specific effort of our time—and really the first of any time." For neither Myrdal did this plan show any special solicitude for individuals, let alone individual rights. Interestingly, it was in his own reflections on the advent of a potentially cosmopolitan economic order—and essentially alone in his writings—that Gunnar Myrdal invoked the United Nations' notion of human rights and fundamental freedoms, commenting on their legalization in the then-new European Convention. In this rendition, Myrdal observed, human rights were a better example of false compromise, since West European countries had reduced the system of international protection they set up for themselves to a dead letter by avoiding entry, neutering enforcement, and containing scope so that it would not even affect still-colonial areas, let alone the whole world. (He might have added that they had also dropped the economic and social rights in their document, even though the earlier Universal Declaration had featured them.) To date, Myrdal concluded, the path of human rights showed mainly that the victory of the nation-state after World War II had thoroughly cut off the prospect for internationalism, leaving behind the nagging but unrealized truth that "*the very idea of human rights and fundamental freedoms carr[ies] with it the concept of universality.*"[29]

Myrdal, however, was never a proponent of an international human rights revolution, even when it finally occurred two decades later. Instead, he concluded it was time for worldwide solidarity out of fear that Marx's prophecies might come true in unanticipated ways. Granted, Myrdal observed, Marx's own followers had in the meantime followed the norm of the developed world and set up socialism in one country, adopting the political economy of national welfare in the East just as surely as had been done in the West under social democratic or Christian auspices. And in that non-communist West, where national welfare had developed partly alongside and partly in response to the Soviet experiment, capitalists had disproved the existence of any law-like process whereby their political economy would dig its own grave. But if nationalism had saved capitalism by eliciting sufficient fellow feeling to support redistributive policy in Western Europe, it was still possible that "Marx's prophecy, which has been proved wrong for the individual nations, may . . . turn out to be an accurate forecast in regard to the relations among nations." This was especially true when it came to the developing areas of the world: they were not being progressively immiserated and "pauperized," as Marxist theory predicted, but their wealth lagged further and further behind that of the well-off countries, which were enjoying explosive growth. If this was the case, the proper response would need to be an internationalism to match the nationalism that had served before. Hence Myrdal's conclusion: "*The concept of the welfare state, to which we are now giving reality in all the advanced nations, would have to be widened and changed into a concept of a 'welfare world.'*"[30]

The basic purpose of Myrdal's work in this era was to blaze the path into that world—an aspiration that readers generally registered. The theoretical core of the argument scaled up analytically from the experience of state planning—shifting from an oppressor state keeping one class dominant over others to a welfare state that shared the wealth—to the kinds of processes that might institutionalize similar effects globally, even in the absence of a world state. To institutionalize such effects would counteract the otherwise expectable process of the rich capturing the lion's share of economic growth, both within countries and in the world as a whole—a process that had been interrupted only once in history, when the welfare state was built to contain inequality on a national scale.[31]

Myrdal was operating beyond even the most visionary assumptions of early attempts, in the 1930s and 1940s, to globalize economic governance, themselves contained at Bretton Woods and after. It had been rare then even for dreamers to make global economic inequality the quandary for international institution-building to confront. Far more dominant was the thought that international economic governance would take the hitherto national campaign for "full employment" global. And two further unanticipated lessons conditioned Myrdal's allegiances by the late 1950s. He worried first that the very early attempts he wanted to extend had broken insufficiently with the still-dominant understanding of "internationalism" as *restricting* economic governance under the banner of free trade rather than *inventing* it in a powerful new form. And second, by the late 1950s, it seemed what really mattered about the 1930s and 1940s was that economic nationalism—sometimes to the point of autarky—prospered and formed the basis for redistributive policy across modular welfare states. If this was so, a brand new internationalism would need to be brought about, one that both more fundamentally transcended the free-trade premises of nineteenth-century internationalism and learned from the welfarist nationalism of the mid-twentieth century to do so—combining the *form* of the first with the *content* of the second. Carr had reached similar conclusions for Europe in 1945, and Myrdal now expanded them for the globe in view of the yawning gap between ever-richer nations and the rest.[32]

The force of these imperatives is most apparent in *Rich Lands and Poor*, one of the first books by a professional economist, or anyone else for that matter, to take up the soon-familiar framing of north-south divergence. It was even more graphically plain in the great emphasis that Myrdal placed on the concept not of individual sufficiency but of international equality. This concept was foremost in Myrdal's lexicon. More than just the explicit topic of *Rich Lands and Poor*, "the equality issue" was the concept Myrdal chose to organize the lecture that he delivered, almost two decades later, upon receiving the Nobel Prize for economics, with the neoliberal Friedrich Hayek in 1974. Myrdal never concerned himself with poverty reduction as an end in itself; rather, he focused on the structures of international economic governance and national income equalization per capita. As a development theorist, his framework was unerringly concerned with state capacity, not individual perquisites (in terms of basic needs or social rights). Even when, late in his career, Myrdal reflected the spirit of the times in titling his last major work *The Challenge of World Poverty* (1970), with the then-novel phrase "anti-poverty" in the subtitle, his text did not focus on the establishment or achievement of minimum provision. Like leaders of the new states before him, Myrdal scaled up the welfare-state promise of equality with even less emphasis on sufficiency—as if that problem would be handled at a lower level of governance than the world economy.[33]

Equality would depend on international governance, but so far "only propaganda forums" had been set up for its advocates. And there was no doubt that the ability to make public claims counted for a lot, providing voice to once-dominated peoples to dispel lingering and opportunistic unfamiliarity with the widening gap between global lives. With decolonization, as Myrdal described it, "the convenience of ignorance" permitted by the distance of global inequality had been lifted, just as had occurred beginning a century before with local inequality. He went so far as to report his "belief that the most important function of international organizations in the present stage of world history is to provide forums where the underprivileged countries can join together in expressing their dissatisfaction." This was a very friendly description of what those countries would shortly proceed to do, culminating in the New International Economic Order (NIEO) proposals fifteen years later. It was nothing short of "a Great Awakening." And unlike any earlier era, including the immediate post–World War II years, an increasingly broad public, not only south but also north, treated rising levels of inequality as a rank embarrassment. "When ordinary people in our developed countries are for the first time made aware of [the] stern facts," Myrdal explained of global inequality, "this experience often has the quality of a revelation to them." As John Kenneth Galbraith observed in his *New York Times* review, Myrdal was much better at making the diagnosis of accelerating inequality than finding the cure for it. Despite Myrdal's optimism, no debate about what institutions would interrupt the divergence of rich lands from poor ensued. In his classic *Neo-Colonialism* (1966), Nkrumah referred directly to Myrdal in issuing a withering verdict on how Myrdal's call to action had been rendered one more hypocritical slogan. "It has been argued that the developed nations should effectively assist the poorer parts of the world, and that the whole world should be turned into a Welfare State. However, there seems little prospect that anything of this sort could be achieved." It fell to the global south to propose the most ambitious scheme for making the notion of welfare world a reality.[34]

AS THEY formulated their plans, the new states also broke the deadlock at the United Nations that had marooned human rights in a non-binding expression of values. Over the years, postcolonial nations nearly quadrupled the number of states that had been around to vote on the Universal Declaration. These new states had a decisive impact, with accelerating strength in the United Nations General Assembly and the parts of the global organization over which that meant power—including the human rights apparatus. And in 1966, committees finalized twin covenants of human rights law that included a treaty on social rights: the International Covenant on Civil and Political Rights (ICCPR) and the International Covenant on Economic, Social and Cultural Rights (ICESCR).

A 1952 decision had split the two kinds of norms—civil and political rights on the one hand and economic, social, and cultural rights on the other—into groups for the purposes of twin legal covenants. Coalitions of the new states, in league with willing allies and led by energetic diplomats such as Egerton Richardson, foreign minister of postcolonial Jamaica, were catalysts in unblocking the project of human rights law, thereby prioritizing global norms prohibiting racial discrimination (and secondarily, religious persecution). Despite the fact that the Soviets, frequent allies in the cause of anticolonial resolutions in the United Nations, acted opportunistically, the new states often played the role of broadening their campaigns beyond the terms of Cold War bipolarity. Their signal achievement was the International Convention on All Forms of Racial Discrimination, approved by the General Assembly in 1965, which in turn provided a diplomatic and political model for the finalization of the general human rights covenants, including the second one on social rights, the following year.[35]

The new International Covenant on Economic, Social, and Cultural Rights (ICESCR), which ultimately came into legal force in 1976, was of obvious significance in global history. By any measure, the most important aim for the new states that sponsored this achievement was promoting the concept of the collective self-determination of peoples. This imperative revived a promise Woodrow Wilson had made at the end of World War I, then confined to the white race, before Franklin Roosevelt renewed it in the Atlantic Charter during World War II, only to consent to Winston Churchill's confinement of it once again. Easily the most significant conceptual contribution the global south made to the origins of global human rights law was to sponsor self-determination not simply as right but as the very first one on the list, signaling that their futures as collective peoples mattered most. But the global south would not merely take self-determination more seriously; it would also give the concept new content, especially by reinterpreting it to have a specifically economic meaning. Its main early move in this regard was to decree that self-determination of a people implies its "permanent sovereignty over natural resources." The principle allowed new states to put an end to the legacy of concessionary imperialism and led to several well-publicized expropriations that nullified contracts depriving countries of profit from the commodities beneath their own ground.[36]

The globalization of other economic and social rights in the ICESCR was an epoch-making event in the broader history of the norms, as a matter of setting standards for the modular reproduction of welfare states around the world, each state struggling to vindicate such rights within its own means. Long after being propounded in early socialism, the right to strike, which not even the ILO had canonized before, finally figured in an international rights document. All of the traditional sufficiency norms concerning adequate standards of safety at work, a decent minimum wage, social security for those too young, ill, or old to work, and mandatory state-provided primary education were reaffirmed. Perhaps the most important novelty of the treaty, however, was an absence: it was the first declaration of rights in world history not to include a protection for property. And it was of tremendous importance for the future that the treaty provided much more detail about the independent existence and importance of rights to food, housing, and clothing as part of a generous "right to an adequate standard of living." It elevated the right to the "highest attainable standard of health" from the 1946 World Health Organization constitution to the canonical status denied it before. But unlike the contemporary first covenant, on civil and political rights, the second covenant, on economic, social, and cultural rights, was deprived of any special monitoring committee. (The treaty was to be supplemented with a monitoring body only in 1985).[37]

For all its importance, the ICESCR was hardly the main focus of anticolonial distributive visions. The new states mainly pursued a new economic order outside the conceptual and institutional framework of human rights. It was far from the case that social rights ever formed the primary ideology of decolonization in the new states or even at the United Nations, let alone met the ambition of the distributive visions of new states for the global scene. The new social rights treaty did not contain any kind of commitment to egalitarian distribution within states, and did not really demand cross-border social justice to meet the sufficiency norms it listed. For all its radicalism, economic self-determination in its treaty form only protected the right of a people not to be deprived by outsiders of "its own means of subsistence." If there was going to be an affirmative obligation of those same outsiders to provide subsistence to postcolonial humanity, or a fuller-blown requirement to achieve a more equal world, it could not come from the text of this right newly guaranteed in law.[38]

The ICESCR did, some later contended, lay groundwork for cross-border distributive obligation to fulfill sufficiency norms, if not for the sake of equality at any scale. Since the novel first article on self-determination, for all its importance, provided no help in this regard, the crucial proviso that each state take steps to vindicate the rights under its own power as well as relying on "international assistance and co-operation" might imply obligations of the global rich towards the global poor. But it was not as if the new states viewed this last clause at the time as a justification for global wealth transfer. Instead, as several diplomats noted in the course of the debates around it, this proviso functioned to anticipate a possible backstop when states were affected by forces beyond their control. "International economic assistance," explained one Mexican negotiator, "could only be supplementary and was mainly a means of counter-acting economic maladjustments arising from external causes." There was practically no hint in the negotiations that anyone might ever place much stress on the minor textual indications that the now globalized social rights fell to all states to fulfill, rather than leaving the poorest states to simply adjust their budgets. Not only did no consensus emerge regarding a serious requirement of redistributive obligation of wealthy to poor states in the origins of human rights law—with the possible exception of the treaty's provision to eradicate hunger, inserted by the United Nations' Food and Agricultural Organization to reflect its global charge. Worse, the arena of human rights did not allow new states to impose obligations on wealthy states to guarantee global sufficiency. As for global distributive equality, human rights law did not envision it.[39]

But far more important, the demands of individual sufficiency the ICESCR outlined for obligation within states paled beside the once quite believable and much more exciting project of demanding worldwide equality among states as a matter of global justice. It was this project that most concerned the postcolonial nations in the very era when human rights law first came on the scene. The human rights diplomacy of the new states meant little compared to their intense and visible investment in global economic reordering. It was increasingly common in the 1960s for the global south to claim that social rights come prior to and are more important than political and civil rights. But this rhetoric was deployed to add legitimacy to the global south's broader economic project, as well as to distract from the rise of authoritarianism in some of the very countries that sponsored it.[40]

THE NEW International Economic Order (NIEO) proposals that offered the dazzling climax of this global project burst into prominence in spring 1974, hard on the heels of the oil shock the fall before. The two events were indissolubly linked, and the NIEO would never have had the visibility it briefly gained without the oil-producing states' brief strategic alliance with its cause and the developed world's anxiety that it portended a regular new occurrence. It felt like the debut—exciting or frightening, depending on the observer—of a geopolitically powerful third-world solidarity that could genuinely transform economic relations. But if it attained momentary though spectacular visibility, the NIEO's origins were hardly recent. And for all of its many contingencies, its emergence proved to be the moment when the globalization of distributive justice first became imaginable to wide swathes of humanity. That imaginative development would be difficult to undo, even once its practical realization became impossible, and defending basic rights and meeting basic needs seemed more than uplifting enough a goal to pursue in an unequal world.

Although difficult to recall in today's neoliberal era of servicing poverty and other inadequate provision, the NIEO was the culmination of a heady time of outsized hopes. A postcolonial leader such as Algeria's Houari Boumédiène, already prestigious for beating an empire, could win significant consensus and attract spectacular notice when he called for his and other fronts for national liberation to transform into a global battlefield for just distribution. The NIEO's sources are often traced to an almost timeless notion of Afro-Asian solidarity, with "the darker nations" achieving a coherent plan and mythical unity at the pivotal Bandung conference in Indonesia in 1955, followed by non-alignment during the Cold War before assorted enemies foiled their plans. In truth, the path from Bandung to the NIEO was anything but foreordained. It intersected the parallel constitution of a Non-Aligned Movement as an alliance of like-minded states (which still exists today) but also diverged from it at critical moments. And in fact the instability of interests, leaders, and states involved in the twenty-year lead-up to spring 1974 is more remarkable than any coherence or unity. Pivotal for all players, however, were subaltern entitlements of sovereign states, beginning with those to natural resources and escalating into claims for just distributional structures between rich nations and the rest.

Instituting supranational legal protections for individuals—including economic and social rights—figured rhetorically or not at all in the kaleidoscope of visions.[41]

The more immediate origins of the NIEO proposals were in a much more concrete and specific formation: the United Nations Conference on Trade and Development (UNCTAD), and the activism of its first secretary general, the dissident Argentine economist Raúl Prebisch. Initially head of the UN's Economic Commission for Latin America (ECLA) before founding the more global body in 1964, Prebisch theorized that a world in which the north manufactured on the basis of the south's raw materials would lock in and indeed accelerate global inequality. This argument led him to argue that Latin American (and presumably, other even less developed) nations should adopt relatively more autarkic approaches to political economy so as to generate indigenous manufacturing sectors to disrupt the downward spiral of dependency. Elevated to the United Nations, Prebisch moved to an alternative vision of globalization whereby commodities traded by the global south could become the motors of an increasingly equal world if fair rules were instituted and poor nations joined forces on the model of a trade union to raise prices.[42]

Even before the NIEO proposals were formally announced, responses to third-world activism were enormously varied, ranging from titillation to horror. A good barometer of change in the 1960s is that the Roman Catholic Church under Pope Paul VI issued Popolorum Progressio (1967). Alongside kindred ecumenical Protestant thinking about the meaning of ethics in a postcolonial world, this encyclical updated Christian social thought for a newly global age, affirming that "the social question ties all men together, in every part of the world." While the encyclical lavished most of its call for love and solidarity on the suffering of the poor, it also acknowledged that "unless the existing machinery is modified, the disparity between rich and poor nations will increase rather than diminish; the rich nations are progressing with rapid strides while the poor nations move forward at a slow pace."[43]

The crisis and obsolescence of the Bretton Woods system after American president Richard Nixon unlinked the dollar from gold in 1971 and replaced that system with one of floating currencies provided a moment of opportunity for orthogonal moves in the global economic governance that Prebisch and others had husbanded as a matter of theory in the prior decade. And when the Organization of the Petroleum Exporting Countries

(OPEC) responded to the Yom Kippur War two years later by quadrupling the price of crude oil, the coincidence that OPEC was a loose affiliate of the NIEO did more than anything else to stoke dreams (and nightmares). "For the first time since Vasco de Gama," one much-cited statement of the moment had it, "mastery over a fundamental decision in a crucial area of the economic policy of the center countries escaped their grasp as certain peripheral countries wrested it from them." What if the oil shock portended a general reconfiguration of global economic relations? One insightful observer called the spate of activism "a hidden turning point in the history of international law." After the NIEO, the conscience would never be the same, even if its heirs who promote the cause of global justice today may not even know it ever existed.[44]

During and after the NIEO's annunciation in a special session of the UN General Assembly and in close connection with a new Charter of the Economic Rights and Duties of States, its primary goal was to devise policies for the equalization of rich and poor nations. The NIEO's diagnosis was harsh. The world's peoples had been involved in one another's affairs for centuries, but it had been on colonial terms. Political decolonization of the globe had barely been finished, and economic hierarchy and predation remained agonizingly entrenched for those who struggled against them and easily visible for those who did not bury their heads in the sand. It was, however, a new day for "interdependence"—one of the NIEO's buzzwords and part of the lingua franca of the age in many different versions. And more and more people, finally aware of how connected the globe had long been, could grant how incomplete decolonization remained, and target the immoral economic hierarchy that (as Myrdal had observed twenty years before) only continued to worsen.[45]

In response, the scaling up of the welfare state took global disparity at the level of nations as the new potential class war with sides to reconcile. Like the proponents of welfare at the national scale, those advocating a new international economic order explicitly abjured revolutionary overthrow in favor of compromise, much to the disappointment of some Marxist commentators. The welfare state metaphor, as for Myrdal before, was popular because it allowed for likening the NIEO to the international equivalent of the "trade union"—as Nyerere most frequently put it—which allowed weaker actors domestically to strengthen bargaining power and exact perquisites. It was not merely that the new states jealously guarded their own sovereignty and saw the NIEO fulfill their claims to economic self-determination and permanent sovereignty over natural resources, though both national sovereignty and economic self-determination were utterly central to their rhetoric. Rather, the analogies to the NIEO's trade unionization for the sake of a "welfare world" signaled a global social justice that was to work neither through the vindication of individual entitlements nor through violent revolution, but rather through the solidaristic institutionalization of a fairer deal for otherwise weak national parties in relation to strong ones. As the Dutch international lawyer B. V. A. Röling, one of the brightest in his field in the decades after World War II, observed, "The guiding concepts in [the] NIEO are in many respects of the same character as the guiding principles which were accepted in domestic law. In both fields the question was whether a law of liberty should be replaced by social law. . . . It meant the universalization of principles that were already applied in the 'welfare state.'"[46]

As already on a national scale in the postcolonial states, the NIEO distinctly emphasized equality in the scaled-up welfarist package, now in an internationalist key. Not sufficiency—especially not for individuals, of whom presumably states would take care themselves—but equality among states was therefore the principal goal on which the NIEO based its demands. All of its policy proposals were justified in the name of this ideal, from massive aid increases to credit on favorable terms, debt forgiveness, and technology transfer. As the NIEO declaration states, the goal was to "correct inequalities and redress existing injustices, making it possible to eliminate the widening gap between all the developed and the developing countries." Similarly, the Charter on the Economic Rights and Duties of States called for "the acceleration of the economic growth of developing countries with a view to bridging the economic gap between developing and developed countries." Both made only the barest mention of individual human rights, and none at all of economic and social rights among them.[47]

The NIEO echoed and scaled up the national welfare state political economy not simply when it came to public authority but also when it came to private actors, sponsoring the first substantial debate in history about the role of multinational corporations in world political economy. According to economic theory close to the NIEO, multinational corporations, if their power went untamed, played precisely the spoiler role towards global distributive fairness that domestic corporations played in national settings before the welfare state set out to subordinate them to a public agenda. Not that its proposals in this regard got very far, as years of "North-South dialogue" followed. But the NIEO succeeded in the 1970s in making plain both the inegalitarian effects of the extant international economic order and the role of private actors within it.[48]

From the beginning, it was easy to see that, as a movement of, by, and for states (or "peoples"), the NIEO made no provision for internal distribution or internal governance in any respect—including when it came to the whole gamut of basic rights. Nyerere insisted that "economic liberation" from an external and oppressive global structure favoring the wealthy required the diplomatic solidarity of poor states and therefore dropping or soft-pedalling concerns about internal human rights practices, however justified they were in pure theory. "For international purposes, we should act together even though internal liberation may not have been achieved by all of us to the same level," he put things euphemistically. "We may criticize tyrannical, brutal, or unjust governments and regimes in the Third World, but we must not do this in the context of the North-South debate." Undoubtedly, there was much hypocrisy in this double standard, as if the only possible response to the growing concern for "human rights violations" in the global south without any attention to global distributive justice were simply to reverse the priorities. But some non-governmental actors supported just that step. Most notably, a group of anticolonial lawyers, inspired by the NIEO, propounded in Algiers on July 4, 1976—the bicentennial of America's Declaration of Independence—a "Declaration of the Rights of Peoples" that proposed to complete decolonization through a liberation of nations and the reorganization of international economic life in the name of equality. The next year, the United Nations General Assembly papered over the divergence between the agendas by proclaiming that "the realization of the new international economic order is an essential element for the effective promotion of human rights and fundamental freedoms and should be accorded priority."[49]

The NIEO came to grief, due to its short-sighted commodities strategy, its coalition of strange bedfellows, and northern responses that ranged from the ambivalent to the oppositional—most definitely including early neoliberalism on the march. If not on arrival, the NIEO was dead by the later 1970s, with the global debt crisis of the early 1980s putting the final nails in its coffin. Its entire approach to the ethics of globalization contrasted starkly with the neoliberal political economy that soon ascended as the "real new international economic order" of the age and since. And in almost every way, the NIEO was also the precise opposite of the human rights revolution that took off in close proximity to its annunciation. Heir to postcolonial visions of distribution, the NIEO prized equality over sufficiency. The beneficiaries of that equality would be the new nation-states in relation to their wealthy betters, and individuals in their relation to one another across the globe through the proxy of state representation. The agent of such distributive fairness was a movement. But it was primarily a movement of states, not non-governmental forces. Just as the human rights movement would present itself, the NIEO was internationalist and globalized concern for the sake of the unjustly treated. Poles apart from the human rights movement, however, the NIEO targeted unfair distribution and prioritized material equality in ratifying rather than undermining state sovereignty, and it relied most on coordinated diplomatic power, not naming and shaming, to broker change.[50]

But human rights were the wave of the future. Would human rights law and movements ultimately offer a comparable attempt to scale up the welfare state to the world stage? They would certainly make far more room than postcolonial visions of distribution for economic and social rights for individuals, as well as for attention to their basic needs. But with human rights in ethics and neoliberalism in economics arising, with the national welfare state in crisis and with initial visions of a more ambitious globalized welfare nipped in the bud, the ideal of equality died. The ideal of sufficiency was left to subsist alone.

5

Basic Needs and Human Rights

"Is the satisfaction of basic needs a human right?" Development economist Paul Streeten asked this question in 1980, but it would not have made sense even a decade before. That year, Streeten was just finishing up his first stint at the World Bank, which had recently committed itself to lending to countries around the world with the aim of fulfilling the "basic needs" of their populations, such as food, shelter, and the like. But now an international human rights revolution was sweeping elite discussion across the world, and the question of what, if anything, the two agendas had to do with each other seemed pressing. "Are minimum levels of nutrition, health and education among the most fundamental human rights?" Streeten asked. "Or are human rights themselves basic needs?"[1]

It was all very confusing. A generation younger than his Swedish colleague Gunnar Myrdal and in his orbit (Myrdal was godfather to one of his daughters), Streeten was far more representative of a succeeding phase of imagining global progress. Growth with the prospect of scaling up the welfare state into a "welfare world" gave way to the fulfillment of the so-called basic needs of individuals on a global scale. But individuals, it was turning out, had basic global rights too. As Streeten and many others were well aware, the 1970s saw two major parallel revolutions, which came from entirely distinct origins but which ended up intersecting. Almost overnight, "basic needs" became the fixation of development thinking, especially in international circles and projects. It is hard to believe, but global poverty had simply not existed before as a policy area, and the turn to basic needs brought it to the center of development expertise and the concern of an increasingly large public. Meanwhile, and likewise suddenly, human rights surged to prominence on the global stage as a reformist cause, championed by social movements and integral to the diplomatic agendas of states. Like two waves crashing into each other, the twin surges of basic needs and human rights hardly canceled each other out. There was some interference, but much common motion. The results were spectacular.

No study of how human rights became our highest ideals can neglect the 1970s era of their breakthrough. The main reason that breakthrough occurred was the search for a new moral culture of idealism and activism as the Cold War entered its second half: nothing seemed to justify the violence that both sides and their clients brought to the world, and the assertion of the most basic entitlements of individuals around the world made new sense. But when that human rights revolution is brought into an even broader history of the modern struggle over the ideals for the distribution of the good things in life, a more complicated and interesting story about the period emerges. A new transnational activism concerning free speech, imprisonment, and torture ascended in visibility, but the tentative intersection of human rights with economic matters—thanks to the basic needs revolution—proved fateful for the future. Many activists newly recruited into the transnational activism facing down the depredation, imprisonment, and torture of totalitarianism in Eastern Europe and authoritarianism in Latin America placed the whole problem of a broader social justice on indefinite hold, or dropped it altogether, in order to focus on personal freedoms. Yet a few redefined social rights in terms of a global subsistence ethic. In the new situation of the 1970s, the dream of a welfare world simultaneously achieved its highest visibility and was definitively shattered as a neoliberal turn began instead. Development as the redemption of collective nations began to ring hollow, and an egalitarian welfarism or socialism for the compromise or reconciliation of classes was giving way to idioms of individual entitlement—an expectation basic needs and human rights shared with one another, as well as with the coming neoliberal revolution whose triumph no one yet expected. The rise of the basic needs paradigm in development thinking, along with its intersection with the concurrent human rights revolution, starkly reveals how visions of sufficient distribution supplanted any notion of material equality from an early date—not least because American political leaders and non-governmental advocates were most enamored of the consolidation of the rights and needs concepts.

Connecting the two could work to lend basic needs the prestigious status or obligatory character of human rights, but in the process, the break with welfarist interpretations of social rights, which had once been associated with egalitarian duties, was immense. It was no longer a 1940s attempt to build a welfare state for citizens, but a new version of humanitarian concern now directed at the global poor, suddenly discovered as an aggregate entity. Intervening campaigns against poverty in various wealthier states were globalized, but with the effect of displacing the dream of welfarist equality. In the 1970s, confidence in such an outcome no longer seemed available, neither within states nor on a newly global stage. And the same occurred in development circles, once the notion of equalizing growth for the formerly colonized world seemed incredible.

Whether in the form of prioritizing basic needs or globalizing social rights, global sufficiency's rise as an imperative was too perfectly timed to avoid the conclusion that rights and needs were really attempts to ethically outflank the more ambitious global equality that postcolonial states themselves proposed in the "New International Economic Order" (NIEO) demands of 1974–75. An emphasis on sufficiency looked to many like a consolation prize for the abandonment of equality. Committing to a vision of sufficient fulfillment of basic needs tacked between the outrage of ongoing penury in a postcolonial world and the costly prospect of egalitarian justice that the same postcolonial world proposed. As the pursuit of global social rights got underway, though its full endorsement awaited the end of the Cold War, the distributive ideal of sufficiency alone survived, and the ideal of equality died.

THE HUMAN RIGHTS revolution occurred almost *ex nihilo* in the 1970s. There had been talk and even treaty making in the United Nations since the 1940s, but it testified more to states colluding to protect one another. No serious move had ever been made to fulfill the organization's promise in its charter to institutionalize not simply peace but justice too. The lone exception of the increasingly outcast state of South Africa aside, human rights rhetoric at the governmental level had remained stillborn, and no state had a visible human rights policy. That changed in a series of stages, above all as new social movements of the 1960s were winnowed down and those movements defined in terms of human rights burst into consciousness across the next decade. Amnesty International, the first high-profile human rights non-governmental organization in history, won the Nobel Peace Prize in 1977, the same year that the American president Jimmy Carter committed his country to a new human rights policy, in part to cleanse the stain of Vietnam from the national image.[2]

Easily the most extraordinary fact about this human rights revolution, from the perspective of ideals about how to distribute the good things in life, is that, with some key exceptions, it unceremoniously purged attention to economic and social rights, to say nothing of a fuller-fledged commitment to distributive equality. It was a striking contrast to the spirit of social rights in the era of national welfare, when they were not only integral to human rights overall but linked to egalitarian idealism and outcomes at the national scale. Now, as if the promise of the Universal Declaration of Human Rights (1948) had never been about national welfare, it was remembered as a charter meant to save the individual from the state's depredations of civil liberties rather than to empower the state to make individual flourishing and equality a reality.

Given that economic and social provisions were canonized in the documents and had been as central to the coming of the national welfare state as they were absent from the new transnational mobilization, it is surprising how easily the reversal was achieved. Perhaps two main reasons explain this shift. For one thing, especially in the global north, Cold War assumptions had long since damaged the 1940s communion of civil and political with economic and social rights, through the sheer force of insistence and repetition. And then, the new visibility of human rights ideals occurred as activists, disillusioned about the failures of socialism, the violence socialist politics sparked, or both—including in socialism's postcolonial forms—embraced their roles, conceiving of "human rights" as a morally pure form of activism that would not require the exaggerated hopes or depressing compromises of past utopias.

Graphic evidence of the turn away from socialism and the skepticism toward social rights comes from Peter Benenson and Aryeh Neier, the respective founders of the first prominent global non-governmental organization and of the major American one concerned with human rights across the period. Despite having stood as a candidate for the Labour Party several times in his earlier life, when Benenson founded Amnesty International in the 1960s, he explicitly understood it as an alternative to socialism and set in motion a pattern that led the group to confine its attention to a narrow focus on political imprisonment. It added torture to its bailiwick in the 1970s and the death penalty in the 1980s, shifting to poverty only after the millennium. "Look on the Socialist Parties the world over, ye mighty, and despair," Benenson explained to a correspondent in justification of his emphases. Part of the reason for his depression was his own serial losses in election campaigns, but he also admitted, in the Christian idiom that frequently crept into his work, that "the quest for an outward and visible Kingdom is mistaken." For the founder, human rights activism was much more about saving the activist's soul, rather than building social justice.[3]

American Aryeh Neier founded Human Rights Watch in the 1970s with an exclusionary attention to political violations in left- and right-wing regimes. Despite his early political awakening, thanks to the six-time socialist presidential candidate Norman Thomas, and his past as the president of the labor-affiliated Student League for Industrial Democracy (which later became Students for a Democratic Society), Neier nonetheless chose a class-free civil libertarianism as his definitive mode of politics. Given that the American Civil Liberties Union, over which he presided before co-founding Human Rights Watch, had ascended to prominence by departing from the class politics that originally birthed it, Neier's Cold War stewardship of liberties and rights confined his attention to basics like free speech and a free press. Human Rights Watch functioned primarily to transfer such single-minded civil libertarianism abroad, with funding from foundation grants that singled out state repression rather than pursuing a more contentious social justice. Through the end of his career in the organization, Neier fought bitterly with anyone who tried to make room for distributive justice, including as a matter of social rights, tirelessly invoking the Cold War liberal Isaiah Berlin's distinction between negative liberty and positive self-realization in his defense.[4]

On a broader view, however, these representative developments within the two most visible northern human rights outfits allowed for many exceptions, especially among the beneficiaries of the earliest transnational human rights politics in the 1970s, activists in Eastern Europe and Latin America's Southern Cone. Attention in both areas focused overwhelmingly on state depredations to the right to life and to liberty of thought and action. While the coalitional basis of the strategy of indicting governments for betraying their own promises to follow constitutional and international law required socialists to mute or soft pedal their ideals of material justice, they did not simply abandon them.[5]

For a long moment in the middle of the 1970s, in fact, a broad mushrooming of socialist groups embraced human rights, including in democratic countries that had repressed leftist agitation. In France, "radicals had equated the struggle for rights as mere reformism, but by the early 1970s, state repression had compelled them to adopt democratic struggles as a fundamental axis of their political work. This did not mean that these groups abandoned violent revolution, the overthrow of capitalism, or the dictatorship of the proletariat as final goals, or that they confined their efforts to the narrow field of parliamentary politics." In Colombia, something similar obtained, as revolutionaries such as the authors of *El Libro Negro de la Represión* (The Black Book of Repression), a documentation of state violence, invoked human rights norms to highlight it, while claiming that the entire purpose of such ideals had always been for the sake of vast political transformation. From early modern revolution to the present, the aim was "to 'popularize' the contents of the Rights of Men for those who hold them, without evading the revolutionary consequences of such consciousness, but actually seeking such effects." The point is not to overstate how open socialists were to rights language. For example, the new liberation theology in Latin America building on the globalization of Catholic social thought of the 1960s turned against rights as it became more radical. And the allergy to framing social justice in terms of rights remained strong wherever Marxism endured as an intellectual or popular idiom. But this hardly meant that the human rights revolution of the era ruled out other possibilities.[6]

In the Soviet Union's Eastern Bloc and the Latin American Southern Cone, where dictatorship ruled, socialists saw no reason to abandon their socialism and no contradiction in joining broader coalitions of dissent, whether at home or as emigres. In the formation of the storied Czechoslovak dissident group Charter 77, the most prominent reform communist to join, Jiří Hájek, was quite insistent that human rights activism involved no relinquishment of his socialism. The Soviet Bloc countries had treated the Universal Declaration with ambivalence, Hájek wrote, but had participated fully in drafting the human rights conventions and solemnly ratified them. (Hájek's Czechoslovakia did so as they came into legal force.) Such facts "banish the doubts of the active socialist-motivated citizens of the Warsaw Pact [i.e., Soviet Bloc] countries, and dispel any fear they might have that the implementation of . . . those documents might be viewed as falling outside the scope and framework of socialist society, or even regarded as hostile to it." In fact, he added, "socialist society is far better equipped than any other society to realize this unity [of political and civil rights with economic and social rights] and sustain it." The same was true of the group's spokeswoman, Zdena Tominová, who agitated for right consciousness while calling for world socialism as late as 1981, during a trip to the West and before her expulsion from Czechoslovakia became permanent.[7]

Opposition to communism in Poland became world famous in the summer and fall of 1980, as the smaller Worker's Defense Committee (KOR), founded in 1976, exploded in prominence and size as "Solidarnósc." It was no accident that this happened thanks to a self-conscious workers' movement engaging in classic strike activity at the Lenin shipyard in Gdańsk, even if its politics were "apolitical" and avoided outright challenge to the regime out of situational necessity and strategic choice. At the start, before the involvement of intellectuals and Solidarity's transformation into broad-based democratic opposition, its twenty-one demands began by insisting on the now internationally guaranteed right to strike, and the rest concerned sufficiency guarantees and especially price controls in the midst of the era's economic crisis and the regime's rationing polices. For much of his suddenly global audience before the 1981 crackdown, electrician Lech Wałęsa was above all a workingman—albeit "a new kind of trade-unionist, not only for Poland but also for the world in general," as one contemporary explained it.[8]

Broader egalitarian aspirations were likewise held by many Latin Americans who fled repression in Chile and Uruguay after 1973 and Argentina after 1976, when coups occurred in each place. Besides those who arrived in more hospitable climates for socialism, there were examples even in fledgling American networks. The economist Orlando Letelier, former Chilean government minister under democratic socialist Salvador Allende, called for the restoration of human rights in his country after his government was toppled and he fled to the United States. But before his outrageous assassination in a car bombing in Washington, D.C. in 1976, Letelier also decried the neoliberal policies pursued by junta leader Augusto Pinochet. Hired by the left-leaning Institute for Policy Studies in the American capital, Letelier was in fact spearheading its project to support the NIEO at the time. Depending on the place, the contiguity of human rights and socialistic aspiration remained live for a while. It would have been appalling to Letelier, as to East European "socialists with a human face" who called for Marxist humanism, to learn that decades later it seemed most plausible that human rights had shared the same lifespan not with the renewal of socialism but with neoliberal policies and unequal outcomes almost everywhere. How that occurred is an intricate problem, but one prism is how human rights were connected with global distributional politics from the beginning through the romance of the concept of "basic needs" in development circles.[9]

INTERNATIONAL development on a global scale had always been a minor affair compared to the projects that the elites of each postcolonial state shouldered to launch growth and build modernity in their own countries. In the tradition of colonial development schemes, in 1949 the United States committed to bringing a better way of life to the world in Harry Truman's storied Point Four program. The West European countries did the same as their imperial designs were slowly displaced, and the United Nations and other international organizations formed their own units and projects as well. The funding for such ventures always remained minimal. Americans were notoriously stingy relative to their wealth—not meeting the United Nations' expectation for foreign assistance, though it never approached even one percent of national income. A persistent track record of Europeans doing proportionately better began rapidly with their economic recovery after World War II and decolonization, yet all told, the amounts never exceeded a tiny percentage of northern spending. And with Americans in the lead, these amounts were often linked to security imperatives.[10]

Through the 1960s, under the sway of a shifting theory of "modernization," Americans were more than more willing to justify and support authoritarian rule as a necessary shortcut to the material preconditions of modern prosperity—a preconception that often led them to prettify some of their least defensible policies, as in South Vietnam during the war. Even then, global development generally took the form of "technical assistance" and advice, helping national elites formulate and execute their grandiose plans for national launch. Despite a massive amount of pain inflicted in the name of future progress, growth was unequal both across the world and—above all—within postcolonial countries. Despite the fact that the United Nations had dubbed the 1960s the "development decade," there was a widespread sense that something had gone awry. When the World Bank commissioned former Canadian prime minister Lester Pearson in 1968 to ratify business as usual, many critics of his commission took the opportunity to cry foul. The poor countries were not catching up, and in the face of this "widening gap," it was also plain that the strides they were making still left their own poor behind.[11]

Even in cases where national growth did occur, in the 1970s it suddenly became troubling how unevenly distributed it was. For development economist Mahbub ul Haq, the verdict on all this was grim, even as the UN made the 1970s the "second development decade" to try again. Born in 1934 in Punjab, Haq had done his training in England and the United States before serving his Pakistani government in the 1960s and then moving to the World Bank in 1970 to direct policy planning, where Streeten was his deputy. In Pakistan, Haq's own views had been orthodox: start national growth, through a combination of state planning and free market policies, and tolerate massive inequality, on the theory that the results would (someday) reach the masses. The conditions for a future welfare state might only come about by exacerbating division in the short term. The trouble was that, by the 1970s, it was generally agreed that what little initial growth such strategies prompted—especially when they took the form of developing indigenous industry to provide cheap substitutions for Western imports—worsened not merely national but international inequality, and it did not appear that they would ever improve the lot of the poor. In fact, not only were the poor nations falling ever further behind, but the poor within those nations often fared worse too. The main results were to entrench the power and wealth of tiny elites, and Haq became notorious for denouncing the handful of twenty-two families that had come to control Pakistani commerce in all sectors. In a piece that became well-known in part because Indian prime minister Indira Gandhi was found to have plagiarized it in a policy speech, Haq concluded: "The very institutions we created for providing faster growth and capital accumulation frustrated later on all our attempts for better distribution and greater social justice." Disarmingly, from his new Washington, D.C. outpost, Haq concluded it was time for a major rethink.[12]

Like his university friend and later Nobel laureate, the Indian economist Amartya Sen (who popularized and refined many of his friend's ideas), Haq spoke from within a mainstream development economics that he shifted profoundly. He did so from the cynical perspective that it was not worth dreaming about a welfare world that was never going to come to pass. Poverty alleviation suddenly emerged as a prime imperative precisely on the ruins of false expectations. There was not only no relatively quick fix (as the NIEO seemed to demand) for countries struggling to grow rapidly only to see themselves fall ever further behind, but also no distant millennium in which a fundamentally unequal would ever correct itself. "The pursuit of elusive present-day Western standards," Haq decided, "cannot be reached even over the course of the next century." Acceptance of global inequality was the beginning of wisdom. "The gap will continue to widen and the rich nations will continue to become richer." It was "hopeless" to expect the reversal of that trend. A mere two years before the NIEO achieved unprecedented visibility for a protest against expanding global inequality, Haq concluded that global sufficiency was the best available hope.[13]

Sometimes celebrated for mastering the obvious if heartrending fact that individuals suffer now, Haq was in fact making a momentous ethical choice between material equality and basic provision. The new goal was to give up on international disparity in order to help the world's poor now. Development for the sake of basic needs was still primarily a governmental agenda, rather than cause for private engagement. But it took a large step toward the moral precincts of the contemporary human rights revolution in directing attention toward immediate personal suffering rather than indefinite collective liberation. "The objective of development must be viewed as a selective attack on the worst forms of poverty," Haq insisted in 1971, the scales having fallen from his eyes. "We were taught to take care of our GNP [gross national product], as this will take care of poverty. Let us reverse this and take care of poverty . . . worry[ing] about the *content* of GNP even more than its rate of increase."[14]

Haq spoke of basic needs from the start, but he was initially vague about what precisely a direct antipoverty agenda implied. He flirted as much with recommending that third-world states strive for a minimum income as with identifying a list of fundamental necessities in order to aim to ensure their provision. And he never described these necessities as human rights. Indeed, when Haq later initiated plans for the now-famous "Human Development Index" after moving to the United Nations Development Programme in the 1980s, it was for him a way of simplifying outcomes and supplanting the mantra of gross national product with a measurement of equal clarity rather than a refractory set of heterogeneous needs and rights to fulfill. In his own mind, the abandonment of international inequality as a problem did not entail a total loss of interest in national inequality. But it was usually appended as an afterthought to the fulfillment of sufficient minima when it came to food, health, and services. "Development goals," he explained in a classic 1972 address, "should be expressed in terms of the progressive reduction and eventual elimination of malnutrition, disease, illiteracy, squalor, unemployment, and inequalities."[15]

There was nothing conceptually new about "basic needs" in 1971–72. In Western intellectual history, some set or other of fundamental needs was long since a commonplace way of gesturing toward the content of a minimally adequate life, and indeed was far older than any theory of rights. Needs had been far more central, in particular, to socialist traditions (especially Karl Marx's own thought) than rights ever were. And the "human needs of labor" had therefore been debated in the origins of welfare states, most notably in English reformer Seebohm Rowntree's early twentieth-century agitation to attend to the poor in industrial cities. For all their familiarity, however, the concept played the signal role in global development thinking of displacing national growth as the index of development and reaching individuals with their needs directly. Pundits in the 1970s often traced the roots of the needs approach to the psychologist Abraham Maslow (who propounded an abstract hierarchy of human needs in 1943) or to the Indian economist and state planner Pitambar Pant (who had joined the growth consensus in his home country but called early for baking in strategies to afford minimum provision). On the brink of their fame, there was nothing intellectually revolutionary about "basic needs." What mattered was how that concept could serve as a mantra that led the field away from its prior doctrines—and for its sternest critics, opposing and palliating the global south's demands for worldwide equality.[16]

In part this was because, certainly at first, little more was involved than a gesture toward what national and international development had so spectacularly missed. Were basic needs "concept or slogan, synthesis or smokescreen?" asked Reginald Herbold Green, an American development economist who was close to ecumenical Protestant discussions and adviser to African countries before he became a founder of a development institute at the University of Sussex. "It is amazing how two such innocent, five-letter words could mean so many different things to so many different people," even Haq acknowledged. The remarkable fact was that, for all its ambiguity, basic needs ricocheted across the intergovernmental and intellectual space, albeit in slightly different versions. The other premier site of basic needs visions, even as the Bank moved to canonize its own, was the International Labour Organization (ILO). It announced basic needs within its "World Employment Program," which had begun in the 1960s as a rubric for the organization to reinvent itself for a postcolonial world. It had been devised after World War I in the developed countries, as a reformist answer to the Soviet Union, and with most of its aims—a humanized workplace and even a right to strike—achieved, the ILO now moved on in search of a new mission. Its first move had been to intervene in reform under late-imperial rule, to push through the abolition of forced labor, and to begin to approximate northern labor standards. In a postcolonial world, it was forced to shoulder a different and more complex task of participating not in the northern welfare-state project but in the southern development one.[17]

At this most influential and pivotal moment in its trajectory after World War II, the ILO did not associate basic needs with human rights. Its turn to basic needs came out of the recognition that it made little sense to adapt a strategy devised for northern industrial conflicts without recognizing the entirely different organization of labor and production in the global south. In the several years leading up to its World Employment Conference in 1976, therefore, the ILO broadened out, officially to place employment in its proper setting, but in reality to offer a full-scale development approach of its own. The conference was the most visible moment during the years of 1975–77, when "basic needs" took the United Nations system (of which the ILO is loosely a part) by storm. Haq was a massive influence in these years, and Sen consulted for the World Employment Programme during the formulation of its report. For the ILO, devising conditions for full or at least fuller employment remained essential, but in a setting in which food, shelter, and clothing along with essential public services were basic needs that development must achieve first and soon. Employment was a means to these ends, not merely an end in its own right. Much vagueness in the ILO's vision remained, though it called for beneficiary participation in the strategy to avoid the risk of top-down imposition. And while it held out the prospect of flexibility, the ILO anticipated the Bank's policies in arguing that the genius of "basic needs" was setting an absolute minimum of essential goods and services that would have the virtues of universal application and easy measurement. "Basic needs can be relative as well as absolute," the conference declaration explained. "In the present situation, however, it is both legitimate and prudent to concentrate first on meeting basic needs in the absolute sense." The wretched of the earth had simply waited too long for help to reach them.[18]

What the World Bank began to flirt with and the ILO propounded, various non-governmental groups ratified in the same period, in what contemporary observers considered a nearly celestial convergence of normally competing agendas. Shortly after becoming a baroness, the English economist and influential public educator about north-south issues Barbara Ward chaired a session in Cocoyoc, Mexico in fall 1974. The session led to a widely publicized declaration insisting that "human beings have basic needs: food, shelter, clothing, health, and education" and that "any process of growth that does not lead to their fulfillment—or even worse, disrupts them—is a travesty of the idea of development." Perhaps most interestingly, the Argentine geologist Amílcar Herrera led a team funded by the Fundación Bariloche that proposed that the wealthy end their "overconsumption" in order to fulfill the basic needs of the global poor. Announced in 1976, his report was alone in the explosion of basic needs discourse to connect the wildfire search for "agreed floors" to remedy poverty with "an essentially egalitarian income distribution" as a distant goal. But like all the other proposals, it was primarily directed, in an era of many neo-Malthusian fears of overpopulation, at challenging the premise that statist growth could suffice for the future of humanity.[19]

Despite the swift proliferation in these years of basic needs rhetoric across the spectrum of intergovernmental and non-governmental discussion, the World Bank became most closely associated with them as the former U.S. Secretary of Defense Robert McNamara, during the Vietnam War, rebooted the institution as its new president after 1968. Despite McNamara's proximity, before his appointment, to Great Society visions in the Democratic Party, it took Haq's influence after 1970 to bring home to McNamara the importance of a direct attack on poverty. The World Bank's activity transformed under McNamara's direction, thanks to more generous lending. The institution's outlays going directly to poverty remediation around the world rose by a factor of six (from 5 to 30% of its overall programs) over the course of the next decade. All the same, at first the Bank budged only slightly to a position known at the time as "redistribution with growth," before moving in the mid-1970s to assert ownership of the basic needs paradigm.[20]

In McNamara's evolving thinking over the crucial first decade of his stewardship of the Bank, he was far more apt to refer to "absolute poverty" as the global scourge. The notion that there was some itemized schedule of necessities to which the Bank's lending should be partly targeted emerged slowly and never fully ousted the imperative of continued growth. Indeed, the crisis years of 1972–74, during which growth targets were often missed due to widespread drought and high oil prices, caused McNamara considerable consternation, in part because the worst-off suffered most. And he was not above worrying moralistically about the need for global "equity" as the activism that culminated in the NIEO was making worldwide structural justice fodder for headlines. All he meant, however, was that inequality was unacceptable to the extent that the poorest were not benefited by it to some extent, or were actually made worse off. He was perfectly frank to the Bank's governing board on this point in September 1977: "For developing nations to make closing the gap [between them and wealthy nations] their primary development objective is simply a prescription for needless frustration." As Haq had argued, abandonment of chimerical global equality allowed achievable goals. "Unlike 'closing the gap,' reducing poverty is a realistic objective, indeed an indispensable one," McNamara explained. Not coincidentally, it was in this same address that basic needs most clearly entered McNamara's rhetoric. "The attack on absolute poverty—basic human needs and their satisfaction—cannot be forgotten, cannot be forever delayed, and cannot be finally denied by any global society that hopes tranquilly to endure."[21]

Part of McNamara's own reasoning was candidly preventive: a world with escalating disparity in income and wealth that did not at least provide a floor of protection for the indigent was ripe for disorder. After his humbling failures directing the Vietnam War, he was, after all, an old hand at grappling with discontent once it escalated into the impossible form of open insurrection. "Too little, too late is history's most universal epitaph for political regimes which have lost their mandates," he now sagely observed. In stages from 1970, McNamara's move to a more and more explicit antipoverty agenda for the Bank reflected the insight that "policies whose effect is to favor the rich at the expense of the poor are not only manifestly unjust, but in the end self-defeating." But there was also much heartfelt rhetoric about the moral necessity of providing a sufficient minimum. It did not require a radical transformation in lifestyles in developed countries, he assured his Washington audiences repeatedly. It did require them to take seriously their age-old religious injunctions. "The rich and powerful have a moral obligation to assist the poor and the weak."[22]

In these decisive years, McNamara came nowhere near the Bariloche radicalism that conditioned basic needs fulfillment for the worst-off on decreasing consumption for the privileged (though he did constantly if somewhat halfheartedly call for more foreign aid beyond the fraction of one percent of national income then canonized as obligatory). Even more important, the World Bank was widely seen as defining basic needs downward, even as it acted to be their premier standard-bearer in international affairs. Ultimately, for all the talk of a plurality of basic needs that did justice to the many-sidedness of human fulfillment, the Bank's true contribution was to monetize a basic minimum measurement to test whether continuing growth benefited the most glaringly poor. Even as it was doing so, the main legacy of McNamara's Bank was to abet the rise of third-world debt that spelled the doom of the NIEO's advocacy for global equity and prepared the way for structural adjustment programs later.[23]

The sheer radicalism with which the development community turned on national growth strategies spoke in large part to the new ethical proprieties of wealthy observers of a world which their prior schemes had seemingly not served well or, as with Vietnam, had clearly made worse. And while a few in the debate preserved a concern for equality within developing nations as the whole purpose of shifting antipoverty strategies, the main effect of the departure was to narrow the optic to sufficiency. Under the reign of "basic needs," development focused on short-term sufficiency targets within nations, thus displacing short-term national growth strategies that postponed both sufficiency and equality alike. Meanwhile, in envisioning the future of the nations of the global south, the embrace of the concern with basic provision almost never went along with a comparable stress on international distributive equality. Indeed, the former was deployed against the NIEO's version of the latter.

WHEN MCNAMARA announced his commitment to the basic needs of "individual human beings," the young Australian human rights lawyer Philip Alston noted somewhat sarcastically that the World Bank president "might have added that they are all the subjects of internationally recognized human rights and that they are all being denied those rights." From the camp of needs and from that of rights, suspicion was a natural attitude: how the two concepts were connected and whether they connected at all were not at all obvious. A territorial dispute of experts ensued.[24]

Paul Streeten was caustic when it came to the risk that human rights would muddy the independent revolution in favor of targeting the fulfillment of the most basic needs. Born in Vienna in 1917, Streeten never fully left behind the youthful socialism he learned there. Forced to live through the triumph of reactionary Christianity after 1934, he fled during the Nazi takeover four years later. As an émigré, he fought for the United Kingdom in World War II before training at the University of Oxford, where he spent most of his career between academia and government. Before moving to the World Bank in 1972, he had already worried that "human rights" were simply not portable to the global south except as distant aspirations; it was up to governments there to supply first material prosperity of the kind that had allowed for economic and social rights to be announced in the drive to welfare states. Unapologetically, Streeten liked to cite Bertolt Brecht's dictum that *"erst kommt das Fressen, dann kommt die Moral"* (first comes the need to eat, and later comes morality). What he meant was that food did not magically appear from being named a right; it had to be provided first for its beneficiaries to usefully have any moral claims to make. Preaching "the eradication of poverty in the near future," Streeten started with "absolute" deprivation as an economist's rather than lawyer's challenge. Biological needs were the main priority, with larger ends coming later—subsistence before any broader sufficiency. However ordered, the list of priorities would still necessarily have to be traded off against each other and alternative ends, and sometimes postponed if better later outcomes were achieved by doing so. It was not, Streeten maintained, as if basic needs ousted the necessity of making hard choices and picking winners. ("It is possible to eradicate poverty rapidly while the rich get richer even faster," Streeten correctly observed.)[25]

Streeten never changed his mind about the mistake of conflating basic needs with social rights—perhaps precisely because rights disguised the economic realities of the task of raising people to a sufficiency line. After witnessing the human rights revolution in the later 1970s, he still insisted that it made little sense to adapt the notion of absolute individual entitlements beyond their core uses to criticize state repression. The most one could responsibly say is that every individual has a right "to a minimum share in scarce resources"—certainly not "an equal share." Rather, at most morality allowed individuals to claim only as much fulfillment of basic needs as appeared feasible after dropping the utopian expectation of fulfilling all of them. Others in development theory were somewhat more generous, seizing the opportunity provided by the rise of human rights to buttress basic needs.

"Needs are not the same as rights," observed the English economist Frances Stewart, a close colleague of Streeten's. "Making basic needs into human rights adds two elements to the basic needs approach. It increases the moral weight of and political commitment to their fulfillment, and it gives basic needs fulfillment some international legal status, the extent and nature of which depends on the nature of the supervisory and enforcement mechanisms associated with the rights. Potentially, the legal status conferred on basic needs adds a very important additional instrument to ensure fulfillment of these needs." With more religious passion than strategic angling, Reginald Green, the Christian development thinker, urged that needs and rights were "basically part of a unifying self-sustaining whole."[26]

There was intellectualism in Streeten's less conciliatory response, but also territorialism: having the human rights revolution affect the explosion of concern about basic needs would accord at least some authority to another group of experts than development economists themselves. Alston, the human rights lawyer, returned the favor by insisting that these concepts were not the same, and that his brand of expertise when it came to distribution was not simply redundant to the concerns with individuals that development economists were now taking on board. For his part, Alston insisted how distinctive human rights law is. It is a matter of binding obligation, and its standards might only overlap with "a comparatively hastily drawn up statement" of basic needs "possessing only a limited degree of international persuasive significance." In a comprehensive analysis, Alston laid out the areas of harmony and dissonance between basic needs and human rights, acknowledging that due to its recent emergence, the former explicitly covered some desiderata such as water and some categories such as migrants that the latter did not explicitly. The risk that a basic needs approach could "degenerate into a technocratic programme devoted to the attainment of subsistence levels of consumption" was a main reason, however, to keep social and economic rights in view—for their more generous vision of sufficiency than bare subsistence. Similarly, the impossibility of restricting human rights to material needs in particular (as some interpretations of basic needs allowed) remained their critical use. The Norwegian scholar and peace studies founder Johan Galtung responded less guardedly and took the rise of basic needs and human rights as an opportunity to announce new items on lists of both. "Casual assertions that particular needs have in fact been translated into human rights may create a damaging climate of skepticism as to the value and validity of existing human rights guarantees," Alston worried, citing the then-recent assurance by a United Nations body that tourism was both a basic need and human right alike. Ultimately, Alston concluded, the sheer popularity of basic needs meant it might be strategically opportune to hitch the wagon of international rights to them, fulfilling rights under another guise given their non-enforceability as law for the moment.[27]

It was Amartya Sen, however, who provided the most interesting case of the significance of the move to basic needs. Although he was not to engage human rights for a while yet, he did so *de facto*, and his move to do so revealed mainly his own contestable priorities at the time rather than a transcendent moral insight. The evidence shows clearly, after all, his central priorities adjusting in 1973–76 when he embraced the positions that have made him an icon in an age of sufficient distribution and human rights. Born in East Bengal (now Bangladesh) in 1933, and schooled in Rabindranath Tagore's educational ambiance at the Santiniketan commune in West Bengal, Sen's earliest interests, after taking his economics degree as a stellar undergraduate and graduate student at the University of Cambridge, lay in the new theory of "social choice." Nonetheless, thanks to the influence of some of his Indian and English economics mentors, such as the Marxist Maurice Dobb, Sen devoted his dissertation and first book to quasi-socialist development economics, offering his own theory of how to achieve growth and national launch. As late as 1972, he conceptualized the problems of needs and poverty within a larger framework of material inequality. Only after 1973, closing a period of writing about national inequality as he passed through various American and English universities, did Sen turn his attention to poverty and deprivation.[28]

Hired by the ILO as a consultant in the early 1970s, as part of its World Employment Programme, Sen was on the ground floor of the basic needs movement. But he theorized it in a very different way than Streeten. The world food crisis of these years brought back memories of the Bengal famine of 1943, which he had witnessed as a boy. In response to the loss of a million men, women, and children to starvation in his now Bangladeshi home province, Sen called for more precision in theorizing poverty while stressing the conditions for and prevention of the worst deprivation that occurred in famine. For Sen, although he was hired as part of the ILO's broader program, these events focused the mind on shorter-term visions, especially on how vesting entitlements (in effect, rights) to provision in individuals would likely lead them to seek the sufficiency necessary to survive even disastrous harvests and other events that implicated an "irreducible core of absolute deprivation." Not attention to the extent of food or the growth of population, but rather "guaranteed minimum values of exchange owing to the social security system" would do most to avert famine and penury.[29]

Sen did not yet conceive of these entitlements as rights, but in effect he was on the road to doing so. Sen's focus on subsistence in famine and the straits of poverty generally was not simply hived off from his continuing thinking about national inequality. Before the world food crisis, he had insisted on their interrelationship, but now he emphasized that "inequality . . . is . . . a *distinct* issue from poverty." Sen also negated any interest in international inequality. His sole mention of that concern through the age of the NIEO's rise and fall was to remark that "in some discussions one is concerned not with the prevalence of poverty in a country in the form of the suffering of the *poor*, but with the relative opulence of the nation *as a whole*." But he bypassed those discussions, except to share in the Harvard University economist and NIEO skeptic Richard Cooper's remark that it "falls uncritically into the practice of . . . anthropomorphizing nations . . . as though they are individuals and extrapolating to them on the basis of average per capita income the various ethical arguments that have been developed to apply to individuals." With collective ethics on the periphery, including inequality among nations, vesting entitlements to basic needs in persons is what would now matter.[30]

THERE WAS no lack of infighting among the proponents of basic needs and human rights, and those proponents were not above intellectual or strategic compromise with one another. But for all their interest, both basic needs and human rights look in retrospect like they functioned to redefine hope for the global south and to help circumvent the NIEO proposals that most observers felt were dangerous or wrongheaded demands from the global south itself. Although the NIEO introduced the unprecedented ambition to take welfare equality global, its most ethically sensitive vulnerability was its neglect of internal distribution of the good things in life within countries. And the NIEO's opponents struck hard.

Like repeated outbreaks of global famine, the fears of "limits to growth" on an overpopulated planet that pervaded the decade were clearly an important reason for the coming of basic needs and the understandable imperative to ensure that ordinary people did not get lost in the crisis of prior statist growth programs. But the NIEO was the historically unique factor, not ongoing poverty and death, outrageous though they certainly were. The sudden revulsion at the fact that that postcolonial visions of distribution lacked basic provision for individuals arguably said as much or more about the horrified as about the horror. As one insightful observer put it, the spiking anxiety about the global poor in World Bank and other circles mostly followed from "*their* past neglect of what a number of Third World governments and many development economists [there] have for a long time taken to be a major area of concern." A new sense of priorities followed from a "changed climate of opinion in western countries." The final end of colonialism after several hundred years, and direct intervention by the United States, became not a moment of opportunity to set things right, but a projection of guilt for the failure of sufficiency on those demanding equality too.[31]

As twin visions of minimum provision, neither basic needs nor human rights thematized national inequality on the brink of its explosion as a wrong apart from poverty, or international inequality as an evil that states might reasonably combat. Most important, then, is to register how much awareness existed, at the inception of the human rights revolution, of what focusing on basic needs and human rights alike portended for the struggle to propound globally egalitarian norms. In case anyone was confused, immediately after the NIEO burst on the scene, the Aspen Institute convened a series of groups to propose "a new international economic order *to meet human needs*." "Nations are not people," its report concluded, sounding a common theme about where the global south went wrong. "Alongside the 'gap' between the average citizens of poor and rich societies, equally significant 'gaps' were becoming obvious *within* countries. . . . It is high time that the world community come together to set agreed floors under individual human needs." By the late 1970s, in turn, it was routine to attack basic needs as a transparent rationale for bypassing the NIEO demands and locking in servicing the poor as the fundamental task in the global south, each country doing so on its own in informally dependent and unchanging relationship to its former colonial masters.[32]

Meeting in Belgrade in summer 1978, the foreign ministers of the non-aligned movement voiced a nearly universal suspicion of the sudden interest in the basic needs of individuals. Not that minimum provision for all was unimportant—it was even pressing—but it needed to be viewed "as one of the many priority objectives for national policy, and not as a substitute for authentic development." And "at the international level," even more important, "this strategy should not obscure the urgent need for fundamental change in the world economic order." Even in the United Nations Commission on Human Rights, Indian delegate Vijaya Lakshmi Pandit (Jawaharlal Nehru's sister and a stalwart proponent of the principles for decades) insisted that "equity and social justice were primary requisites for the implementation of economic, social, and cultural rights everywhere." Consequently, she worried that "the basic needs strategy has been used as an excuse to imply that the only problem of developing countries is [providing] a minimum necessary for subsistence." "Poverty cannot be eradicated by isolating it from the system," the Pakistani intellectual Altaf Gauhar added bitterly, "any more than disease can be cured by suppressing the symptoms. And this is what is wrong with the 'Basic Needs' approach."[33]

To be sure, there was no reason a concern for using some of their surplus to address grinding poverty and starvation could not fit in the NIEO agenda of the postcolonial states. In expert fora, such as one convened by UNESCO in 1978, the precise relationship of basic needs, human rights, and the NIEO were the subject of an outpouring of earnest discussion. What held true in theory did not necessarily follow in practice, however, especially since basic needs had never been applied to accelerating northern consumption alongside southern poverty. Galtung insisted that, given "the way the BN approach has been launched, and applied predominately *only* to the Third World, the Third World has every reason to regard it as a ploy for side-tracking the world economic issue raised by the NIEO." More than this, it was not implausible for the new states to fear that, like human rights, basic needs were going to be one more means of eroding their hard-won sovereignty. "In the light of past history, the First World's disavowal of interventionist intentions does not carry conviction, nor does its protestation that the BN approach will not have any unintended consequences," Galtung summarized.[34]

True, some treated basic needs as a valuable supplement to the NIEO, none more interestingly than Haq, the figure most responsible for the coming of "basic needs" to development economics, after he declared the dream of global equality a fantasy. How Haq's engagement with the NIEO in the mid-1970s squared with his insistence earlier, before expert audiences, that the whole rationale for a turn to basic needs was that the south would never catch up to the north never did emerge with much clarity. Unlike Sen, however, Haq agreed with the popular rhetoric of the time that "the search for a new economic order is a natural second stage in the liberation of the developing countries." "It is my own conviction," he added resentfully in Sweden in November 1974, a few months before the NIEO declaration, "that the developed countries simply do not care . . . what happens in the Third World." In response to the bromide that "the Third World has to reconcile itself" to the existing international order, Haq responded that "the Third World *is* the future international order." And in the mid-1970s, Haq's arguments for the redistribution, if not directly of income and wealth, then of "future growth opportunities" was occasionally noticed in the global north.[35]

Haq understood something like the NIEO to be the international equivalent of the coming of the national welfare state, achieved once again through strategic pressure from below. "On the national level," Haq explained in 1975, "a turning point was reached in the 1930s, when the New Deal elevated the working classes to partners in development and accepted them as an essential part of the consuming society. On the international level, we still have not arrived at that philosophic breakthrough when the development of the poor nations is considered an essential element . . . [yet] we may be nearing that philosophical bridge." This time around, pressure from below was provided by dissident states as the functional equivalent of trade unions: entities that represented individuals, who could not exert sufficient power on their own for change. And by the end of the decade, Haq wrote sensitively of how the stampede of development experts and donor nations, not to mention the United States government, to care for global poverty was understandably leading in the global south to alarm about distraction from a fuller-fledged agenda. By 1980, it had gone so far as to put at risk the compatibility of concerns for international and intranational distribution, global equality and basic needs. That basic needs were so diversionary, Haq affirmed, was predictably causing the global south to "throw out the baby with the bathwater."[36]

Positioning himself as an impassioned Third World intellectual, Haq in the end sought a uniquely balanced and conciliatory position, adopting an ethical rage at global inequality without ignoring national distribution and governance. He participated in the founding of the Third World Forum, an association of global southern intellectuals, and chaired its task force on thinking through a new international economic order. Somewhat subversively, Haq went so far as to observe that the risk of rebellion within states—of which McNamara warned, as a rationale for more generosity—applied globally too, and for the sake of equality, not just sufficiency. But as the NIEO waned, Haq increasingly concluded that "the real task of development lay back home" and indeed, "no degree of international agitation can ever obscure that fact; no amount of international resource transfers can ever substitute for national decisions on fundamental reforms." He added:

> The intellectuals from the third world face a cruel dilemma here. If they stress the issue of reform of national orders ahead of the international order, they run the risk of providing a convenient excuse to the rich nations to postpone serious discussions on the reform of the present world order as well as of losing the support of their own national governments. Yet what can possibly be gained by greater equality of opportunity internationally if it is denied to the vast majority within the national orders?

Streeten, Haq's fellow World Bank economist, agreed that the overriding necessity was to explain that basic needs by no means interfered with the NIEO. In fact, putting them together saved each from its own worst pathologies: basic needs from "degenerating into a global charity program" and the NIEO from serving postcolonial elites alone. For all their promise, however, such rhetorically conciliatory attempts to make basic needs get along with some version of the NIEO were not representative.[37]

Since it was only rarely invoked in relation to distribution in any form, the human rights revolution was even more likely than basic needs to be seen as a nefarious plot against the global south's egalitarian gambit. There was not even much subterfuge about it: human rights were often openly advertised as a means to seek the weak point of the NIEO nations, delegitimizing their ethical claims by stigmatizing their holdover "British socialism" and political misrule, as the American Daniel Patrick Moynihan did in a widely read *Commentary* article and then as United Nations ambassador. As with human needs, there were some who hoped that human rights could save the third-world project from itself while also making it more acceptable to the north. They were likewise unrepresentative. Some began to devise a new "right to development" that wended its way through United Nations fora. According to some of its proponents, such as the Indian international lawyer Upendra Baxi, making development itself a right would bring the global south's demand for global equity inside the emergent human rights revolution, which would in turn save the basic needs concept from locking in the dominance either of first-world elites globally or of third-world elites locally. "Linking [basic needs] to human rights principles might also go at least part of the way towards allaying the legitimate fears which have been expressed about the notion of basic needs from the viewpoint of the Third World," Alston wrote.[38]

But if the consolidation of basic needs and human rights served multiple possible agendas, easily those most apt to consolidate human rights and basic needs were Americans in general and the American government in particular, in order to harmonize visions of sufficiency even as they watched the NIEO passing unmourned or even danced on its grave. Driven by Minnesota Congressman Donald Fraser, the 1973 Foreign Assistance Act—also notable as the country's pioneering human rights legislation, which denied foreign aid to states that unjustly imprisoned political enemies—directed monies toward food production, nutrition, and education, according to what were dubbed the "new directions principles" in American development policy. This reorientation, driven by familiar realizations about the stagnation of the global poor, intersected with the international discourse around basic needs. It was arguably given a major impetus by Secretary of State Henry Kissinger's initially conciliatory response to the NIEO at its most threatening, notably at his high-profile September 1974 address to the United Nations General Assembly on "interdependence." There, Kissinger recognized that global development needed a fix and turned to "appease" the global south with promises of increased food aid even as he angled to contain and divide the third-world movement, pioneering the enduring American strategy of responding to a call for equality with a gesture toward subsistence. What looked like policy reorientation to some, of course, looked like another excuse for more negligence to others. As one analyst observed, "For some bilateral donors, a BHN [Basic Human Needs] approach is perceived to be more clearly humanitarian and is perhaps more likely to be supported by a domestic constituency that does not generally view foreign assistance as a major priority."[39]

Within a few years, Americans were the first to connect basic needs and human rights in any widespread and systematic way. Until the end of the decade, when security concerns once again trumped humanitarian ones in foreign aid (with Egypt's and Israel's allotments soaring) and new president Ronald Reagan upended the country's new human rights policy, "the basic needs and human rights orientations of U.S. foreign policy began to develop in tandem." It was in this context that American spokesmen, both within and outside of government, began to gesture toward economic and social rights as part of the clarification of Jimmy Carter's new policies. In his historic Notre Dame University commencement address on human rights policy, in May 1977, Carter made sure to mention "the new global questions of justice [and] equity," acknowledging the desirability of "equitable trade" to "help the developing countries to help themselves." But he reminded his audience that "the immediate problems of hunger, disease, [and] illiteracy are here now." Above all else, there was Secretary of State Cyrus Vance's nearly simultaneous affirmation at his own much-remarked spring 1977 address, at the University of Georgia, that the human rights his administration's epoch-making policy would cover included "the right to the fulfillment of such vital needs as food, shelter, health care, and education." Added in the last draft of the speech, "more by accident than design," the critical verbiage nonetheless overjoyed those who wanted America's human rights policy to become more than a new anticommunism. Deputy Secretary of State Warren Christopher repeated the same language before the American Bar Association that summer. And at the same time, Vance spoke before the ministerial meeting of the Organization of Economic Cooperation and Development (OECD) formalizing that "new directions" now meant the "basic human needs" notion that had percolated from elsewhere.[40]

Strikingly, American observers and non-governmental organizations were also tempted to unify rights and needs. "When human rights advocates . . . express concern not only about mass arrests and cases of mistreatment, but about economic rights as well," wrote the academic Patricia Weiss Fagen the next year, "they, in effect, speak of meeting basic human needs." In a similar vein, Richard Falk, a Princeton international lawyer, proposed to "speak of basic needs as human rights." Legal activist Peter Weiss, and the left-wing Institute for Policy Studies of which he was a part, charged that the United States only talked the talk of human rights and basic needs, rather than enacting policy. "An infinitely larger number of the world's people are suffering—actually suffering—from 'consistent patterns of gross violations' of their fundamental rights to work, food, health, shelter, and education, their rights, in short, to *live* their lives instead of struggling for their existence," Weiss explained in a September 1977 speech, "than from violations of their rights to freedom from torture, arbitrary detention, and censorship of the press." If the United States purported to care so much about human rights violations, why was global poverty not a similarly obligatory imperative of policy? Basic needs were rights.[41]

Despite Kissinger's rhetoric under caretaker president Gerald Ford, American policy toward the global south in the Carter administration both embraced basic needs more authentically rather than cynically and opposed the NIEO's more egalitarian demands, mostly by letting them wither on the vine rather than through Kissinger's Machiavellian scheming. In his OECD address in summer 1977, Vance made very clear that "the North-South Dialogue is about *human beings* [and] a fuller life makes sense for *people*, not just states." Rather than Vance, in any case, the guiding spirit proved to be Polish émigré Zbigniew Brzezinski, who as Carter's national security adviser proceeded to adapt the American response to the north-south crisis forged under Kissinger, avoiding the NIEO more thoroughly but focusing on global misery slightly less strategically. Carter made clear early on that he would have no truck with any kind of global redistribution. "I'm not in favor of taxing the poor people in our rich country to send money to the rich people in poor countries," he explained in the first months of his administration. But his years in power marked a more fulsome embrace of basic needs against the background of his storied promotion of human rights. Drawing on the work of the Overseas Development Corporation, a Beltway institution founded in the 1960s that had bruited the basic needs concept over the mid-1970s, Carter openly stressed the notion as a palliative alternative to NIEO demands. Rights and needs were worth talking about; equality, not so much. Not that the American governmental consolidation of basic needs and human rights ever went very much beyond rhetoric, but both functioned to define a basic minimum of protection in an era when, despite its visible decline, the egalitarian NIEO still struck policymakers as radioactive. By either basic needs on their own or in experimental consolidation with human rights, the American response to claims of equality with the consolation prize of professing commitment to sufficiency was clear.[42]

AMERICANS TENDED to be the least apt to seek conciliation with the NIEO's demands, but others were more generous. A decade after the Pearson commission, McNamara suggested to Willy Brandt, the former social democratic chancellor of West Germany, that he chair a new commission to review where development stood, which issued its high-profile results in 1980. This body was radically different, especially in its inclusion of representatives from the global south and in its rhetorical engagement in the ongoing "north-south dialogue." Brandt certainly hoped it would be a blow for the idea of "global social democracy," and he worked in proposals to tax the world arms trade in order to redistribute some of its profits. But unlike a less visible report by the Dutch socialist and the first Nobel Prize winner for economics Jan Tinbergen four years earlier, which had appeared much closer in time to the NIEO and urged much more radical steps (including reduction of global inequality), Brandt's results were less divisive. While his report certainly called for much-expanded foreign aid in the form of increased outright transfer and fairer trade arrangements, it was focused not on global inequality but rather on global poverty as the highest priority. It addressed food as well as employment and health as "elementary needs" (although it drew some fire for failing to call for their fulfillment by the time of the millennium). By the time the commission was done, the pressure the global south had brought to bear on the northern conscience was quickly evaporating. Appearing on the heels of the Soviet move into Afghanistan, the Cold War was in the process of rekindling. And, although brittle from the first, any third-world position now seemed weak beyond easy redemption. Soon after, some were declaring the "end" of "the third world" at least as "a political alternative."[43]

By the end of the 1970s, the transnational human rights movement had been born as an epoch-making phenomenon. Amnesty International had organized anti-torture activism and enjoyed an apex of visibility, while East European dissidents and Latin American victims had become world-historical moral icons in new alliances with transnational movements. Jimmy Carter's human rights policy had been born and debated. Not all advocates of human rights turned a blind eye to distribution, let alone relinquished their transformative ambitions when it came to economic fairness. Yet by 1980, human rights were far along in their transit from principles of an egalitarian welfare package for fellow citizens to aspirations of global sufficiency for fellow humans, and their early encounter with development thinking in general and a relatively minimalist interpretation of "basic needs" in particular was lubricant for the slide. Human rights might have survived the period defined in some other way, but as they lost their association with the national welfare state and became much more familiar in arguments about the most exigent global depredations, the rare instances that they were seen to bear on distribution reimagined them in the spirit of global antipoverty. The optic of basic needs proved critical to this process, and both basic needs and human rights arose for many and served for all as focal points for a turn away from distributive equality, both within nations and above them, as socialism began to enter decline and the NIEO's demands were bypassed.

6

Global Ethics from Equality to Subsistence

"Whatever the other consequences of the demands by the Third World for a new, more egalitarian economic order, one thing is clear," an intelligent observer of the vicissitudes of the New International Economic Order (NIEO) across the 1970s noted at the time: "those demands have given rise to an unprecedented debate on the subject of global distributive justice." The invention of what is now called "global justice" in philosophy occurred alongside contemporary events and reflected shifting agendas as the field made its own move from equality to sufficiency. The first book in history propounding something like a philosophy of human rights on a worldwide scale consummated this move. It is not always true that philosophy captures its own age in thought. In this case, however, it did, providing an indispensable perspective from which to register the rise and fall of the New International Economic Order and its utopia of worldwide equality, before a human rights movement focused on sufficiency reset the limits of optimism for what proved to be a neoliberal age.[1]

No such thing as "global justice" in distribution of the good things in life existed in mainstream philosophy until the decades after 1945, and the postcolonial states led the way in broadening the terms of social justice to the world. But while defending both equal and sufficient distribution of the good things in life on a worldwide scale became possible in philosophy, the new theories that resulted in philosophical circles had radically different fates. The egalitarian option—known since as "cosmopolitanism" to its advocates and critics—is still utopian and unimaginable as the standard of a movement in a neoliberal age. Pursuit of global subsistence rights, by contrast, has enjoyed impressive practical support along the same timeline, not least in the form of an international human rights movement dedicated to securing the most basic features of livelihood. The trajectory of philosophy in the pivotal few years of the invention of global justice reflects the origins of our practical situation more or less perfectly.

American philosopher John Rawls's *A Theory of Justice* (1971) had reflected many premises of the dream of national welfare during World War II and after, not least by calling for communities of justice to achieve material equality, if with special attention to the fate of the worst off. From the perspective of the era that followed, however, the book is illustrative for a new reason: Rawls's restriction of distributive justice to boundaried states and peoples, which had gone without saying in the era of national welfare, suddenly became controversial, as developments in the course of the 1960s and 1970s challenged its self-evidence. Rawls's thought registered the assumptions of national welfare on the brink of crisis, or memorialized hopes for their further extension when they were about to be eroded by a neoliberal revolution. At the beginning of the 1970s, the rise of international ethics in the face of scandalous famine inaugurated a novel emphasis on the ethics of global destitution, which would redefine "human rights" in the era since.

The demands of the NIEO for global equality, in its brief moment of prominence, prompted the appearance of the theory of so-called "global justice"—the scaling up of Rawls's egalitarian national welfare state so that it became notionally worldwide. Not the abjection and poverty of the global south but its agency and challenge caused what Gunnar Myrdal had first called the "welfare world" to come to contemporary philosophy, if not to the globe since. On the grave of the dream of equality, however, a proposal to pursue the sufficient minimum of social rights took off, as a subsistence ethic for the globe transformed the conscience. Untethered from the NIEO, philosophy had the power on its own to memorialize unavailable egalitarian utopias in a neoliberal age. Allied to the new human rights movement, however, when philosophy prioritized a palliative ethics and meeting "basic needs," it successfully canonized a new subsistence ethic for an unequal world.

FOR ALL the innovative aspects of the book that proved the swansong of national welfare in the United States, Rawls's *A Theory of Justice* took up a surprisingly conventional picture of international affairs. Rawls assumed that the parties to his version of the social contract lost their classes, bodies (including genders), and cultures, but the national units of the historical world persisted in the so-called "original position" from which he derived his principles of justice. In a brief discussion, Rawls postponed international affairs to a second-stage contract undertaken by state parties resulting in conventional minimal principles of world order. Human rights were unmentioned, and there were no distributive obligations. In short, it was an illuminating testament to the staying power of the post–World War II national framing of the aspiration to welfare.[2]

Ethical theory had never been lacking, but in the postwar era, as early global justice theorist Onora O'Neill mockingly commented, it had been concerned with "genteel examples of the minor dilemmas of life (walking on forbidden grass, returning library books)" and failed to take up "the harshest of 'real world' moral problems." The Vietnam crisis galvanized it and prompted the creation of mainstream political philosophy nearly from scratch starting around 1970. In debates on the civil disobedience and conscientious objection of American youth, global justice was already lurking, but as the troops were drawn down after 1968, a far wider picture came into view. As Brian Barry, a talented political theorist trained at Oxford University who eventually wrote on global justice himself, later commented, "the Vietnam war was unquestionably the crucial external stimulus," just as the publication of the "extremely long, poorly organized, and stylistically undistinguished" *A Theory of Justice* counted as the internal cause of the spike in the field. The characteristic themes in the early phase of international ethics, however, concerned war specifically, notably atrocity abroad and civil disobedience at home. Obviously, mainstream Anglophone philosophers were hardly the first globally to understand the questionable morality of the American Cold War or to criticize it on theoretical grounds. More important, the moral philosophizing unleashed by the Vietnam War really did not lead to the immediate invention of "global justice." This suggests a need to search further into the 1970s for the propitious moment.[3]

In two rapidly crystallizing geopolitical contexts in the immediate aftermath of Rawls's book, the global approach to justice he had excluded suddenly became imaginable. One was the so-called "world food crisis," which became apparent just as the Vietnam War was being wound down. The Australian philosopher Peter Singer's classic essay on famine, easily the most influential intervention on far-flung moral obligation both in that decade and since, originated in reflections on the displacement and hunger following the devastating cyclone and successful independence bid in what became Bangladesh in the brutal years of 1970–72. But this was mere prologue to the crisis of the several years thereafter. It stoked continuing interest in destitution and prompted philosophers to debate with one another how best to justify deterritorialized obligations to aid. It would be a serious mistake to reduce global justice to a sentimental response to distant suffering, however. Alongside the specter of hunger, the egalitarian NIEO rose and fell, which inflected the invention of global justice with nearly equal power.

"As I write this, in November 1971, people are dying in East Bengal from lack of food, shelter, and medical care," Singer began his landmark essay, which appeared in the third issue of *Philosophy and Public Affairs*, the intellectual epicenter for theories of global justice, in spring 1972. The child of Jewish refugee parents from Vienna, Singer had studied in Oxford and was a young instructor there. His own interest in faraway starvation, which he wrote much more about only after the Cold War, was a subsidiary theme in his writings of the period, but in virtue of its serendipitous timing, the effect of his early article was monumental all the same. In its few pages, Singer argued for an ethically radical conclusion in a series of disarmingly simple steps. First, suffering and death are bad. (Often taking up utilitarian positions, in his initial foray Singer actually did not specify why they were bad—he did not feel he needed to do so.) Second, if someone can prevent such bad consequences "without sacrificing anything of moral importance," it is her moral obligation to do so. Introducing his memorable analogy of a child drowning, whom any reasonable moral actor would save (and would never abstain from saving just because of some minor cost like soiled clothes), Singer also insisted that distance made no difference to the assessment. Singer clarified that he further believed that any moral actor was required to sacrifice up to the point that anything of *comparable* moral significance came into play—not just her inexpensive clothes but her stacks of money—yet the weaker version of Singer's thesis was so revolutionary that he was content with it. The implications of his straightforward premises, as Singer knew, demanded vastly increased philanthropy. "The whole way we look at moral issues—our moral conceptual scheme—needs to be altered; and with it, the way of life that has come to be taken for granted in our society."[4]

However powerful, Singer's venture was new mainly in bringing the philosophical tradition into connection with a much older humanitarianism in a novel postcolonial situation. All along, since shortly after the death of its founder Jeremy Bentham in the early nineteenth century, a utilitarian version of consequentialism had had tight links to global affairs because its chief votaries were supporters—and not infrequently servants—of the British

Empire. Empire was not gone in Singer's day, but it fought its last battles in the 1970s in Portuguese central Africa, bloody struggles on which Anglophone philosophers did not comment because they had moved on from the default support of colonial projects that once characterized the larger societies in which they lived. Singer's deployment of consequentialism for global ethics thus mattered much more because the world had become postcolonial while philosophy was cloistered than because there was no precedent for his views. Indeed, in his paper and throughout his later career, Singer framed the practical problem as one of how much philanthropy morality demanded from the wealthy in the world. To the extent that he did so, his argument fit in a familiar logic of humanitarianism, which erupted in the transatlantic sphere once again in response to secession crises both before and after the independence tragedy in East Bengal (subsequently Bangladesh) that motivated Singer's paper.[5]

And there were other features of Singer's paper that left a great deal of room for further thinking. He homogenized foreign suffering regardless of its cause; its roots in endemic poverty, natural disaster, and civil war were apparently not philosophically relevant. Singer's approach, despite its very general framework calling for global consequentialism, was explicitly framed to single out for attention the most grievous wrongs, whether natural or political, for succor. Singer's approach was egalitarian, of course, in the sense that it took all human beings as equal—with their suffering equally worthy of concern. But he consciously distinguished his argument from what might ensue if one applied his principle across the board instead of merely in response to horrendous spectacle, and made no general call for equality of distribution of the good things in life. In this crucial sense, his essay framed international ethics as a matter of lessening evil. Singer's ethics then and later dictated not institutional criticism of the world order—whether of postcolonial geopolitics or global distribution—but personal charity. As a first step, at least, the point was not even a governmental or mobilizational politics of subsistence, let alone global distributive equality. Rather, Singer made ethically pertinent alleviating the most visibly dire need, presumptively through one's personal checkbook.[6]

The crystallizing circumstances in the late Vietnam era that made Bangladesh of sudden interest to philosophers, and might otherwise have made that interest evanescent, were to continue thanks to the world food crisis that followed in 1972–75. Grain prices spiked and a wave of hunger killed millions, including one million in Bangladesh (again), as well as in Ethiopia and the West African Sahel. The causes were complex and included weather, large rises in Soviet grain imports, and persistent agricultural policy in some countries, like the United States, that subsidized some farmers not to grow grain to keep prices higher for others. The United Nations called a November 1974 summit in Rome known as the World Food Conference to address the calamity. Little was done, however, to create international famine response, although both particular governments and non-governmental charities acted; instead, new United Nations arrangements were envisioned to bring support to small farmers worldwide, who were hit hardest by forces beyond their control, like the weather pattern and global economy.[7]

As discussion continued amid headlines of scandalous global death, philosophers learned enough to be much more suspicious than Singer had been in 1971 of reigning fears of a worldwide "population bomb," and they soon treated corresponding programs of population control with more skepticism. But the philosophy of global justice really came into its own when arguments for a politics of subsistence rights and an institutionalization of global equality were propounded. The first argument, though it awaited the human rights revolution of the later 1970s to become full-blown, had roots in the immediate aftermath of Singer's essay. Onora O'Neill, the daughter of a high-ranking British diplomat hailing from Northern Ireland (and later a baroness), took the critical early step. She had earned her doctorate in philosophy under Rawls and taught at Barnard College in the period, beginning her career as a defender of socialism, penning a popular article defending Karl Marx's dictum that ethical distribution takes place "from each according to his ability, to each according to his need." Long after she stopped referring to Marx, in fact, O'Neill oriented her thought around the duties that needs prompt—but within a couple of years these were explicitly long-distance needs thrown up by the world food crisis.[8]

In "Lifeboat Earth," her own milestone essay published in *Philosophy and Public Affairs* three years after Singer's, O'Neill offered a vision of entitlement to subsistence as a matter of individual right rather than part of a vaguer and broader theory of bad consequences to avoid. "[F]rom the assumption that persons have a right not to be killed unjustifiably," O'Neill explained, "the claim that we have a duty to try to prevent and postpone famine deaths" followed. It did so more narrowly, O'Neill thought, and therefore uncontroversially than in Singer's approach. It was not just one piece of a vast global cost-benefit analysis. O'Neill's trouble with Singer's approach, she indicated, was its overbreadth. To say that moral actors had to help prevent bad things, assuming nothing important (or nothing comparable) had to be sacrificed in doing so, was so general a principle that in reality it required a massive calculus about where to start—not a specific focus on the truly important rights or needs. Even more important, famine deaths were not external and remote: the key fact, for O'Neill, was that in a newly "interdependent" world, we were related to people whose most basic rights, starting with their right to live, it was our responsibility to protect. The situation went beyond interdependence: O'Neill was in touch with growing claims that affluent citizens of developed economies were actually *at fault* for famine (although she registered no awareness of the NIEO proposals of postcolonial states oriented to global egalitarian reform of the same moment). Even so, she took it to be her task to explain, not the historical background or political remedy to famine, but why it violated individual rights.[9]

Oriented to visible famine, the new ethics of global hunger, whether based on bad consequences or basic rights, did not venture beyond the case for global moral obligations in the most exigent cases. But O'Neill's approach proved indicative of where the field would proceed, in its attempt both to offer a rights-based theory and, albeit more implicitly, to connect theories of justice beyond borders to the unfolding reception of her teacher Rawls's approach.

ETHICAL INSIGHT into absolute destitution made justice a matter of intensifying philanthropic obligation, beyond mere charity but still a matter of palliation. Soon, however, this seemed simply too narrow for several mainstream philosophers. They wanted to make the international system a topic of inquiry into just social relations—as if it were possible to view the globe itself as just the sort of "basic structure" that Rawls had seen as the setting of just social relations in the national welfare state. In short, philosophers propounded their own vision of a "welfare world." Here, the NIEO was to matter profoundly, for just as the world food crisis broke out, the global south also became the source of an open and quite shocking revolt against prevailing global hierarchy. And by the mid-1970s, once the vivid memory of starving children had passed, hunger and poverty became absorbed into an unprecedented (for philosophers) discussion of global inequality generally. Late 1976 saw the pioneering ethicist Henry Shue assert that just food policy was inseparable from fundamental principles of global justice, and leading philosopher Thomas Nagel argued similarly, in response to Singer in the same year, that "charity is not enough" since "the ethical aspects" of the hunger are simply "part of the general problem of global economic inequality."[10]

For their propositions about the priority of egalitarian principles of international distribution over specific conclusions about food policy, both Nagel and Shue cited the momentous essay Charles Beitz published in *Philosophy and Public Affairs* in 1975, which anticipated his dissertation at Princeton, completed in 1976, defended in 1978, and published in 1979 as *Political Theory and International Relations.* A peripheral graduate student in the 1970s, Beitz turned out to be of tremendous importance in the long run. According to his Princeton friend Samuel Scheffler, at the time Beitz's topic "was sometimes met with what I fear may have seemed like a kind of polite condescension, for [it] struck most of us as a bit peripheral to the main issues raised by Rawls's theory." But now it is apparent, he continues, that Beitz "helped to invent a new subject, the subject of global justice, which is today one of the most hotly debated areas within all of political philosophy." Though he was only in his twenties, global justice was "the house that Chuck built," as surely as the broader revival of liberal political thought that Rawls sponsored is "the house that Jack built." Like Shue, who had preceded him in the program by a few years, Beitz and therefore global justice were a product of Princeton's interdisciplinary program in political philosophy. For Shue this mattered because "few established philosophers . . . could have known enough about politics, especially international politics," to get very far.[11]

It was also the case that Beitz hoped not merely to debate Rawls but also to draw on his own prior history of activism to argue for a preexisting movement in the world that he found exciting. A graduate of Colgate University and a pupil of ethicist Huntington Terrell during the Vietnam War, Beitz worked for Terrell the summer after his college graduation, in a program funded by the Institute for World Order, to help construct the field of peace studies. Terrell's pacifist leanings (his wife was a lifelong Quaker) led him to early membership in the academic movement, but after graduation, Beitz looked as if he were choosing a more activist path. His first publication was a coedited collection of readings based on this course and answering to the widespread hankering at the turn of the 1970s for a spiritual reorientation. He then worked with a friend to generate a broader guide for those whom the New Left and campus activism had inspired to change the world, starting at home. Only a brief concluding section of *Creating the Future* (1974), Beitz's co-authored mass-circulated "guide to living and working for social change," concerned global politics. It barely focused on distributive justice, but it did denounce a global hierarchy in which "all good things flow to the north or simply circulate within it." Professing a "tenacious faith" in change from below, Beitz and his co-author recommended that those longing for renovation engage in consciousness raising and systemic criticism. "If you are somehow inclined to be a planner, and philosopher, a visionary, a poet, see if the idea of global society is not worthy of your prolonged creative energy."[12]

But Beitz was forced to choose a vocation in the midst of a waning of the New Left; as for so many, it would be as an academic. As Beitz had already registered in the preface to his guide for activists, it was "the ebbing, not the rising, of the tide of change" that set parameters for radicalism now. Philosophy as a career, and not merely his arguments in it, was a way of sheltering crashing hopes. Beitz's decision to enroll at Princeton (after a brief stint at the University of Michigan) and his choice once there to move away from the more progressive professor Richard Falk—even if he embarked on his paper on global justice in Falk's seminar—are illuminating. And the passage of time convinced him that the true problems in the world were not so much or only military, but also and mainly economic. "Questions of war and peace," Beitz had written right out of college, "are far more profound than the traditional questions asked of international relations; they are bound up with the roles that each individual must choose to play in the world, with his or her personal fate and moral identity." In his inaugural article, Beitz now noted that the recent focus on war and peace had "too often diverted attention from more pressing distributive issues." Beitz's project slowly registered the collapse of the New Left in the decade after 1970, but there was a closing window when the NIEO sparked his project of making the philosophical case for the globalization of egalitarian justice.[13]

Put simply, it prompted Beitz to globalize Rawls to justify the demands of globalized egalitarian justice. What the Vietnam War was to liberal political philosophy generally, the NIEO, alongside the world food crisis, was to global justice particularly: the sensitizing event or rude awakening that precipitated a change in consciousness and the birth of an academic field. Because the NIEO fit an even more general sense that the time had come to elevate the redistributive sensibilities of the welfare state to the globe, it mattered most. In 1971, John Lennon asked his listeners to imagine a world beyond countries and hierarchy (and property), while in his own hit the same year, the folk star Cat Stevens sang of dreaming of the world as one.

The next year, Apollo 17 astronauts took a picture of the earth from space, known as "the blue marble," that prompted unprecedented consciousness of unity on an integrated planet. "The brief record of man's industrialising and modernising efforts suggests that, at certain critical moments, the political decision to abandon total reliance on largely automatic market mechanisms for distributing economic opportunity and income and to put in their place some system of distributive justice has given the whole society the chance of a new start," observed Barbara Ward, easily the leading popular writer on global economic affairs of those years, in her submission to the UN's food conference. "It is possible that some such turning point has been reached in the larger arena of the world and, for the affluent powers and groups, the most vital issue in survival is their ability to accept new standards of sharing."[14]

It is perhaps unsurprising, then, that the explosion of consciousness concerning world economic unfairness pushed against the limits of Rawls's *Theory of Justice*, then and since at the center of philosophical debate about the nature of social justice. But it always takes an individual to notice, and Beitz was that person. A few others before him had noticed the implausibility of postponing world affairs to a second-stage contract, but Beitz became most identified with and spelled out the critique of Rawls's rationale for allowing the nation-state to be treated as analytically and politically freestanding, even in what Rawls termed "ideal theory." The criticism did not turn on the ethical significance of a prior violent history (including colonialism, whose importance the NIEO emphasized) in producing the peoples and boundaries that are morally arbitrary from the perspective of cosmopolitan universalism. Instead, Beitz targeted Rawls's assumption that each nation was *self-sufficient* enough to be treated separately analytically and have its own social contract (and then state borders) politically.[15]

In response, Beitz made two main arguments. First, the unequal distribution of natural resources worldwide forbade the simplification of treating global justice as a second-stage problem. Second, and more boldly, Beitz claimed that it was simply false to suppose that it was possible to disentangle states, especially for the purposes of a contract governing distributive justice in an age of multinational corporations, capital flows, and economic "interdependence." Beitz argued that no one familiar with the empirical situation of the world in the 1970s—or at least the new perceptions of interdependence then—could conclude that entering separate state-based ventures in social justice was possible at all. "If evidence of global economic and political interdependence shows the existence of a global scheme of social cooperation," Beitz affirmed, "we should not view national boundaries as having fundamental moral significance." The analytical expedient of proceeding directly to state-based contracts having failed, it followed that a global bargain would take place. If Rawls's difference principle—allowing for distributive inequality only to the extent it helped the worst-off—applied, it did so in the first instance to world economic relations. "The state-centered image of the world has lost its normative relevance because of the rise of global economic interdependence," Beitz concluded. "Principles of distributive justice must apply in the first instance to the world as a whole, then derivatively to nation-states." While Beitz soon called his alternative "cosmopolitan," he also effectively admitted that both his arguments followed much more from contemporary sources than from any texts in the philosophical tradition. Leaving aside the French Revolution's apostle of humanity Anacharsis Cloots, Beitz furnished the first proposal for a global social contract in history, and it called for worldwide distributive equality.[16]

Beitz later referred to that term he used, *interdependence*, as "part of the argot" of the era. He was right. The NIEO had offered its own definition of interdependence as a fact about world politics mandating its prescriptions for justice: when it came to basic principles, the NIEO declaration referred to it alongside sovereign equality and self-determination. "The true meaning of interdependence," the Non-Aligned Movement insisted at its Lima meeting in 1975, the year of Beitz's essay, must "reflect unequivocally the common commitment to build the New International Economic Order." But the "true meaning" of interdependence was far from clear—and some worried that it could cover all manner of sins. Writing in *Commentary*, Robert W. Tucker, perhaps the most assertive American critic of the NIEO, decried "a new sensibility" among "liberal intellectual elites" which welcomed the drive for "interdependence" as a replacement "for a world in which the hierarchical ordering of states seemed natural and inevitable." He referred as much to domestic sympathy, such as the "Declaration of Interdependence" that historian Henry Steele Commager drafted for wide circulation in 1975 as a bicentennial update for America's founding principles, as to the NIEO itself. Tucker detected a new premise in the wind—one of "collective responsibility of universal application that heretofore has been applied only within the state and then only in this century (and in the United States only in the last generation)." And he sagely explained why it was leading well-meaning Americans astray, among other things into apologetics for third-world despots who were hiding domestic oppression behind the camouflage of moral agitation for global economic fairness. Yet even Henry Kissinger, in a United Nations speech offered in late 1974 for an America back on its heels after the oil shock (and Vietnam), called for interdependence in response to crisis.[17]

When Beitz cited the worldwide maldistribution of natural resources as a response to Rawls's account, the NIEO's exceptional prominence drove the argument even when Beitz volunteered to improve it. The global south's own approach had been to claim that nations enjoyed "permanent sovereignty over natural resources," in order to attack the legacy of concessionary imperialism by voiding old extraction contracts or by expropriating multinational corporations of their ownership of precious things underneath the postcolonial soil. In 1975, Beitz treated that view as ethically flawed, even if potentially justifiable for the moment. It made more sense, he wrote, not to radicalize the principle of national sovereignty by extending it to natural resources, but rather to undermine the expectation that nature's accidental gifts were anyone's to own, especially since many postcolonial states suffered not the legacies of concessionary imperialism but the bad luck of poorly endowed territory. All the same, Beitz, signaling his support for the NIEO, ended by mitigating his worries about its natural resources principle on the grounds that it often made sense locally and temporarily, albeit not across the board and for all time, "to defend developing nations against resource exploitation by foreign-owned businesses and to underwrite a national right of expropriation."[18]

When it came to the NIEO's call for global distributive equality, by contrast, Beitz's support was full-throated and uncomplicated. The NIEO was on ethically firm ground in demanding global institutional reform of the economic system for the sake of more egalitarian outcomes. Invoking its bill of particulars, Beitz clearly indicted the preeminent function of multinational corporations that, along with prevailing trade rules, created a dynamic in which "value created in one society (usually poor) is used to benefit members of other societies (usually rich)." Even more revealingly, Beitz, like O'Neill, relied on dependency economics, the school of thought widely believed to explain why global arrangements hurt the plight of the worst off countries, to conclude that "poor countries' economic relations with the rich have actually worsened economic conditions among the poor." In view of these facts, Beitz emphatically concluded, "Rawls's passing concern for the law of nations seems to miss the point of international justice altogether." Similarly, Beitz wrote that Singer's approach "appears to miss the point: any effort to produce a permanent shift in the international distribution of food would require drastic changes in the institutions through which the prevailing international distribution of wealth is maintained." As Beitz concluded in 1975, "The duty to secure just institutions where none exist endows certain political claims [i.e., the NIEO's] with moral seriousness. . . . When the contract doctrine is interpreted globally, the claims of the less advantaged in today's non-ideal world—claims principally for food aid, development assistance, and world monetary and trade reform—rest on principles of global justice."[19]

Like his article, Beitz's *Political Theory and International Relations* of four years later—though mostly written by 1976, it underwent two rounds of revision before publication—began its discussion of international distributive justice with an epigraph from the NIEO Declaration emphasizing interdependence. But much transpired as Beitz finalized his account, and he changed his mind about a great deal. For one thing, the human rights revolution, associated with Jimmy Carter's election to the American presidency, intervened. Where Rawls had not used the phrase "human rights" in *A Theory of Justice*, after 1977, his followers began to do so. More important, the high tide of the NIEO in the context of which Beitz first imagined a global social contract in 1973–75 had passed. While faithful to both of his original arguments for global equality, Beitz now worked to present them much more clearly as *an alternative to* rather than a regrounding of the NIEO's claims. These alterations are worth as much attention as the original arguments, because they indicate something of the spirit of the later 1970s, which was to leave global equality utopian, even as the goal of according minimum or sufficient distribution to suffering humanity emerged as more durably credible.[20]

Beitz now turned to a fascinating indictment of what he called "the morality of states" and the claims of collective self-determination headlining NIEO ideology. In his original article of 1975, Beitz appended a passage referring favorably to a people's right to self-determination—noting its violation in America's interference with Salvador Allende's Chilean experiment in democratic socialism. He also suggested that a theory of global justice could furnish reasons absent in Rawls's non-interventionist approach for the international community to defend popular self-determination. Beitz's mature text of 1979, however, took as its central purpose not simply the plausibility of globally fair distribution but a version of it that meant that the NIEO's rationale of self-determination—and perhaps the NIEO itself—had to be abandoned.[21]

Beitz concluded the NIEO's call for equality, vague about exactly what its rejection of colonialism in the name of collective "self-determination" entailed, survived philosophical scrutiny only as "a means for promoting conformity with principles that would be agreed to in a hypothetical social contract. . . . Self-determination is the means to the end of social justice." But the beneficiaries of that justice are *individuals*, rather than the *peoples* or *states* which the NIEO insisted on equalizing (though, in its defense, only in proportion to their population size). After all, Beitz wrote, "it is the interests of *persons* that are fundamental, and 'national interests' are relevant to the justification of international principles only to the extent they are derived from the interests of persons." And this meant if it cut against empires, or South African apartheid, it was because self-determination cut against any claim of non-intervention supporting unjust regimes, including potentially the new states themselves. "While colonial government is usually illegitimate according to these principles," Beitz observed, "there is no assurance that successor governments will be any more legitimate according to the same principles."[22]

After these materials were added as a preliminary to a case for the rule of globally scaled principles of distributive justice, the results not only differed starkly from the still statist and nationalist premises of the NIEO (a movement of states claiming a national basis for a new international justice). Beitz's adjustment likewise reflected a widespread feeling in the West, crystallizing at just this moment, that postcolonial self-determination claims had gone too far and provided a mask for the internal domination of new postcolonial elites claiming international oppression. This feature of Beitz's argument fit perfectly in the turn against third-world nationalism and its subaltern vision of global reform, a turn that fed into the basic needs approach in development and the human rights revolution as deeply as any other input. As Arthur Schlesinger, Jr. put it in 1977, the breakthrough year for human rights in American discourse, "states may meet all the criteria of national self-determination and still be blots on the planet. Human rights is the way of reaching the deeper principle, which is individual self-determination." Though still hewing to NIEO's goal of equalizing distribution, Beitz wanted to index it to deserving individuals, which he now appeared to worry that the NIEO would never reach, even if it achieved its goals.[23]

Not coincidentally, Beitz dropped many of his originally more radical assumptions about why the NIEO mattered so much. He detached his account from his reliance a few years before on the "dependency" economics that afforded the NIEO its intellectual underpinnings. In his discussion of the urgent claims of economic self-determination so dear to the NIEO (and to which he relocated the original discussion from his article of north-south economic relations), Beitz reconsidered the aggressive charges that the rich immiserated the rest as empirically controversial. He now argued that, from an ethical perspective, the crucial step was to shift to a new framework in which it was not disempowerment of collective state economies but violations of individual rights that mattered. "It is especially unfortunate," Beitz wrote, "that criticisms of dependence have been framed in terms of deprivation of national autonomy." And even if dependency economics were correct, Beitz suggested, it would make more philosophical sense to articulate it in terms of violations of individual rights rather than of neocolonial collective domination. After all, "the objectionable features of dependence—like excessive exercises of state power or large internal distributive inequalities—might be reproduced by an apparently autonomous state." It was a telltale sign that Beitz now agreed with the NIEO's enemies that the third world could not hypocritically contest international hierarchy and go on to mistreat its own citizens. Similarly, retooling his discussion of economic interdependence in his case for a global social contract, Beitz now offered a much less emphatic diagnosis about the function of multinational corporations in promoting global unfairness.[24]

With global justice, Beitz certainly offered an alternative to conservative American observers of the NIEO like Tucker, who worried that well-meaning elites were betraying the American national interest and Western hegemony out of good-hearted humanitarian sentiment positing cosmopolitan obligation. The pressure of expansive solidarity was suddenly considered "a necessary truth that needs no defense," Tucker complained, though it had been "foreign to men's imagination prior to the postwar period." From his perspective, "the material issue is not whether any modern social ethics could pretend to provide enduring justification of existing inequality in international income distribution, but whether there is any modern social ethic that has sought seriously to justify income redistribution beyond the confines of the state." Amusingly, on this point Tucker could cite to his defense none other than John Rawls himself: "In this regard," he added, "it is perhaps significant that the most widely discussed 'theory of justice' to appear in the West in many years has scarcely a word to say on the subject."[25]

In transcending the limits of a national welfare that, even in Rawls's monumental account, had shortly before been the conventional wisdom, Beitz nonetheless moved to a specific "cosmopolitanism." And he elevated into a matter of abstract principle the argument that critics of the NIEO like Tucker offered when they insisted that the alliance's first and foremost goal was to achieve *geopolitical change* in the realm of power rather than *individual justice* in the realm of ethics. In another stormy passage, Tucker wrote: "However the state system is defined that is held responsible for present global inequalities of wealth and power, it is not the state system per se that is condemned. On the contrary, it is primarily through the institution of the state—and, of course, cooperation among the new states—that the historically oppressed and disadvantaged are to mount a successful challenge to persisting unjust inequalities." Where Tucker inferred from this point that calls for global welfare concealed a dangerous power play under the mask of high principle, Beitz took from it the need to replace the NIEO's call for *global equity among states* with one for *global equity among individuals*. For Tucker, "a global redistribution of income and wealth is not to be equated with a 'new beginning' in history if this redistribution is largely effected by, and in the name of, states." For his part, Beitz wrote in an especially clear formulation in a related essay, "The effect of shifting from a statist to a cosmopolitan point of view is to open up the state to external moral assessment (and, perhaps, political interference) and to understand persons, rather than states, as the ultimate subjects of international morality." The respective doubts about states claiming moral equity (and presumably the collusion of subaltern states the NIEO involved) clearly differed—but they overlapped, too.[26]

Beitz never forbade the ethical validity of an international order based on states, but he did change the rationale for it, reducing nation-states to intermediaries, with no moral standing in themselves, between global principles and deserving individuals. In his book and later, Beitz made absolutely clear that the persistence of an interstate rather than global organization might satisfy the dictates of global justice. And when he turned, in *Political Theory and International Relations*, to spell out more fully the implications of the ethical move above states for the world as it stood, the results were (as in Rawls's domestic setting) familiar in policy terms, however revolutionary they were compared to existing reality. As an ethical thinker, Beitz was primarily committed to a novelty and rigor in the way he came to his call for foreign aid as an obligation of egalitarian justice, rather than Singer's call for a modicum of help or some theory of mandated basic provision. But the subaltern internationalism of the NIEO had no place in Beitz's finished form of global justice, which generally went silent when it came to how an egalitarian world would ever come about.[27]

As late as 1981—two years before the global debt crisis that would definitively undo its dreams—the NIEO still elicited some sympathy from Beitz within severe limits. But like many others, he mainly shifted to emphasize that development of "largely indigenous processes" of growth would prove most important. Beitz ruefully concluded that "massive cash transfers *may* succeed only in removing incentives for increasing indigenous food production, and even institutional reforms like those of the New International Economic Order *may* only reinforce the structural inequalities found in many poor societies." Not finding an agent for global equality to his liking, and worried that the third-world program of a welfare world was a mere pretext for domestic repression and unfairness, cosmopolitanism came to philosophy as an unfulfillable dream. "The real dilemma, and ultimate uncertainty, of global egalitarianism is whether a political coalition can be mobilized within the rich countries for completing the picture of which NIEO is only a partial outline," Beitz was left to conclude. "It is hard to be optimistic about the prospects."[28]

THERE WAS no political coalition available for global equality, but one would emerge to aim for provision of basic needs and the defense of human rights worldwide. Beitz's philosophical "cosmopolitanism" emerged as a standing option in the intellectual scenery and came to loom very large in the discipline after the Cold War ended, memorializing a global egalitarianism that remained elusive in real life, much as the equalizing promise of the welfare state receded in a neoliberal age. As human rights politics emerged, a far more practically important form of international ethics was propounded, focusing on global entitlements to subsistence, fully developing the approach that had beckoned in O'Neill's early response to Singer. In the hands of Henry Shue, this enterprise captured the turn away from any egalitarian option in global affairs to work within an international basic needs and human rights framework and to encourage state policy—in particular that of the American state—to take on global misery.

As Beitz himself later recorded, "among the works of political philosophy stimulated by and contributing to" the rise of human rights to "the status of a *lingua franca* of global moral discourse," no other book to date "has proved more seminal" than Shue's. If Beitz's *Political Theory and International Affairs* in some respects memorialized the road not taken, Shue's *Basic Rights*, published in 1980, offered a window onto the one that was. It reflected a moment when a handful of American human rights activists wanted to incorporate an acknowledgment of the basic needs of humanity into their country's foreign policy revolution, and in doing so anticipated today's era of a global human rights movement that cares not merely about state repression but also about sufficient provision.[29]

A courtly southerner from the Shenandoah Valley in rural western Virginia, and a pious Christian growing up, Shue had attended Davidson College in North Carolina before winning a Rhodes Scholarship to Oxford University in 1961. He spent the 1960s there and at Princeton, where he earned his doctorate, "a student deferment away from the Southeast Asian jungles" and writing about conscientious objection, slowly turning against a war he had initially supported on patriotic grounds. Teaching at Wellesley College and never publishing his dissertation, Shue initially wrote respectful interpretive essays on Rawls's achievement. His path to tenure blocked, Shue was invited by his fellow philosopher Peter G. Brown to join the Academy of Contemporary Problems, a short-lived public policy research center initially founded by Ohio State University earlier in the decade. Hoping to verse himself in public policy and possibly to enter politics, Shue worked to organize thinking concerning American food policy in an age of international hunger before he followed Brown to the University of Maryland, where he helped launch the Institute for Philosophy and Public Policy in fall 1976.[30]

This institute was the first of the ethics centers in the United States that married ethical theory and public affairs, and it was the central institution for the invention of global justice, holding pivotal events and publishing landmark volumes. Supported by the Ford Foundation and the Rockefeller Brothers Fund, Brown had founded the center with the explicit mission of informing public policy debate. Its location in Washington, D.C. and the coincidence of its founding with Jimmy Carter's 1977 annunciation of an American human rights policy affected Shue's thinking profoundly. As the institute started up, and with impeccable timing, Shue devised and organized a working group on human rights in American foreign policy that included leaders and staffers from prior congressional activism and non-governmental advocates—the ragtag band that did the work that made human rights eligible for visibility thereafter. He was perfectly positioned to respond when Carter famously announced his administration's storied human rights policy in his January 1977 inaugural address. More than this, the basic needs revolution in development and U.S. Secretary of State Cyrus Vance's May 1977 affirmation that vital needs for subsistence might become part of American policy also were clear incitements to Shue's thinking. Similarly, his associations with Patricia Weiss Fagen and other activists and analysts urging a consolidation of human rights and basic needs paradigms gave Shue a mission: to define basic needs *as* basic rights. As with the rest of global justice in philosophy, for all its abstraction, *Basic Rights* was an artifact of an exceedingly specific time and place.[31]

Close to a decade older than Beitz, and unlike him a latecomer to relating philosophical argument to global politics, Shue embarked on his book in 1977, registering not the early- to mid-1970s of global distributive justice debates but those of the later human rights revolution alone. He thus intervened in a critically different way than Beitz, not galvanized by third-world egalitarian demands, but yoking a very different emphasis on bare sufficiency to the sudden prominence in American and especially Beltway international affairs circles of new rhetorics of basic needs and human rights. Global subsistence, Shue contended in a pathbreaking development, was a matter of human rights. Social rights were not a creature of national welfare, but a justification for international remedies for the worst indigence.[32]

Basic Rights opened with an epigraph from Albert Camus's existentialist novel *The Plague*. Against the "relentless onslaughts" of pestilence and terror, Camus's doctor protagonist had concluded, there was never going to be "a final victory." In the portion Shue cited, this fact made it all the more important to honor "all who, while unable to be saints but refusing to bow down to pestilences, strive their utmost to be healers." The epigraph brilliantly encapsulated Shue's decision, at the opposite pole from Beitz, to seek not a full-scale theory of global distribution, but to focus on "the moral minimum"—"the least," he explained in the book's first line, "that every person, every government, and every corporation may be made to do." He rose in defense of "a morality of the depths," as he movingly called it. "About the great aspiration and exalted ideals," he observed, "nothing appears here. They are not denied but simply deferred for another occasion." The theory of basic rights was supposed to "specify the line beneath which no one is to be allowed to sink." Shue did not rule out the importance of equality and excellence alongside security and subsistence. But in the spirit of Camus's novel—which Shue cited again in closing, exhorting an alliance of human rights activists to the imperative of healing—it would also be fair to say *Basic Rights* was premised on a tragic moral outlook in which the permanence of evil required those who cared about good to seek a simple minimum of protection. Officially, it merely postponed global social justice of the kind Beitz cared most to harvest from the NIEO; but temperamentally, its healer's ethic assumed that there was no perfect or permanent health, only endless disease to succor. (Forty years later, Shue chose the phrase "fighting hurt" to encapsulate the goal of his career.)[33]

Shue's epoch-making gambit was to insist that alleviation of global misery was everyone's duty, correlated with the most basic rights of humans as such not simply to liberty or security but also to subsistence. In making it, he devised novel arguments with quite lasting effects both within and far outside the precincts of professional philosophy. His most abstract but profound contribution was to reconceive what a "human right" is. For Shue, it was always, among other things, a claim that imposed one or more positive duties. To that date, philosophical consensus had held that some rights merely imposed duties on the state (and possibly other actors) to *abstain* from violating them; and in this view it looked like social rights were different in kind, and possibly illegitimate, because they imposed duties to *act* to allow the rights to be enjoyed. Free speech merely requires the state not to interfere with it, while health care demands a state program. But Shue contended that all rights imposed a complex set of duties to abstain and act, and while the set might differ from right to right, there was no categorical difference between "negative" and "positive" rights, as philosophers had frequently believed. Shue's trifurcation of the kinds of duties that every right involves—the duty to not violate it, the duty to keep third parties from violating it, and the duty to ensure its enjoyment—was later canonized in the United Nations as the command to "respect, protect, and fulfill" all human rights. More broadly, more than any other argument, it ultimately swung the philosophical consensus away from default skepticism about social rights.[34]

The reason Shue undertook his philosophical revision of the nature of rights and duties in the first place, however, was to reach the conclusion that there was a set of basic entitlements that included *subsistence rights* as fundamental. No one who said they cared about human rights—as many

Americans suddenly did in the years he wrote his book—could do so without treating subsistence rights as every bit as important as liberty rights, such as the freedom to speak, or security rights, such as the entitlement not to be tortured. "[T]he same considerations that establish that security rights are basic for everyone also support the conclusion that subsistence rights are basic for everyone," Shue insisted. In this regard, Shue was facing down a Cold War philosophical consensus which, to the extent it took up the topic, had either refused to include or hierarchically downgraded the significance of "social rights." This even included Rawls, who had claimed—outside historical or developmental states—that freedom of the person in particular and the basic rights that protected it were to be viewed as prior to and more important than the undertaking of distributive justice. After a transformative trip to Indonesia and the Philippines under the auspices of the United States Information Agency in 1978, Shue was weaned from his initial temptation of reversing Rawls's priorities in order to argue that subsistence was *more* fundamental than liberty or security. His brief encounter with authoritarian development, especially in Jakarta, convinced him that such claims could buttress right-wing rule as much as they appealed to leftists who feared that liberals insisted on freedom in order to postpone welfare indefinitely. Shue had also authored a famous philosophical essay on the immorality of torture that appeared in *Philosophy and Public Affairs*, also in 1978; in *Basic Rights*, he explained that his point was not to "argue that liberty is secondary—only that liberty has no priority." O'Neill, who had first responded to the call to justify the remediation of hunger in terms of the basic rights and not overall welfare, understood the significance of Shue's breakthroughs both in rights theory generally and in vindicating the importance of subsistence specifically, later calling both moves "highly damaging" to preexisting assumptions.[35]

In making a case for global subsistence rights, Shue saw it as his task—much as Beitz and O'Neill had seen it as theirs—to translate dissident insight into the sources of and remedies for postcolonial hierarchy into palatable terms for his audience. In Shue's case, that meant reorienting the concept of "human rights" to which people were already claiming allegiance in increasing numbers. "The original motivation for writing about basic rights," Shue openly commented in his preface, "was anger at lofty-sounding, but cheap and empty, promises of liberty in the absence of the essentials for people's actually exercising the promised liberty." His goal, he continued, was "to make some contribution to the gradual evolution of a conception of rights that is not distorted by the blind spots of any one intellectual tradition." However, the truth is that Shue was not so much the philosophical translator of alternative philosophical traditions as the mouthpiece of dogged healers of the worst suffering in the global south. A onetime candidate for the ministry, after his dissertation, Shue had made an atypical and brief foray into Western Marxism in the early 1970s. However, his reading for *Basic Rights* indicates that his exposure to literature on global immiseration—as well as the crucial trip to East Asia, where he met a nun healing the poor and a lawyer defending them, to whom he then dedicated his book—mattered much more to his choices.[36]

The most potent influence on Shue's thinking, however, came from a local and recent book he read—*The Moral Economy of the Peasant* (1976), by the political scientist James Scott, who happened to be a colleague of Shue's wife. By that happenstance, Shue was introduced to Scott and his work, with its claim that peasants, no matter where in time and space they are, put subsistence at the center of their moral ideals and expectations. The claim had a titanic impact, convincing the philosopher of the preeminence of basic needs and rights. According to Scott, peasants in feudal Europe and colonial Asia organized their villages around providing enough to survive, and their attitude towards authority always emphasized the need to "guarantee *minimal social rights.*" As capitalism and colonialism both threatened their strategies and displaced former feudal authority, Scott maintained, rebellion ensued: outsiders thwarting immemorial strategies of subsistence, as colonial and later new states often did, invited endless trouble for their rule. What mattered to the global poor, Shue stressed, was that "all should have a place, a living, *not that all should be equal*"—a pivotal claim from Scott that Shue revealingly cited not once but twice in his short book. That peasants might want other things, like Christian redemption or secular revolution, had been entertained by Westerners before, but not now. A morality directed at basic subsistence instead of material equality followed, for Shue, not merely in view of right and wrong but also in view of what the global poor ostensibly wanted. And whatever the postponement of higher ideals in the name of the morality of the depths, it meant flirting with the rejection of distributive equality as a relevant moral ideal.[37]

This was a new departure for Shue, testifying to the impact of his reading of Scott and his travels abroad but, above all, to the collapse of equality and the surge of subsistence in a discontinuous moment in recent ethical history. Social justice was globalized and minimized. As late as his 1976 paper, Shue had been quite insistent (citing Beitz) that there was no avoiding the topic of global distributive justice overall for anyone interested in specific policy domains. To bracket it—for example to formulate a food aid or population control policy—endorsed existing injustice, given "our tendency to assume that we are entitled to all our wealth, however gained" as if it was incumbent on poor countries to reduce their population before deciding whether it was fair for them to be poor in the first place. How many human beings India could "carry" or sustain would differ drastically, Shue concluded, if the global south "benefitted from a 'new international economic order.'" Conversely Beitz, in a contribution to a Maryland center conference and volume on American human rights policy, argued—against the grain of the north Atlantic human rights revolution of the 1970s but in tune with basic needs rhetoric—that the philosophical reasons often marshaled for favoring "first generation" over economic and social rights were unconvincing. A theory like Rawls's, whatever its commitment to the priority of liberty from coercion over distributive justice, demonstrated that human rights were best conceptualized within an overall theory of social justice that allowed the two commitments to be balanced rather than ranked in a simple hierarchy. And Beitz's arguments were designed to support the same meliorist policies on the part of northern governments that Shue emphasized; the main difference between them was whether to argue for those policies on grounds of equality or subsistence. Yet Shue's subtle departure from egalitarianism by the time he finished his book was revealing.[38]

Beitz had been sufficiently undeterred by mounting objections to Rawls's difference principle to make his task its straightforward elevation to the world stage. Shue rose in anger, reacting not so much to Rawls's failure to internationalize equality but rather—and much in parallel to earlier critic of Rawls Frank Michelman at the level of the domestic welfare state—to Rawls's failure to argue for an absolute social minimum in directing justice to the moderation of inequality in distribution overall. In fact, Shue's commitment to a rights-based global social minimum broke rather fundamentally as much from Beitz's global egalitarianism as from Rawls's domestic egalitarianism—and he knew it. "Like someone committed to the fulfillment of subsistence rights, Rawls does focus his theory upon the fate of the worst-off," Shue acknowledged. "But instead of providing a floor, or, to change the metaphor, a life-preserver, Rawls provides only a rope, hitching the worst-off (in a rather loose way) to all of the better off." It was true, in other words, that any increase in wealth at the top, on Rawls's theory, was allowable only insofar as it helped at the bottom. "But Rawlsian theory contains no provision that everyone's head must, for a start, be held above the surface of the water," Shue continued. "The Rawlsian difference principle can be fulfilled while people continue to drown but with less and less water over their heads." Social rights mattered as standards of absolute needs, irrespective of the general distribution of income or wealth. If so, Rawls's egalitarian principles were wrongheaded domestically—and simply more graphically on the global scene, where millions could die from hunger every year and more lived in unending penury. Similarly, in his otherwise enthusiastic published review of *Political Theory and International Relations*, Shue was actually quite critical of Beitz's respectful elevation of Rawls's difference principle to the world stage. The fact that *some* principle of global distributive justice existed, as Beitz had demonstrated, hardly meant that it had to be an egalitarian one. In his deference to Rawls, Shue wrote, Beitz had not shown "that a difference principle would be chosen to guide international transfers, even if it would be chosen in the initial Rawlsian national case (as is doubtful)."[39]

As a contributor to global justice discourse, therefore, Shue bracketed or dropped equality in the name of sufficiency, intent on showing that nobody should accept a global justice that did not *at least* vindicate subsistence rights—and that foreign and global policy should concentrate resolutely on that vindication first and foremost. And what Shue did not say was as significant as what he did. Unlike Beitz, by 1979 Shue apparently saw no respectable third-world agenda to either engage or oppose, and no global distributive equality (whether of states or individuals) as its ultimate prize. Unlike Beitz, Shue did not attack a putative ethics rooted in third-world sovereignty; he simply paid its claims no mind. When it came to collective ethics, his concern fell, like so many others' after Singer, on whether compatriots of wealthy nations had special obligations that overrode the exigent claims of outsiders, even to basic subsistence. Shue's victim-orientation in what was the first true work on international human rights in philosophy also functioned to put brakes on the indefinite expansion of obligation that some feared as infeasible. Beginning with O'Neill and continuing in Shue, setting a minimum threshold based in rights, as least as a matter of initial or immediate obligation, allowed a response to charges that global ethics involved moral burdens that were simply excessive. Shue's conclusion was that if America could not be, like Camus's doctor, a "true healer," that it "can at least try to take the victim's side."[40]

169

Oriented by the Maryland center's mandate, Shue closed his book with a series of recommendations for the policies of the United States government, proposing to start with official recognition of subsistence rights. He did not address the United Nations or the international system—though his work was to have its greatest impact there—but the American state alone. Doing so may not have been implausible at the time. Shue was able to cite the very minor assurances within Carter-era Washington, D.C. that the human rights revolution would engage distributive justice. The country, some hoped, might take more ownership over the global situation, in light of the absence of better actors. For many northerners, the United Nations had become little more than a forum for third-worldist apologetics for despotism. An America recovering from the depths of the Vietnam War was hardly an ideal agent of justice, but who else was there?[41]

Hoping to seize this moment of perceived opportunity to redirect the human rights movement and American human rights policy at the time of their inception, Shue recommended conditioning American foreign assistance on the insistence that beneficiary states not deprive their own citizens of their basis of subsistence. He also suggested better regulating corporations operating abroad. But insofar as Shue aimed his philosophy at policy change, events quickly revealed his moment as anything but propitious. In practice, Carter's administration treated the provision of basic needs as rhetorical. Not only the American state, but even the bulk of the nongovernmental human rights movement lopped off economic and social rights from the era of national welfare and from the Universal Declaration of Human Rights as if they had never been—until social rights were laboriously restored (and never to American foreign policy) decades later. And with Ronald Reagan's election the year *Basic Rights* appeared, any belief in the promotion of a global social minimum in the human rights movement must have seemed wholly premature. As one of the earliest of many enthusiastic reviews of Shue's book observed, "The Reagan administration's hostility to human rights activism promises a chilly reception for Shue's arguments for a right to subsistence." Even the northern human rights movement proved immune: Shue would have to wait until the end of the Cold War to see the shifting priorities of that movement take social rights on board.[42]

Shue later dropped his policy recommendations when his book was republished, but they are critical to the moment in which even its most abstract philosophical interventions were framed. It seemed believable, though unlikely, to reorient the human rights revolution of the years during which the book was composed to assume responsibility for distributive justice. But in Shue's hands, and that of the human rights movement that followed, it was an expansion that bracketed inequality as the political crisis to confront in the name of treating the most abject misery as the disease to heal.

WHILE THE succor of faraway suffering (itself rooted in longstanding humanitarian sentiment and practices) and the attempt to vindicate subsistence rights have enjoyed major practical support since, the philosophy of global egalitarianism remains a file in the archives of utopianism. Shue's clarion call for a philosophy of subsistence rights offered a vision of sufficiency across the distribution of the key human goods that anticipated a world in which equality is not a concern or is postponed until later, while bands of Camus's healers operate to bring to the suffering their moral due of subsistence.

The birth of global justice involved a remarkable philosophical consensus about the individualization of the basis of social justice. Whether as a matter of their interests or rights, all the founders argued in terms of the prerogatives of individual persons as the sole foundation of any transnational justice. The more collectivist claims of third-world nationalism or internationalism, like those of the welfare state before Rawls, were abandoned. It was Beitz who—keenly aware of the arguments of third-world political leaders and their very different ethics of collective self-determination—had made this shift most explicitly, aware that there are alternatives to it; but for Shue, too, sympathy for foreign suffering did not translate into any deviation from an individualistic basis for ethics.

Shue clearly registered his awareness that powerful agency is collective. "The burdens connected with subsistence rights," he wrote in a powerful passage redolent of Scott's studies of peasants, "do not fall primarily upon isolated individuals who would be expected to forgo advantages to themselves for the sake of not threatening others, but primarily upon human communities that can work cooperatively to design institutions that avoid situations in which people are confronted by subsistence-threatening forces they cannot themselves handle." His concrete recommendations were directed to the new human rights movement and, through its pressure, the American state. Yet even though—in a remarkable aside in a footnote—Shue protested "the distorting atomism at the heart of liberalism," he, too, erected his argument for the rights to subsistence firmly on individualistic grounds.[43]

It may seem striking that the different options in the age of "global jus-tice" have the selfsame starting point in an exclusionary moral individualism as economic liberalism does, poles apart from the nationalist premises of the welfare state in the global north and attempts to transplant it to the global south in the prior era. In this resolute individualism, the birth of global jus-tice looks like it testifies to the enormous power—and possible limits—of a moment when international human rights in ethics and globalizing market fundamentalism in economics became companions on the road towards the present. Similarly, the version of global justice that found institutional and mobilizational support, with egalitarianism memorialized in books and the goal of subsistence slowly taken up in practice, might have required the ad-justment of neoliberal priorities, but not their relinquishment.

But its ethical individualism and its compatibility in its practically real-ized form with the endurance and explosion of inequality hardly make of global justice a neoliberal cause. The same was to be true of the human rights movement itself, though it shared the same foundations and timeline as the shift in political economy. The unnerving results do, however, pose hard questions to philosophy about whether and how it can truly guide events, just as the human rights movement would struggle within the neoliberal cage it did not build but could not exit. The defense of equality in Beitz, as in Rawls before him, was moving, but if it did little more than let fly the owl of Minerva at dusk, what was its use? We need ethics, but philosophy seemed mainly to register losses by proclaiming a principle of distributive equality just at the time when the welfare state was about to suffer unending waves of assault, and a postcolonial dream of a global welfare was spurned.

What could survive outside of theory was not distributive equality, but a more minimal commitment to sufficient provision and the global basic rights that now justified it. Even then, with global ethics rescuing a cosmopolitan utopia from historical disaster, it has never been altogether clear how great a role its guise of pursuing subsistence has played in making the aftermath at least more humane. The results threw the very value of the ethical enterprise into doubt. To fend off all those who have doubted that ethical princi-ples could ever make much difference, the outcome raised the still-live chal-lenge of how morality as philosophers propound it can change the world rather than mourn or humanize defeats. As Beitz worried in closing his touchstone essay inventing global justice, "If we cannot expect moral theory to provide a firm guide for action, one might wonder whether moral theory has any practical point at all."[44]

7

Human Rights in the
Neoliberal Maelstrom

In late August 1976, before his cruel assassination a month later, the left-wing Chilean economist Orlando Letelier argued in *The Nation* that there was a hidden connection between the political terror causing extreme human rights violations in his country and its new free market policies. Exiled from serving the dream of democratic socialism after President Salvador Allende's death, Letelier suggested the connivance of Milton Friedman and other "Chicago boys"—neoliberal economists in orbit around Friedman's University of Chicago Economics Department—with the repression that the nascent human rights movement was exposing. "Violation of human rights, the system of institutionalized brutality, the drastic control and suppression of every form of meaningful dissent," Letelier complained, "is discussed (and often condemned) as a phenomenon only indirectly linked, or indeed entirely unrelated, to the classical unrestrained *free market* policies that have been enforced by the military junta." The truth, however, was that there was a profound connection. There was no way to separate concern for human rights from attack on the neoliberal source of the violations.[1]

Forty years later, in September 2016, *The Nation* republished Letelier's classic piece alongside documentation proving Chilean strongman Augusto Pinochet's role in Letelier's Washington, D.C. killing. Introduced by left-wing intellectual Naomi Klein, it was now important to claim a different or deeper link between human rights values and neoliberal policies than Letelier had asserted. Since 1976, the economics that had debuted in Chile had gone global, both to a series of other national settings as a result of democratic choice and to international financial institutions that were to impose them, far less willingly, in many other locales as a matter of technocratic expertise. For Klein, in the most popular history of neoliberalism ever written, it was not just that free market politics were inimical to human rights outcomes. It was that human rights movements were to blame for collusion or at least distraction from this truth. Her admiration for Letelier notwithstanding, Klein asserted that human rights imposed "blinders" on the relationship between neoliberalism and terror. "The human rights movement," Klein observed of the Chilean scene, "helped the Chicago School ideology to escape from its first bloody laboratory virtually unscathed." Amnesty International, for example, took a neutral attitude toward root causes, refusing to single out the deepest culprit for the events so as to focus on an informational politics that merely named and shamed incontestable state abuses. "Where the effects of neo-liberal reconstruction began to bite," one of Klein's admirers puts the general case, human rights law and mobilization "leav[e] unchallenged the conditions in which those abuses had become possible." Is decrying the terrors of neoliberalism without mentioning neoliberalism in effect to collude with evil?[2]

That admirer, international lawyer Susan Marks, contends that "the history of human rights cannot be told in isolation from developments in the history of capitalism." If human rights fail to grapple with the causes of state violence, the rise of neoliberalism is part of the explanation why human rights took off as the prime optic for justice locally and globally. "The human rights movement as we know it today took shape during the 1970s," Marks explains. "[And] a rather important aspect of the context for the movement's emergence is . . . the rise in that period of the neo-liberal version of 'private' capitalism, with its now familiar policy prescription of privatisation, deregulation and state retreat from social provision." It is no accident that progressive attempts to pursue human rights across the world have coincided with the "last utopia" of neoliberalism. At the very least, campaigns for human rights distract from the true source of the very evils they purport to oppose.[3]

If few in the 1970s anticipated the neoliberal age that followed, forty years on it seems pressing to reassess how human rights fit into the political economy of their own age of at least rhetorical ascendancy. Nationally, welfare states entered crisis; globally, if a "new international economic order" prevailed, it was one in which market fundamentalism made impressive inroads, with inequality exploding in many nations. Yet human rights enjoyed increasing prominence in that very neoliberal age—breaking out into mass visibility in the 1970s when neoliberalism experienced its first breakthroughs, and ascending to something like a consensus public philosophy in worldwide ethics in the 1990s, when neoliberalism occupied the same status in worldwide economics. The striking correspondence between the two naturally raises the question of their relationship to each other.

Klein's allegation, however, is exaggerated and implausible. It does not fairly or properly position human rights in their neoliberal age. In what sense did human rights "help" neoliberalism make its way? Though sharing the same moral individualism with their economic rival, and the same suspicion of collectivist projects like nationalism and socialism, human rights surely did not bring the neoliberal age about. It was not the job of human rights activists to save Marxism from its theoretical quandaries or the left from its practical failures. There is no reason to think that a human rights stigmatizing "superficial" abuses could not coexist with a more "structural" politics, just as Letelier demanded. Whatever the relationship so far of human rights law and movements to their neoliberal companion, they also brought unprecedented scrutiny not merely to state violence around the world but to the profound failures of states to treat their citizens equally no matter their gender, race, religion, or sexual orientation. Human rights movements also called more and more on longstanding resources—starting with the social rights in the Universal Declaration of Human Rights of 1948—for demanding economic entitlements, from employment to housing to food. And in fact, for all of its sins, what Klein calls the "disaster capitalism" of neoliberalism could sometimes fulfill the wildest dreams of human rights law, as Chinese marketization brought more human beings out of poverty than any other force—certainly including the human rights movement itself—has in history.

None of this means that human rights failed to conform to their neoliberal ambiance. Just as before in its modern career, the notion that individuals have basic rights was shaped by the political economy that always affects so much else in moral ideals and social relations. Human rights had been strongly linked to classical liberalism in the nineteenth century, which meant their deployment as slogans for defenders of free contracts and inviolable property. In the mid-twentieth-century age of national welfare, human rights were recast in the spirit of egalitarian hopes within discrete and exclusionary communities. Finally, neoliberalism once again exerted a strong pressure of redefinition. Never did the language of human rights revert to the narrow protection of contract and property, as in the nineteenth century when Karl Marx denounced the effect and for which Hayek could still wax nostalgic in the 1940s. Although the two movements for human rights and neoliberal policies shared the same abstract lifespan, their concrete relation to each other was far from straightforward in its details across time and space. When their relationship is reconstructed more carefully, taking account of economic and social rights as they were restored to the agenda after the Cold War ended, the argument has to change dramatically.

The older association of human rights with national welfare was surely uprooted by a countervailing trend. Even as human rights were updated for a newly visible brand of cross-border politics as neoliberalism's own version of cosmopolitan globalization took off, they were reimagined as international tools of status equalization, especially when it came to discrimination against women and other subordinated groups. Human rights law and politics, if not to blame for causing or distracting from neoliberal assumptions, were nonetheless condemned to a defensive and minor role in pushing back against the new political economy. The trouble was not so much that human rights obscured a necessary structural politics as that, as latecomers in the new era to distributional concerns of any kind, they stigmatized only the shame of material insufficiency while turning a blind eye to galloping material inequality. Great advances were made when it came to status equality and supranational responsibility, but at the high price of material fairness at every scale, for which human rights law lacked the norms and human rights movements the will to advocate.

It was theoretically possible for human rights law and movements to function so as to make the new wave of governance more humane in the distribution of the good things in life. If sensitized to the need to remediate poverty in the development of the poorest lands around the world and providing the tools to fight austerity policies in the richer ones, where welfare states had already been built, human rights could offer resistance on paper to the worst neoliberal policies. But even in theory, with their moral focus on a floor of sufficient protection in a globalizing economy, human rights did nothing to interfere with the obliteration of any ceiling on distributive inequality. Deprived of the ambiance of national welfare, human rights emerged in a neoliberal age as weak tools to aim at sufficient provision alone. The political and legal project in their name became a powerless companion of the explosion of inequality.

IT IS CRITICAL to begin with a survey across time and space of the appearance and institutionalization of neoliberal thinking. Such a survey raises serious difficulties about the plausibility of establishing any kind of connection—beyond the weak one of common individualism and chronological simultaneity—with human rights law and movements, to say nothing of viewing the two phenomena as complicit with each other. A tour of diverse nations, regions, and, later, international institutions in an increasingly neoliberal era shows how distinctive each situation was across time and space. The worry that the rise of human rights politics offered a problematic kind of distraction from the neoliberal transformations that reshaped the lives of billions must face the complexity that those transformations took place in different places, at different moments, and in different ways.

Letelier was on the mark when he said that neoliberalism visited Chile first before traveling the world. Its intellectual origins went further back, to the heart of the age of national welfare and social citizenship—with its sufficiency provision and constrained inequality achieved through market control or regulation, high taxation, and worker empowerment. From the 1930s, early neoliberals disagreed about much and were beset by uncertainty. The founding of the famed neoliberal Mont Pèlerin Society in 1947 did not stamp out that disagreement; in some ways, it exacerbated it. In fact, at the high tide of consensus around national welfare, neoliberals were almost as vehement in their criticisms of nineteenth-century *laissez-faire* as their opponents were.

The Austrian economist Ludwig von Mises came closest to being a full-blown advocate of untrammeled market freedom. But its younger advocates, such as his student Friedrich von Hayek and German fellow traveler and "ordoliberal" Wilhelm Röpke, were willing to hedge their critique of planned economies within appeals to the importance of state-imposed order, the ends of Christian social morality, and the sufficiency aims of the new welfare states. What they hated was the specter of economic planning. They were not, however, against scripting a role for the state of various kinds. And they were often happy to endorse the value of basic provision when it came to the most vital necessities. In his popular broadside against planning, *The Road to Serfdom* (1944), Hayek had been entirely candid about the compatibility of his liberalism with social insurance and a state-guaranteed basic minimum for food, clothing, and shelter. "There are difficult questions about the precise standard which should be assured . . . but there can be no doubt that some minimum of food, shelter, and clothing, sufficient to preserve health and the capacity to work, can be assured to everybody," Hayek wrote. Of course, Hayek did not rally to the rhetoric of social rights, let alone link them to a larger egalitarian project. Harkening back to the spirit of rights in the nineteenth century, rather, basic entitlements were for Hayek precisely a talisman against state authority rather than an argument for its expansion. He jeered at those who attempted to make rights serve national welfare and commented that "much more consistency is shown by the more numerous reformers who, ever since the beginning of the socialist movement, have attacked the 'metaphysical' idea of individual rights and insisted that in a rationally ordered world there will be no individual rights but only individual duties." It was an insightful comment about just how controversial rights were in the attempt to bring social justice to economic governance in the 1940s, even to its sponsors.[4]

In West Germany, after its founding in 1949, Röpke and his fellow ordoliberals helped shape the fiscal agenda of the new Christian Democratic regime, and the notion of a "social market economy" became the slogan for a hybrid Christian-neoliberal welfare state. Even there, to say nothing of other spaces of national welfare, the full-throated defense of the virtues of the free market remained on the defensive across the world. That changed in only one place with great speed when, after his coup, Augusto Pinochet invited Milton Friedman and other "Chicago boys" to advise on imposing neoliberal economics in Chile after fall 1973. After many investigations of the matter, including when Friedman won the Nobel Prize in economics in 1976, the first neoliberal laboratory clearly linked physical repression and market freedom. Chileans who had studied in Chicago, such as Pinochet's finance minister Sergio de Castro and economic czar Jorge Cauas, were the pivotal actors in implementing the Friedmanite policies. (Notoriously, the Mont Pèlerin Society met in the Chilean seaside resort of Viña del Mar in 1981.)[5]

By the same token, however, the Chilean experiment was unique for its active and intense neoliberal turn. Human rights activism broke out and formed transnational communities of solidarity from various Latin American epicenters starting in the summer of 1973—with the coup in Uruguay several months before Pinochet's. It did prompt the octogenarian Hayek to abandon all faith in the service that "human rights" could give neoliberals. The flame he had tried to guard of a reversion of individual rights to their nineteenth-century use of keeping the "mirage" of social justice at bay was now out. Their novel uses for the sake of placing a justified stigma on Pinochet, whose economics Hayek supported, and on the totalitarian states he always despised were plain. In a fascinating video recorded some three

decades after *The Road to Serfdom*, just as Jimmy Carter made the principles so visible a part of American foreign policy, Hayek recognized that
human rights now implied a kind of cross-border opprobrium, including
on the Chilean leaders who had enthusiastically imposed neoliberal economic policies. In Hayek's considered judgment, human rights in this new
meaning went too far: "The United States discovered human rights two years
ago or five years ago," he commented in the face of the spike. "Suddenly
it's the main object and leads to a degree of interference with the policy of
other countries which, even if I sympathized with the general aim, I don't
think it's in the least justified."[6]

Beyond such ostensible meddling, if human rights somehow abetted or
distracted from neoliberal victory solely by targeting repressive violence,
Hayek did not realize it. More important, to the extent it existed, the phenomenon was localized to one place. The very uniqueness of Chile's early
neoliberalism suggests that "there is no single relationship between human
rights and market fundamentalism across countries and types of rights," and
the complexity of the era since proves it even more spectacularly. Political
terror could come on the basis of other economic policies, both in Latin
America and beyond. More important, neoliberalism thrived in more places
after democracy came. Prey to military rule like Chile, neither Brazil a few
years before nor Argentina a few years after took a strongly neoliberal turn
until their "transitions" to democracy occurred in the next decade. In Argentina, for that matter, the more experimental attitudes of the first post-transition
leader, Raul Alfonsín, gave way to the market friendliness of Peronist Carlos
Menem starting a full fifteen years after the neoliberal laboratory in Chile
was set up. In the 1970s, local activists could easily maintain their belief—as
Letelier certainly did—in the compatibility between human rights and social
justice (indeed global socialism). Far more important than Klein's allegation
that human rights in the 1970s distracted from neoliberalism, therefore, was
how the relationship of the two changed in the later 1980s as authoritarian
regimes fell and new polities emerged. In Argentina, and in the startling postcommunist wave in Eastern Europe, the most troubling relationship between
human rights and neoliberalism occurred not under dictatorship but in the
creation of freer societies. Even then, it was highly dependent on chronological specifics and local circumstance.[7]

IT IS WORTH focusing on the Eastern European case for the critical reason
that, unlike under the right-wing Latin American regimes, the transition

to democracy from communism implicated the long-term viability of socialism. Letelier had invoked human rights in the spirit of his democratic socialism. A parting of the ways between them, however, began under communist rule in the 1970s, when appearance of human rights movements helped put state socialism on trial. Intentionally or not, the distinction made then between human rights politics and a broader social justice proved fateful for the future, especially once communism fell so unexpectedly at the close of the next decade. Although East European regimes sometimes garlanded themselves as paragons of social rights promotion, a dissident critique of state socialism that had no equivalent elsewhere oriented most of the new human rights movements to political liberties but also sapped the possibility of a socialist sequel to the critique of the socialist state. This gave Eastern Europe its prime significance in the global history of how human rights moved from an idiom of national social justice to a powerless companion of global neoliberalism. Even in Latin America, a wave of democratization that had barely begun by the events of 1989 was powerfully inflected by the fall of communism. This set up a global moment in which freedom increasingly implied civil liberties on the basis of market freedom alone—an equation that human rights law and movements would do depressingly little to shake. This was even true in India. In that country's mid-1970s state of emergency, Indira Gandhi had taken advantage of her powers to clarify in the country's constitution that it was a socialist state. Only two decades later, the end of the Cold War changed everything, and Finance Minister Manmohan Singh moved to neoliberal policy reforms in 1991–92, in the shadow of a worldwide ideological abandonment of socialism.[8]

The fundamental dynamic was that the obstacle of state socialism was cleared by the ascendancy of human rights in Eastern Europe, with a large portion of the global left taking their lessons from events there, although almost none of their sponsors intended to pave the way for a neoliberal sequel. As socialism slowly departed the world, human rights came to appeal as the central language of justice. After its participation in the creation of welfare states, socialism had become and long remained the most identifiable language of material equality, and its departure explains more than any other factor why the age of human rights was also the age of neoliberalism: it was no longer the age of a socialist left. Data show clearly that, in all languages, people began to speak of socialism less and less as they came to speak of human rights more and more, with points of inflection in both trajectories at the same moment in the mid-1970s, the one falling below and the other rising above in 1989 and after. But rather than allowing the identification of human rights as a market fundamentalist language, it was far more the case that proponents of human rights took it upon themselves to solve one problem, leaving its aftermath for later. The critique of state socialism for its oppressions proceeded for two decades as if nothing would ever take its place. In fairness to state socialism's critics, almost no one imagined neoliberalism would.

When dissidents against their East European socialist states inadvertently undermined what had been, West and East, the chief ideological bulwark against inequality, it was hardly with the goal of bringing that inequality about. One reason was that dissidence nearly always took the form of "apolitical" coalition-building, even when self-styled socialists participated. Nearly all dissidents defined their tasks as moral, the better to avoid frontal challenge to the regime, treating state critique as the sole refuge of opposition. They necessarily abjured a programmatic and political style of engagement that propounded a vision of what a truer social justice might look like instead. It was not just an abandonment of the threat of revolution that had done much to prompt redistributive bargains in Western welfare states (and legitimated dictatorship as it was fulfilled in Eastern ones). If no politics were available for the time being, then socialist commitments were also in abeyance.

If a "disenchantment of socialism" accelerated in the period, at first more profoundly in its East European homelands than abroad, it proceeded through a strategy of avoidance more than a direct critique. However it occurred, it removed a condition that subsequently both allowed and forced human rights into the position of companion to neoliberal economics. True, some dissidents explicitly argued that attempts to build a socialist state, whether revolutionary or not, posed distinctive risks of horror. No possible version of socialism, they insisted, could fail to produce terror. In doing so, they extended a moralistic anti-totalitarianism invented for a critique of a very specific regime into an attack on the plausibility of socialism in any guise—as if human rights had not been one of the idioms for the invention of social citizenship only a few decades before. But despite such zealots, it was more the case that the success of a politics of distributive equality was slowly placed beyond the reach of imagination even when dissidents saw no need to repudiate the communist welfare state as a matter of ethical principle.[9]

The Czechoslovak hero Václav Havel, for example, denied that his own version of anti-politics totally lacked positive content. But he asserted that

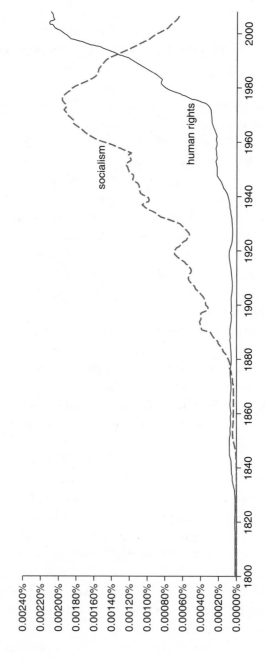

The comparative prominence of *human rights* and *socialism*, as reflected by the percentage of English-language books in which the terms appear each year. Graph generated via Google Books Ngram Viewer.

it was on the basis of fundamental human "needs" in a "hidden sphere" that grandiose hopes in politics had to be rejected for now, precisely because such hopes played into the hands of power. "The less political policies are derived from a concrete and human here and now and the more they fix their sights on an abstract 'someday,'" Havel explained, "the more easily they can degenerate into new forms of human enslavement." The allusion to needs was not a commitment to a politics of sufficient provision: it was too hazy for that, and it primarily explained the basis on which dissidents could mount a moral critique of the otherwise totalizing state. But it also left no room for a politics of egalitarian distribution. Neither socialist nor neoliberal, at worst it proved easy prey for those who sidelined the former and institutionalized the latter.[10]

No doubt the most remarkable case for the dynamic of socialism's recession in the midst of a moral critique of regimes for human rights violations occurred in Poland, because its uniquely large mass-workers movement, in globally visible dissent in 1980–81, nevertheless left it open to neoliberal "shock therapy" after communism ended. In the origins of the Solidarity movement, dissidents such as Jacek Kuroń, who had once been revolutionaries critical of bureaucratic socialism in the name of Marxism, joined eagerly. It is notorious that others were pushed by their dissent beyond socialism. The onetime Marxist humanist philosopher Leszek Kołakowski—critical of Marxism but still a democratic socialist in the early 1970s—was the most prominent example in exile. In Poland itself, the dissident Karol Modzelewski abandoned earlier revolutionary notions, but hardly embraced savage capitalism. Already by the mid-1980s, after the imposition of martial law, younger dissidents such as Adam Michnik and others reflected that the trade-unionist form of solidarity in which Polish dissent had arisen had to be dropped if a space for reform ever reopened, offering "one of the most stinging indictments of working class activism ever written by an ostensible supporter." Yet such a rare human rights activist, open to liberal thinking later, was mainly significant in the communist period for exploring common ground with Roman Catholics and converging with them in critiquing the regime's human rights violations without focusing on the bread-and-butter issues that deeply concerned the trade union rank and file of opposition networks. In Poland, as elsewhere in Eastern Europe and Latin America, human rights movements had to be built from such coalitions, and distributional commitments were easily sidelined in practice.

Neoliberal ideology was the furthest thing from the minds of those who made fateful tactical choices.[11]

The consequences of the negative politics adopted by coalitional dissident movements and the increasing privilege they accorded to civil liberties were only apparent when communism fell in 1989. Even then, popular discourses in the pivotal early months sometimes crossed into a new concept of revolution that would save socialism for the masses in a democratic and non-violent state. "The dispute in our society today is not for or against socialism, but about the form of socialism," one Czechoslovak spokesman explained in that year. "Socialism is not after all the heritage of functionaries, who want to preserve their privileges. . . . Socialism is the heritage of the citizens of this country." This leaves the puzzle not of how human rights could abet neoliberalism, but of how the latter could rush into the space changed and partly cleared by the former.[12]

Across the region, as elsewhere, neoliberalism had its own advocates, with much greater outside help than those who promoted some socialist sequel to state socialism. Those who concluded that individual freedoms, including economic ones, mattered most exerted power to make externally recommended marketization particularly rigorous. The Freedom Union in Poland, the Alliance of Free Democrats in Hungary, and the Civic Democratic Alliance in Czechoslovakia dropped concerns about class—including complaints about emerging inequality—in the name of entrenching markets. Politicians who primarily won fame for their association with human rights politics suddenly found themselves commanding the destiny of nations, despite their prior denial of any political agenda. Both in Eastern Europe and Latin America, it was typical for anti-authoritarian icons to find themselves the charismatic faces of policy choices they may not have advocated or even understood. Others were quickly marginalized. Neoliberalism succeeded to different extents and for contingent reasons at a critical turning point.

The extreme case of Poland illustrated how fast and stark the neoliberal turn could become during the heady romantic days of liberation. But it also demonstrated that it was contingent, not due to a die long since cast by human rights. Critiques of socialism may have done their work among some intellectuals, and Solidarity leaders in the critical moment of 1989–90 opted for elite and market-friendly politics, spurning labor's calls for a different path, with more popular opinions sidelined. Although they had been so fundamental to dissidence in Poland, there as elsewhere, trade unions, in the name of which socialist states had ruled, were not in a strong position to alter outcomes. Even so, the neoliberal victory there was not due to the inherent neoliberalism of all those who had opposed communism before but "much more the result of a specific course of events in the summer and autumn of 1989." In any case, strategies of liberalization very different from Polish shock therapy were tried, and results were comparably diversified. Sometimes, as in Hungary, the transition was slower and took place under the auspices of former communist elites rather than dissident icons.[13]

Often, impressive growth occurred, but it was uneven—almost nonexistent, for example, in Bulgaria. And trailing only Latin America among the more developed regions of the globe, Eastern Europe became more unequal more quickly than anywhere else. Different economic approaches, along with many other factors, laid some of the groundwork for nationalist and religious backlash that later devastated the very democracies East Europeans set up, even as the new inequalities they introduced were never undone. It was an unfortunate spectacle. But concluding that human rights movements in the later Cold War abetted the results, especially in the East European cases, is like blaming the doctors fighting one disease for not realizing the patient would soon suffer from another. They are above blame for their Cold War critique of the totalitarian state. Their obsession with old problems as if new ones could not follow them once the Cold War ended, however, is another matter.[14]

Democratization and neoliberalization in Eastern Europe, Latin America, and elsewhere in a so-called "third wave" were bound up with the extraordinary prestige of the idea of human rights, mainly because the latter failed to be effectively dissociated by any actors from the triumph of market values, as inegalitarian dynamics took root. But it mattered far more that neoliberal votaries did their own work. If dissidents famed for opposing the prior regime occasionally served as charismatic faces, the diversity of the backgrounds of the neoliberal politicians themselves proved more determinative of outcomes in different places. Unlike Havel, his neoliberal rival Václav Klaus had served as a central bank functionary under communism; others even had leftist pasts they abandoned. Most vividly, the Brazilian intellectual and later president Fernando Henrique Cardoso transformed from Marxian critic of "underdevelopment" during the era of his country's dictatorship into an advocate of human rights and neoliberal reform alike in post-transition political life. Once again, the harshest verdict is that the human rights icons and movement were not attentive to the inegalitarian consequences of neoliberalization, including long-range ones that eventually became flagrant. Having honed their vocation of stigmatizing dictatorship, champions of human rights were simply out of position to register the fateful economic developments that were in fact setting the terms of the future.

Human rights—including social rights—were embedded in post-transition constitutions. In the early years of new democratic regimes, however, domestic and especially transnational human rights movements concentrated on admittedly thorny issues of dealing with prior elites, most often through lustration in Eastern Europe and punishment in Latin America. They demanded the protection of fledgling norms of free speech and free associations, even as previously nationalized industries were privatized (in ex-communist Europe, sold off in fire sales to future oligarchs) and neoliberal prescriptions were institutionalized through an alliance of external policy makers and local politicians. As the neoliberal transformation occurred, human rights movements were busy doing other things. An entire field of "transitional justice" theorizing pathways to democracy was founded that, with rare exceptions, disregarded or marginalized distributive questions and paid no mind even as the conditions for inequality were laid.

After this early moment of transition, human rights movements and legal regimes focused on the backsliding of new democracies that once seemed so promising, as authoritarian victories and populist anger accelerated. Especially with the growing strength of regional human rights protections— whether an inter-American system of human rights or the European Court of Human Rights, whose jurisdiction eventually extended over all but one of the former Eastern Bloc countries—both national movements and regional authorities attempted to defend the political and civil rights essential to democracy. They did not, however, try to enforce any dictates of distributive justice. This was true whether it came to failed hopes in Russian democratization under Boris Yeltsin giving way to Vladmir Putin's autocratic tendencies, anticipating a much larger wave of East European illiberalism, or the mixed picture of Hugo Chávez's early Venezuelan populism after 1999. The European Convention of Human Rights, restricted to civil and political liberties, exploded in significance in the 1980s and especially after the Cold War ended, in tandem with the construction of a common European economic space that provided liberal political norms to accompany the push of liberal economic precepts eastward. This legal project of extending human rights in the European east was the historical companion of "second wave neoliberalism," which involved the largesse of massive foreign direct investment in many East European states (Poland especially), tremendous inequality, and ultimate backlash. But despite the broad and early negligence of distributive politics, none of the regimes and movements that promoted human rights in these regions were neoliberal enterprises per se, and their blame was not so much abetting the romance of market freedom as failing to cry foul about its likely effects when the time was ripe to do so.[15]

THE CLASSIC geographies for activism since Eastern Europe and Latin America made human rights famous are especially illustrative of how the new politics accompanied but did not significantly abet neoliberal transformations. The Anglo-American and later western continental European transition to market fundamentalism, where there had been and still is no dictatorship, presents a quite distinct set of peculiarities that make the relationship between human rights and neoliberal victory even less plausible to assert.

With due allowance for the fact that the United States had shunned social rights, with no socialist or social democratic party to advance redistributive politics, these were places that had taken considerable steps toward a welfare state under democratic auspices offering sufficient provision and egalitarian citizenship—although all were equally beset with discrimination in provision based on gender and race. But unlike the despotisms of east and south during the later Cold War, transatlantic countries and especially the two Anglophone nations of the United Kingdom and the United States enacted new policies without attracting the censure of new human rights movements, which were largely focused abroad while national welfare suffered reversals at home. Well-known for its failure ever to establish fundamental economic protections, and with anticipations during Jimmy Carter's presidency, the United States would take its own neoliberal turn after Ronald Reagan's 1980 election from a state that had once featured higher taxation, more intrusive regulation, more generous social programs, and relatively more egalitarian outcomes. The United Kingdom provided a far more striking case, given its historic Labour Party and more devotion, both rhetorical and real, to the goals of sufficiency and equality in a modern welfare state. But in neither place did human rights arguments or movements prominently enter the equation; the most that can be said is that both countries, like those of Western Europe, hosted the lion's share of the private activists and developed new foreign policies that focused on violations of basic civil liberties abroad, even as solidarity withered at home.

In Western Europe, socialism remained strong into the 1960s and continued to make a central place for egalitarianism in popular belief and socialist thought. British Labour Party intellectuals in the Cold War such as Hugh Gaitskell were less sure than before that welfare required planning, but material equality remained a sacred cow. His experimental follower, the high-flying Anthony Crosland, could celebrate in his *The Future of Socialism* (1957) the great strides in sufficient provision and income equalization that "capitalism" had shockingly allowed; indeed, he could declare that both goals were close to achievement at home. As time wore on, however, the egalitarian concern of Labour thought became a matter of "retreating visions," with the dark years of the 1970s, including deregulatory moves by Carter's Labour opposite James Callaghan, leading to Thatcher's election and neoliberal policymaking. Continental European countries did not follow suit so nakedly. Few recall that something called "Eurocommunism" was all the rage in these years. And François Mitterrand was elected prime minister in France on a forthrightly socialist program two years after Thatcher's election, even if he turned in a new direction not long after. But all were forced to contemplate major transformations of welfare arrangements.[16]

The articulation of various "third ways" in the reform of welfare states, however, did not take place under the sign of human rights, and as they were put into practice, sufficiency protections were by and large respected. For that matter, compared to nearly everywhere else on Earth and especially Thatcherite Britain, continental Western Europe was to protect the strides it made in equalizing income after the Great Depression from the tides of neoliberal prescription—which exposed its countries to regular complaints from neoliberals that they had doomed themselves by not reforming their welfare states enough. The West European welfare state trajectory was surely not one in which human rights law and movements played the role of distraction from "disaster capitalism" nor even that, as in Eastern Europe or Latin America, of breeding inattention to economic fundamentals as human rights paved transitional roads to post-authoritarian market freedom. Continental West Europeans participated with gusto in the construction of human rights law focused on global hotspots and especially the fate of the global south, while tenaciously preserving welfare arrangements at home. For them, the slow activation of the European human rights system was mostly a separate event from neoliberalization; the outcomes of budgetary, fiscal, and tax policy on the two sides of the English Channel were too different to permit any other conclusion.

health were. To the extent that social rights were made legal demands in national settings, activists mainly sought judicial enforcement of social rights in court, a star-crossed endeavor that garnered massive attention but rarely paid off. But finally and most of important of all, human rights had no commitment on their own to material equality, and they coexisted with a new political economy of hierarchy that they did not disturb.

Economic and social rights had been on the defensive intellectually in global institutions, and only the Cold War allowed the consensus to shift. It was far more common for even those favorable to human rights to worry that economic and social rights had become an apologia for third-world brutality than it was to devote serious efforts to advocate for them and find adequate institutions to vindicate them across the world. Already in 1986 the United Nations human rights commission appointed Slovene Danilo Türk, later the president of his country, to be special rapporteur for economic and social rights, a thematic mandate that split in the following decade into a number of expert monitoring positions for the status of different such rights, old and new. Easily the most visible sign of the shift to a new agenda occurred, however, only once the Cold War ended, and the Vienna Conference on Human Rights in 1993 allowed for a reset on governance projects. The conference proclaimed that economic and social rights were "indivisible" from political and civil liberties, and that there was no way to be for the latter without endorsing the former. This essentially papered over the major disputes in the prior several decades about the relative importance and priority of different kinds of rights, not to mention how little consensus there had been in the 1940s that individual rights were the proper way to formulate human aspirations.[22]

What was really occurring was the detachment of social rights from the welfare state project that had birthed them. The International Labour Organization, not really having recast itself as a human rights outfit in either the 1940s or the 1970s, did so with aplomb after 1989, continuing its traditional promotion of labor rights within the auspices of a relaunched international human rights agenda. The transnational promotion of labor rights in terms of "core standards" under the ILO's post-1999 "Decent Work Agenda" offered multiple pathways and provided some tools to resist the egregious outcomes of globalization, even as others volunteered to interpret them in market friendlier ways. But in all of their versions, these enterprises operated in the absence of the original project of national welfare: balancing class power to shape some better (including more equal) outcomes. What remained was the goal of making the world more humane, without otherwise challenging neoliberal globalization.[23]

There was, in short, a basic modesty in how human rights governance intruded into economic affairs. Some forged arguments that neoliberal "privatization" in particular ran afoul of human rights law protecting basic provision. More illustrative of the shift was the mainstream thinking concerning precisely the private multinational corporations that were empowered as public governance was beaten back in a neoliberal age. Gone was any notion from the age of national welfare that corporations serve the public good. Proposing a globalization of welfare, forces associated with the NIEO in the United Nations had attempted to ensure that multinationals were not neo-imperial continuations of the old concessionary imperialism, but their project to elaborate a code of conduct for such entities failed due to opposition. In the successor age of international human rights, advocates debated how to subordinate corporations to global norms in order to prevent and punish their involvement in (sometimes, sponsorship of) the worst forms of atrocity, which was an entirely different—and in many respects far lesser—aspiration. Bickering occurred about how legal to make that case, but it was more revealing that corporations were being asked to steer clear of the worst violence, not even to work to guarantee basic provision on a global scale.[24]

Modesty also described nongovernmental forces capable of providing augmented pressure from the sidelines of governance. Since the end of the Cold War, the mainstream international human rights movement has generally envisioned a large zone of compatibility between its values and "globalization." During the heyday of neoliberal triumph in the 1990s and even after, most spokesmen insisted that the values of international human rights could guide or "tame" globalization if and when it goes wrong. It would do so by developing and deploying a toolbox of legal and other standards to correct and "civilize" an era of transnational market liberalization that has generally improved the human lot. Even as domestic trade unions waned in support of more full-spectrum entitlements, northern transnational activism surged when it came to new global causes. Neither with the 1999 protests against the World Trade Organization—the famous "Battle in Seattle"—nor the galloping protests after the 2008 financial crisis did transnational movements ever primarily articulate their grievances in terms of human rights. The same was the case in national settings in the most affected lands, especially in Latin America before and after the *marea rosa*, or "pink tide," and later in southern Europe, where grassroots mobilization and some governments opposed neoliberal policy. Newer and traditional non-governmental international human rights activism never really committed to offering an alternative to the globalization free markets were providing, even as they began agitating slowly, in the name of sufficient provision and within strict limits.[25]

Illustratively, the first international non-governmental organization concerned with economic and social rights globally, the Center for Economic and Social Rights, was founded in New York in 1993. Perhaps the most storied group, Amnesty International, ultimately moved to distribution as part of its reorientation away from northern leadership to allow its currently far-flung membership (including in the global south) more local guidance over activities. When the Bangladeshi lawyer Irene Khan became secretary general of the group in 2001, she argued for attention to global poverty as a human rights concern. Meanwhile, Human Rights Watch, the premier global watchdog group in funding, refused to countenance the viability of economic and social rights due to the dogged allegiance of its founding director, Aryeh Neier, to human rights as civil liberties. Even after he departed the organization in 1993 to head the Open Society Foundations, under his longtime successor Kenneth Roth, Human Rights Watch still gave desultory attention to economic and social rights. Roth explained that only when clear discrimination took place, rather than less easily shamed structural injustice, could the informational politics of his organization make a difference. To the extent the human rights non-governmental organizations later burgeoned across the global south, they almost always refused to exclude economic and social rights, in a stark departure from their northern opposite numbers. No human rights NGOs, northern or southern, emphasized inequality for its own sake.[26]

The strictest and most insuperable limit that new concerns with social rights faced also defined them most profoundly: there was no way successfully to argue for distributive obligation except within each state's borders. Even after the global social rights law in the form of the International Covenant for Economic, Social, and Cultural Rights came into force in 1976, for those states that ratified it, the treaty was deprived of any prospects of enforcement for a long time. The companion treaty protecting civil and political liberties called for a Human Rights Committee to interpret the treaty and monitor how well states have done living up to its norms, and most states also ratified a companion protocol giving that committee power to hear individual complaints. In contrast, it took more than a decade for an equivalent committee to be created for the economic and social rights treaty, and only a few states agreed, two decades thereafter, to submit to a mechanism allowing that committee to hear complaints against them. Once online, neither that body nor anyone else was ever able to seriously undermine the expectation that the treaty's sufficiency provisions would have to be fulfilled exclusively through the reorientation of each state budget, in a national rather than transnational distributive space. In its most crucial early interpretation of the treaty, in 1991, the new Committee on Economic, Social, and Cultural Rights observed that "international cooperation for development and thus for the realization of economic, social and cultural rights is an obligation of all States [and] is particularly incumbent upon those States which are in a position to assist others in this regard." To date, nonetheless, there has been no serious erosion of the assumption that states are on their own to fulfill the economic and social rights of their citizens. Not that conscience was not globalized, and the attention and work of nongovernmental organizations moved to economic and social rights in a massive wave after the Cold War. But the law could not suggest much more than demands, within rich states, to keep neoliberal austerity at bay and, within poor states, to adjust inadequate budgets to roll back a bit of misery. With the bid to institutionalize an international law of global equality dead practically on arrival in the 1970s, in the neoliberal age, international law furnished no redistributive tools among states, and few activists or governments tried to build them. Whatever the globalization of charity in the age of neoliberalism and human rights, there was never any globalization of social justice, even for the sake of basic rights of subsistence.[27]

The assertion and pursuit of economic and social rights slowly drifted away from their conceptualization as backstops for a project of class politics oriented to white male workers across the North Atlantic, to become adjuncts of concern for the most indigent on a global scale, notably on the African continent. The mobilization of conscience that human rights nongovernmental organizations attempt to channel made them adjuncts of the much more longstanding call for humanitarian philanthropy that the global rich might give to the global poor. As the glory years of transnational activism focused on Eastern European and Latin American repression passed, Africa became the next privileged site of human rights consciousness. It has been as central in the 1990s and since for thinking about the purposes of the enterprise as it had been peripheral before. In the process, great strides were made both in specifying what any particular right might demand— standard-setting, in the jargon of the field—and in making room for new rights that figured hardly or not at all in the age of national welfare. But the very emergence and transformation of norms also illustrated the increasingly humanitarian logic of social rights when they were unconnected to a more global distributive move, even for the sake of basic provision.

Good examples were provided by the rights to food and water. The one had already garnered a reference in the Universal Declaration of Human Rights of 1948. But as a template for the national welfare state calling for rising standards of living, that document was primarily directed to the perfection of advanced citizenship rather than the humanitarian difficulties of global suffering, which in any event were problems by and large falling on the empires of the time to manage. The Food and Agriculture Organization of the United Nations was set up in 1945, for example, unrelated to the concept of human rights. After the inclusion of a more specific right to food in the international social rights treaty in the 1960s, the world food crisis of the 1970s sparked major efforts on the norm in the 1980s and since. In the face of recurrent drought, an even more novel right to water was crafted.[28]

The right to health—and the broader movement to pursue global health as a human right—provides a final example of how norms were elaborated as part of an expansion of humanitarianism after decolonization, in a world in which originally imperial global health enterprises were retained amid profound continuing hierarchy. Despite the language of a right to the "highest attainable standard of health" as far back as the World Health Organization constitution in 1946, it was not really until the 1990s in the midst of the HIV / AIDS crisis that some public health experts, especially the enterprising Jonathan Mann, began to rethink the endeavor in terms of human rights. It was a bid to give outrageous need more visibility, but ultimately global health remained the philanthropic and technocratic enterprise it had long been and still is. When movements for access to medicines allowed drugs to be made available far more cheaply, or even conditioned access to markets for pharmaceutical companies on distribution of their products for the worst off, it could amount to millions of dollars of cross-border wealth transfer. Some, such as famed activist Paul Farmer, temporarily recast their prior heroic interventions to remedy illness in some of the most unpropitious circumstances as human rights campaigns—insisting that the phrase really meant a challenge to inequities of power, not to mention of wealth on a global scale. So far it has not happened, and an unrepresentative Farmer soon thought better of reforming human rights in the way he initially demanded.[29]

The turn to a canon built from renovated and newfangled social rights was inseparable from a historically unprecedented and unquestionably noble enlargement of humane sensibility. But this enlargement had to work across hierarchical lines of wealth and power without challenging them, bringing the notion of human rights into increasing proximity with older traditions of humanitarianism, and forcing advocates to relinquish the midcentury egalitarian premises of citizenship in the face of so vast a spectacle of misery that sufficiency seemed quite enough to strive for. What was left, when it came to the distributional aspirations of human rights, was the goal of basic provision on a national scale, especially the project of its judicial enforcement there.

THE TURN to national judges to seek enforcement of basic provision in distribution of the good things in life was predetermined by a multitude of factors. The judicial turn, seeking vindication of norms originating in the drive to national welfare, nonetheless departed radically from it, reposing hope in an agent for enforcing basic provision that had never been tried. Unlike in the older period, it was no longer popular to assume that the state-managed class compromises of empowering labor and managing their disputes with capital if bargaining broke down would best protect individuals from the worst economic outcomes. The moment of social rights constitutionalism after 1945 had been in the spirit of majorities demanding national welfare, including material equality, after total war. Now the notion of a right, including a social right, was associated with those likely to lose out in competition for power and interest representation and with those who might need judges to defend their rights *against* majorities. Far outside the domain of socioeconomic protections for the worst off, heroic judges had been sweeping the progressive imagination for two generations. After 1989, practices like judicial review of executive action and legislative enactment—once American idiosyncrasies—conquered the world in the age of American geopolitical ascendancy. Commentators strongly influenced by neoliberal ideas, such as the University of Chicago law professor Cass Sunstein, initially argued against even including economic and social rights in constitutions of newly democratizing states, because they might interfere with pro-growth protection of property rights. He lost the argument, but only to those who hoped that, in the midst of a neoliberal age, the time was now ripe for constitutionalism to extend to social rights defended by judges.[30]

Back into the 1960s, the Harvard professor Frank Michelman had pioneeringly argued that constitutional law was appropriate for attention to a social minimum that his colleague, the philosopher John Rawls, had omitted from his *A Theory of Justice* (1971) in outlining a theory of just distribution. Michelman pressed on fellow lawyers the argument that the American constitution, even without amendment, might authorize judges to enforce such a minimum. The argument did not succeed. When Michelman proposed it, other radicals were even more ambitious, viewing the U.S. Constitution's Fourteenth Amendment as a device for prospective claims to greater class equality. After the election of Richard Nixon, the U.S. Supreme Court swung permanently to the right, and distributive justice, on the brink of recognition, disappeared from U.S. constitutional law. Standards of sufficient provision were never constitutionalized and furthermore were subject to "welfare reform" and ideological wrangling—and material inequality exploded in the country. When 1989 came, however, the project of making economic and social rights judicially enforceable for the losers in politics became fashionable elsewhere. Constitutions around the world nearly all included the rights, and intense interest crystallized around the possibility of their judicial enforcement. The most famous setting, where Michelman and many others sought hopes for a judicially enforced minimum of provision, was South Africa, where the post-transition constitution of 1996 ushered in an original approach to how courts could help the best-off economy in Africa provide its citizens a decent living as a matter of right. What had begun for Michelman as a friendly amendment to an egalitarian project prospered as an end in itself in the age of human rights. As material equality cratered in so many nations, including a South Africa where the African National Congress in power abandoned land reform and allowed the country to be transformed by neoliberalism, judicial protection of a sufficient minimum drew extraordinary attention.[31]

In legal terms, the mission to find a judicial role for social rights faced difficult obstacles. In some constitutions, economic and social rights did not have the same level of enforceability as traditional protections or were not even formally rights, but rather "directive principles of state policy." And the international treaty protecting them had disabled enforcement at the start, because states only agreed to "progressively realize" economic and social rights, which implied they need not be enforced to the letter anytime soon. But the same 1990 treaty interpretation by the Committee for Economic, Social, and Cultural Rights that had hinted at cross-border obligation to fulfill a sufficient minimum was more insistent about the need to open a new judicial front. The Committee offered the notion that economic and social rights have a "minimum core" that human dignity requires immediately. In other words, within many norms of sufficient provision, there was a subsistence floor: a minimum within a minimum. The whole right might take a long time to fulfill, but the minimum core allowed and cried out for judicial enforcement now.

An exciting period of experimentation followed, especially after the South African Constitutional Court's decision in 2000 to side with Irene Grootboom, a litigant who claimed that her constitutionally and internationally guaranteed right to housing was being violated. The court enforced the right by obliging the government to do something rather than nothing—while leaving what that meant open for democratic and political decision-making. Copious ink was spilled on the decision, in part because its modesty struck a number of Americans as providential, not only because social rights were a non-starter in their own constitutional law, but also because they felt they could teach lessons from their own experience of how counterproductive "judicial activism" is. They had seen managerial intervention for the sake of social reform fail badly in their own country as the domestic civil rights movement reached strict limits. In contrast, when judges kept to their role as adjuncts of vibrant social activism, forcing the fulfillment of social rights on political branches of government, more impressive results might ultimately obtain.[32]

In some countries with greater capacity and wealth, the idea of a judicially enforced social minimum had great appeal and could play a potentially remarkable role. Long creative in judicially enforcing national welfare commitments, because its 1949 constitution named the country a "social state," Germany's Federal Constitutional Court proclaimed after the Cold War that the value of human dignity implied that every citizen had a right to an *Existenzminimum* of subsistence. And across the former communist divide in Hungary, already in the 1990s citizens of the new liberal democracy turned to courts to stave off neoliberal "welfare reform" proposals, citing the post-transition constitution's social rights provisions. Other East European countries, however, saw judges interpret constitutional rights so as to clear obstacles toward marketization. And after 2008, when the financial crisis drove austerity measures in European welfare states with predictable victims, human rights norms and laws provided frustratingly little help, with occasional exceptions (in Lithuania and Portugal, for example).[33]

Popular movements—such as the campaign for a right to food in India, which made litigation part of a broader strategy—were exciting examples of citizenship politics that revealed a progressive role for legal enforcement in specific circumstances. Yet the broader successes of the rapid influx of economic and social rights into the human rights movement after the Cold War were depressingly hard to locate, despite intense efforts to find legal footholds for their vindication. Observers doubted there was any empirical basis for thinking that constitutionalizing economic and social rights had made a difference to national budgeting processes. And in the midst of a data-driven vogue among scholars of seeking to prove positive effects of international human rights law, economic and social rights law generally went missing from the measurement. Most disappointingly, it turned out that the South African example, initially so exciting on doctrinal grounds, had proven not only faulty—Irene Grootboom never received the remedy that judges had "forced" on political branches of government—but also unrepresentative of broader patterns of social rights enforcement. It was, of course, remarkable in itself that judges could seem not defenders of order and property but an emergent voice for the poor. However, turning to the judiciary rarely served the worst off, since reaching it generally required literacy and organization. Pensioners battling any budgetary reorientation to free funds for other purposes were able to induce courts in Latin America and elsewhere to lock in their entitlements. For this reason, social rights adjudication functioned far better to maintain the middle class against the stripping of privileges than it did to succor the most miserable. To identify the claims of and offer remedies to the truly indigent, the internationally developed concept of a "minimum core" to each social right proved of less use than many originally hoped.[34]

THERE WAS no doubt, in sum, that human rights politics had been altered by economic and social rights advocacy after the Cold War, but in the end its sufficiency norms generally had nugatory or paradoxical effects, especially under judicial stewardship. While some progressive and Marxist observers concluded that neoliberalism had finally revealed the bitter truth about human rights in general, others claimed that salvation was to be found in a recommitment to economic and social rights. This insistent vision ignored the fact that while human rights movements had set out to achieve material sufficiency, their mixed if not negative record in doing so took place against the backdrop of the loss of standards of material equality. After all, even if legal or mobilizational techniques for vindicating rights to a sufficient minimum in provision of the good things in life were ever achieved, it would not guarantee a modicum of material equality, which was in fact the chief casualty of the neoliberal age.[35]

Even when it did work, correcting globalization under the flag of human rights meant building a floor of protection in the distribution of the good things in life, without concern for the explosion of inequality nationally or its entrenchment globally. It is most pivotal, for this reason, to turn from how human rights did with sufficiency in the face of the new political economy to the fate of material equality in the same era. The most generous conclusion was that it was unfair to expect them to succeed at a goal they almost never tried to adopt and whose abandonment defined the age of neoliberalism and human rights perhaps most deeply. Human rights did not abet neoliberalism, but precisely because the human rights revolution has at its most ambitious dedicated itself to establishing status equality with an ethical and actual floor of distributive protection, it has failed to respond to—or even allowed for recognizing—neoliberalism's obliteration of the ceiling on material inequality.

Human rights law and movements strove for a greater amount of valid social pluralism than ever defended. If the struggle for basic provision paled beside this priority, it is because human rights legal and political activism conformed to the largest trends of its time. After the 1960s, developed welfare states in the North Atlantic simultaneously welcomed more different kinds of people as their beneficiaries and suffered crises of solidarity in material terms. Poles apart from the 1940s, when they were in orbit around the political economy of welfare states, the notion of human rights since the 1970s has been bound up with a neoliberal shift from a politics of unprecedented redistribution for privileged actors in national states to an accommodation of "difference." A struggle for recognition of identities beyond those of white males challenged the narrow terms of established welfare states, but only in the age of state retrenchment and redistributive failure. Women, once silenced in their families, and those once acceptably stigmatized on the basis of race, sexuality, indigeneity, or disability demanded and sometimes won fairer treatment. It was only worrisome that, in a world-historic breakthrough of increasing recognition, everyone was treated more equally than ever before, except materially.

In the global north and especially in Anglo-America, trajectories were graphic. Women, massively excluded from the work force, had been viewed as part of the framework of progressive social policy of welfare states as part of male breadwinner families, with due allowance for social provision for exceptional cases. After the 1960s, this concession to patriarchy began to be lifted. Now the most abject on account of their gender (or race) were increasingly recipients of enlightened social policy, even as the rich consolidated more and more gains. Subordination of such groups remained glaring, and progressives were not wrong to focus on it—especially since the center and right insisted more and more that not state assistance and social interdependence but "personal responsibility" must prevail as self-help. The renovation of the welfare state in the name of status equality, especially in employment, required heroic struggle. But material equality began to suffer; worse, models of social reform that refused to sever class inequality from the agenda of progressive change were contained or destroyed.[36]

Human rights law and movements matched and followed the trend. It is shocking, in retrospect, how little they were originally concerned with status discrimination, even though the Universal Declaration had straightforwardly prohibited it. How women later became new agents and objects of the human rights revolution in a neoliberal age can serve as a shorthand for dramatic campaigns against status discrimination and for a new form of inclusionary global development. Almost no progressive social justice movements in history—from premodern religion to modern nationalism and socialism—had made the equality of women prominent in their challenge to hierarchy. With some exceptions, mainly in the history of socialism, quests for material justice had consisted largely of movements of, by, and for men, most definitely including the global south's bid for an egalitarian New International Economic Order. Feminists in Mexico City to mark International Women's Year in 1975 were appalled by the negligence of the interests and rights of women by those such as Iranian princess Ashraf Pahlavi (sister of the ruling shah) who insisted that only national development and international reform would serve them. ("We women united," American feminist Betty Friedan explained, "to insist that women's equality couldn't wait on a 'New Economic Order.'")[37]

In the 1970s, when feminist movements exploded immensely and there was still a radical socialist feminism, a traditionally male-centered human rights movement was challenged. A treaty called the Convention for the Elimination of All Forms of Discrimination against Women was negotiated late in the decade, coming into legal force in 1981. It has always wanted for state agreement and enforcement, but it remains easily the most transformative human rights treaty ever envisioned, demanding a reach into the "private" realm and thus an attack on patriarchal relations not just in employment and politics but also in families and homes. Startlingly, it enjoined states to "take all appropriate measures, including legislation, to modify or abolish existing laws, regulations, customs and practices which constitute discrimination against women."[38]

But, like most other movements in the neoliberal era that followed, feminism redirected the human rights revolution within a dominant framework in which fair distribution became distinctly secondary and development was imagined to be available in free market terms. After the Cold War, it became impermissible for human rights law and activism to omit women from their ken. The United Nations human rights apparatus engaged in unprecedented informational campaigns, and both states and mainstream pressure groups such as Human Rights Watch finally took on board gender discrimination in their bureaucracies. A host of more exploratory non-governmental organizations north and south grew up to seek new approaches to pursuing burgeoning international and regional human rights for women. By the time the American first lady Hillary Clinton remarked that "human rights are women's rights, and women's rights are human rights" at the fourth United Nations World Congress on Women in Beijing in 1995, it was official orthodoxy in the field. Many countries had already made exceptional progress in integrating women into the workforce, which continued in the two decades that followed, while Western Europe alone surged ahead when it came to women's parity in holding political office. In European human rights, both nationally and regionally, antidiscrimination law prohibiting gender subordination slowly developed as perhaps the most exciting and visible body of norms that the region's newly empowered judges might enforce.

In a quite sudden development after the Cold War, a movement that had in the 1970s prioritized women's equity rediscovered corporal violence as the most burning challenge to face. It was almost inexplicable that the internationalization and reimagination of women's rights as human rights had omitted sexual violence, despite an extraordinary commitment to correct private subordination. Now in the 1990s, at the Vienna World Conference on Human Rights and elsewhere, a global imperative to focus on suffering bodies surged overnight. It bridged divides tearing apart a movement now of, by, and for women—but ones in radically different situations across the globe. In international fora, national settings, and different movements, priorities shifted. Premier feminist Catharine MacKinnon, who had pioneered sexual harassment law in the 1970s, could now ask the question "Are women human?" to force the criminalization of atrocity since the 1990s to take seriously all of its victims, especially of rape in wartime. Sexual violence very specifically was the easiest kind of discrimination to address independent of material distribution, locally and globally, and it often seemed plausible to do so as a matter of foreign "culture." Activists north and south who had themselves struggled to incorporate attention to gender violence now could worry that it was displacing all other feminist causes, especially when it detached violence from local and global distributive contexts.[39]

No reformers opposed the meteoric success in bringing attention to gender violence, north or south, but some did worry that it recapitulated old orientalist stereotypes and that new campaigns were disconnected from larger goals. A first-world feminism, more and more successful in combating employment discrimination in wealthier economies even as material inequality skyrocketed, looked across the global wealth gap it could not surmount, except to stigmatize the worldwide culture of intrusion into women's bodies, from genital mutilation to unpunished marital rape and honor killing. Similar choices were made in the massive revival from the late nineteenth and early twentieth century of concerns about trafficking in women across borders. It pit long-dominant enthusiasts of the regulation of sex work and "the new slave trade" against skeptics, who worried that the campaign (especially when it urged the criminalization of prostitution) simultaneously worsened their material plight of women while ratifying oppressive understandings of female virtue. But, as Friedan had suggested at the very beginning of the campaign to internationalize women's rights, women's fortunes had often been mortgaged to the logic of postponement that structural justice projects had supposedly required. In response, singling out the fate of women's bodies for attention now was an ideological and strategic choice to be selective. It was almost inevitable that material equality lost importance in the process.[40]

As with neoliberalism's emergence and rule in general, what its critics took to calling neoliberal feminism differed profoundly across space and time. And it was far from the case that the exciting new feminist activism in human rights after the 1970s inevitably scanted distributional issues. But unlike the socialist feminism that was increasingly a distant memory, it argued for equalizing women with men, without a broader approach to the distension of the income curve in many economies, as the rich proved the truest victors of the period and global inequality was not a primary concern. Beside the antidiscrimination law in wealthier countries, the turn to women's rights as human rights faced the enormity of global hierarchy far less frontally. Insofar as it did so, it tracked a development agenda that long since had begun to take on a feminist optic to single out the centrality of women to any project around basic provision and especially poverty. The importance of women's specific plights had already received new attention in the course of the 1970s basic needs movement, since among its other sins postcolonial development regularly treated women as the least important beneficiaries of growth. The pioneering Danish economist Ester Boserup initiated salutary change in optics in the 1970s, which led increasing numbers of practitioners to adopt gendered lenses for their global task. Over the 1980s and 1990s, development placed women ever closer to the center, now with a massive expansion of the non-governmental sector and the rise of non-governmental initiatives like the microcredit revolution, both of which fit well with neoliberal assumptions.[41]

From multiple perspectives, women became some of the chief beneficiaries of the human rights era, and no prior ideology (other than feminism itself) had served them better. Their earlier treatment as adjuncts of nations—and husbands—in the political economy of the welfare state north and south changed drastically. But the form of their benefit was the pursuit, in the north, of status equality of individuals rather than distributive equality of classes and, in the south, of sufficiency initiatives in a new women-sensitive development that broke with any concern with international inequality. One contrarian explained that "lack of a widespread acceptance of the doctrine of state accountability for economic justice" was itself unacceptable, if it meant that increases in status equality went along with declines in material equality within nations. As for the world, she continued, women's rights as human rights had entered "the geopolitics of debate without being able to shift the . . . rules that privilege some nations as more sovereign than others." But such criticisms of the reigning form of feminism were bypassed.[42]

As the new political economy took hold, it was most demonstrably and graphically national rather than global material equality that was the fundamental casualty from the 1970s to the present. Late in the day, the French economist Thomas Piketty caused a ruckus in demonstrating that Anglo-American countries especially had undergone a stark reversal from the contraction of income inequality in the middle of the twentieth century to the return to near–Gilded Age and late-Victorian levels of income capture by the top earners. It was equally obvious, though much less scandalous for transatlantic audience, that in the developing world, inequality increased even more rapidly, especially in China and India after their turns to market liberalization. The victories of both societies, especially China's, in remediating poverty made it indisputable that the predominant trouble with neoliberalism was not poverty but inequality. It also made clear that there was not so much collusion of human rights in the "disaster capitalism" of neoliberalism, but rather that neoliberalism could help human rights movements attain some of their most cherished ends. Human rights law and movements remained important to indict both the shortcomings of such developments as well as China's notoriously repressive government—for many remained in poverty or had their socioeconomic rights violated in more specific ways. But human rights law and movements possessed no capacity to reject the profoundly unequal manner in which successes in vindicating some of their own norms of basic provision were achieved. In the age of neoliberalism, the greatest embarrassment of human rights legal regimes and activist movements has been that they did little to promote the achievement of sufficiency that occurred, while lacking any ethical norm or practical capacity to indict the galloping inequality that came along with it.

Drawing on diverse sources of foreign economic thinking, Chinese leaders after Mao Zedong's death and Deng Xiaoping's ascendancy engaged in market reforms. The state that had once claimed to adapt socialism to local conditions now institutionalized "neoliberalism with Chinese characteristics." The peripatetic Milton Friedman visited in 1980, but equally if not more important to Chinese leaders were late-socialist versions of neoliberalism. Many are still surprised to learn about these theories, such as the vision of "market socialism" developed by the East European and later émigré socialist economists János Kornai, Ota Šik, and Włodzimierz Brus, all of whom consulted for the regime. Thirty years on, the results were plain, in a remarkable salvation brought to hundreds of millions who had previously languished below the World Bank's extreme poverty line. India enjoyed nowhere near as great success in remediating poverty. Its democratic system did allow for a number of successful legal campaigns, especially around food access and security, under a constitutional court willing to read what had been economic and social directive principles in its constitution into the more binding right to life. It came in second to China for the greatest rate of increase in domestic inequality across the period. When it came to Africa, nothing remotely comparable happened. The structural adjustment policies it suffered led to familiar doses of international advice about how to cope (sometimes from the same authorities imposing the pain), development expertise about how to spark change after the failure of earlier fashions, and an escalation of humanitarian aid, especially under the auspices of the new private "philanthrocapitalism."[43]

No one should celebrate the Chinese and other victories against extreme poverty, of course, without acknowledging how hard it is to prove such findings. The rousing story of how many people existed in extreme poverty, defined as living on less than one dollar or so a day, was frequently told without mentioning that it left the lion's share of beneficiaries in the category of "severe" poverty, living on only slightly more. Still, the overall gains showed that marketization could in some circumstances fulfill the wildest dreams of human rights activism and law, and even when it did not, it was sometimes open to modification so that it at least promised a more humane globalization. It took a fight across the 1990s, but the Washington Consensus neoliberal policy toolkit was updated to build in "social safety nets," justified in terms of human rights or not. But such policies generally balanced their commitment to sufficient provision with continuing recommendation of straitened governmental budgets, and never aimed at any restoration of some of the material egalitarianism that the coming of the national welfare state had once made vivid.[44]

NOT THAT no voices within the human rights community entertained such revisions. "Unless we can effectively bridge the gap between the realm of human rights and economics," observed Theo van Boven, then the UN human rights division head, at a 1980 seminar, "we risk the pursuit, on the one hand, of an international economic order which neglects the fundamental human development objectives of all our endeavors, and on the other, of a shallow approach to human rights, which neglects the deeper, structural causes of injustice." Easily the most prominent attempt to retain some optic on global fairness in the neoliberal age was the so-called right to development, propounded by the United Nations General Assembly in 1986.[45]

Its origins stretched back to the 1970s, and was best interpreted as an attempt to save some of the NIEO impulses from the wreckage and to re-think global equality as human right. Unlike the collective right to self-determination that had become part of the human rights law in the 1950s and 1960s, but which had concentrated on postcolonial freedom from ex-ternal interference (including a people's right to its own means of subsistence), the right to development followed the NIEO in targeting unjust international hierarchy as *itself* a human rights violation. But while it meant a great deal to its proponents and elicited much verbiage in United Nations fora for more than a decade, it failed to gain traction, a victim of its foes and its vagueness. Like the right to self-determination before it, the right to devel-opment was widely regarded as pernicious, as many human rights activists interpreted it as a shield against criticism of sovereignty, especially given its promotion by states seeking a rhetoric for their interests in a new world in which human rights rhetoric were now high fashion. As with self-determination, it struck many as not merely politically dangerous but conceptually confused. "In a just world, underdevelopment would not be permitted," one of its slew of critics irritably remarked. "But this alone by no means establishes, or even strongly suggests, a moral *right* to develop-ment." For other adversaries, it was little more than another high-minded excuse for unjust internal dynamics in postcolonial states. The human rights phenomenon owes much of its currency not merely to the fact that postcolonial states required opprobrium for their perceived misrule but also that their essential distributive project targeted international equality while ignoring national hierarchy—not least when it came to women. In the absence of the powerful geopolitical project it memorialized, the right to development could muster little more than monitory rhetoric concerning unjust global dynamics. With the right to development as the exception proving the rule, global inequality simply went missing from human rights politics in a neoliberal age.[46]

In his role as special rapporteur in the years straddling the end of the Cold War, Danilo Türk, the Slovene human rights lawyer, still considered economic and social rights part of the new world of structural justice envi-sioned by the NIEO proposals, and along the way gave income inequality among nations (not within them) brief scrutiny. Still, starting in his pre-liminary report, even he understood the main goal to be the eradication of "extreme poverty," and he focused on the value of human rights in mounting resistance to policies that did not help solve that problem. While attention to inequality was not totally absent into the 1990s—notably when a mandate on income inequality and human rights was created for Chilean José Bengoa, who went on to discuss rising domestic and not merely global inequality—it disappeared soon after. Even before it went missing, approaches to attacking the problem increasingly revolved around equality of opportunity within markets rather than equality of outcomes imposed by social constraint on markets.[47]

It was really only twenty years later, in the aftermath of the spike in consciousness around national inequality under neoliberalism, that the human rights community returned in any significant way to the fray. As for so many others, Piketty and populism finally prompted a rude awakening. At the very least, the moment was opportune for a plea for indispensable relevance, with only rare self-criticism and self-examination about how the human rights era and the neoliberal one coincided. Alston, appointed to the mandate on extreme poverty and human rights that emerged as a vestige of Türk's original work, alongside the United Nations roles since created for experts on individual social rights, suddenly turned his attention to inequality in 2015. Doyen of the field, Alston's prime worry seemed to be that Piketty had returned inequality to the center of widespread intellectual reflection, but no one had bothered to mention human rights as the reason to care or as the basis for a response. Illustratively, the weight of his attention fell now—in a complete reversal from Türk's day—on national inequality rather than global inequality. And for him, it was crucial to see human rights as the proper response to it, at least when it reached "extreme" form.[48]

Alston acknowledged forthrightly that "there is no explicitly stated right to equality, as such, under human rights law." Equality was best understood, within extant frameworks at least, not as an end in itself but as a means to the other ends established by economic and social rights. Put another way, if "extreme inequality" were shown to be causally related to "extreme poverty" or to the violation of other rights, then the law indirectly demanded more equal outcomes. In any case, the inequality in question concerned means or outcomes only insofar as it affected opportunities—which is the kind of inequality Alston supposed everyone could agree about, even citing Hayek to his defense. It was a powerful argument at least to the extent it suggested that in any real-world scenario, human rights norms on the books from the Universal Declaration on, even though never calling for distributive equality, in fact required some constraints on inequality. Along with

Alston's report, a broader conversation slowly began about the role human rights could play in the inequality crisis.[49]

Despite the explosion of inequality, the rise of sufficiency gains, even if due substantially to China and typically measured in income or purchasing power rather than human rights fulfillment, was cause for celebration as "the greatest escape" from the ills of poverty humanity had ever known. For neoliberals themselves, inequality was simply the price to pay for that result. Few human rights activists may have been personally satisfied with that answer, and not merely because it appeared too self-congratulatory when so many in every country were still left in grinding penury. While there was no debate about the trend toward increasing national inequality in both developing and developed economies in the neoliberal age, the question of whether global inequality improved or worsened was more contentious— both harder to measure and more ethically fraught. Unlike the heady days of the NIEO, there was a much less visible emphasis on income and wealth gaps across the world. Over a few years, thanks largely to the empirical findings of economist Branko Milanovic, it became popular to assume that globalization's great virtue, even if it came at the price of worsening in-country inequality, was the equalization of the world.[50]

To the extent it was happening, it was slow and spotty, and the very worst off were still stranded. Especially with its private form, equalization under neoliberalism was a far cry from the welfare world model the NIEO had promoted before its rival neoliberal globalization set in. Even as the rich soared and destroyed any modicum of egalitarian fairness in most countries, it was difficult to anticipate equalization of standards of living around the world across any time horizon, and not only because of the unique circumstances of the Chinese and (secondarily) Indian successes. It is still the case today that most inequality is due to differences of average income between countries, not within them. As one economist observed, it remains far better to be poor in a rich country than rich in a poor one. Although human rights seemingly presuppose that humanity is one, they had emerged as the highest ideals there are in a world that is, and will indefinitely remain, profoundly unequal. Caught unawares by the consequences of inequality, especially when it took the form of populist backlash, human rights movements faced a frightening present and future of upheaval. It was unclear whether they could defend their own principles in the storm, let alone calm it as neoliberalism passed from strength to strength.[51]

Conclusion: Croesus's World

Imagine that one man owned everything. Call him Croesus, after the king of ancient lore who, Herodotus says, was so "wonderfully rich" that he "thought himself the happiest of mortals." Impossibly elevated above his fellow men and women, this modern Croesus is also magnanimous. He does not want people to starve, and not only because he needs some of them for the upkeep of his global estate. Croesus insists on a floor of protection, so that everyone living under his benevolent but total ascendancy can escape destitution. Health, food, water, even vacations—Croesus dispenses them all.[1]

In comparison with the world in which we live today, where not many enjoy these benefits, Croesus offers a kind of utopia. It is the one many believe was foreseen in the Universal Declaration of Human Rights (1948), and it has become our own, with the rise of the international human rights movement in the past half-century—especially now that this movement has belatedly turned its attention to the economic and social rights that the declaration originally promised. In this utopia, it is no longer a matter of haves versus have nots. The worst off have enough. But they are in a yawning hierarchy, far beneath the have mores.

We increasingly live in Croesus's world. Tiny numbers of rich people dwarf the rest in their wealth, and some national settings have been trending toward absolute inequality, even if the global picture is more complex. It now goes without saying that any enlightened regime respects basic civil liberties, although the struggle to provide them is unending. Croesus hates repression, not merely indigence. He would never consent to a police state. He views the atrocities of war and occupation with horror; he glows with outrage when the word "torture" is mentioned. And he also considers it scandalous, even as the sole inhabitant of the top, to live in a world of destitution at the bottom. Croesus's generosity, then, is as unprecedented as his wealth. How could anyone trivialize what Croesus has to offer?

Many of our ancestors would have demanded more. Any direct commitment to material equality—a ceiling on the wealth gap between rich and poor—is as absent from the Universal Declaration, and the legal regimes and social movements that take it as their polestar, as it is from Croesus's mind. Human rights guarantee status equality but not distributive equality. Nothing in the scheme of human rights rules out Croesus's world, with its absolute overlordship, so long as it features sufficient provision of the good things in life.

In itself, Croesus's magnanimity seems deeply flawed—immoral even— if it coincides with some of the widest inequality ever seen. This is the point of the thought experiment: Human rights, even perfectly realized human rights, are compatible with inequality, even radical inequality. Surprising though it may seem, there turns out to be no contradiction between drastic material inequality and fulfillment of basic provision. Our question is whether we should continue to idealize Croesus's world as we make our own world more like his every day.

From the short-lived Jacobin state to the mid-twentieth-century welfare state in its North Atlantic, Latin American, and postcolonial versions, the political economy that accompanied the Universal Declaration of Human Rights committed nations to a new form of social life. It was a politics struggling to achieve sufficient minima for a wider set of privileged citizens than ever, as well as a modicum of socioeconomic equality among them. Out of the experience of misery during the Great Depression and the solidarity of World War II, along with the communist threat, capitalist states signed on enthusiastically to national welfare. For their parts, communist states in Eastern Europe established welfare states of their own devising, and frequently socialistic postcolonial states tried to follow suit. Although ruined by gender subordination and horrid racism, it was the most materially egalitarian political economy modernity has seen. The late philosopher Derek Parfit recently claimed that it is best to sequence our commitments to build a minimum floor of protection and to institutionalize a ceiling on inequality. Starting with one, in theory, by no means precludes reaching the other. But the lesson of the age of national welfare is that the struggle to advocate both sufficient protections and more equal outcomes, in order to do justice to both, is not to be sequenced but to be made simultaneous, with all the difficulties that pursuing two ends at once inevitably involves.[2]

The ideal of welfare never implied only protection for the weak. It condemned the libertarian premises of nineteenth-century capitalism, championing the state's role to intervene for the sake of the common good, whether in the name of the reform of capitalism or communist revolution, Christian democracy or secular socialism. The consensus to moderate and reverse (though never eliminate) nineteenth-century inequality showed across the policy landscape, from antitrust to tax policy, not to mention state intervention into production or ownership of its means. It is perhaps because human rights offered a modest first step of sufficient protection rather than a grand final hope of material equality that those rights were broadly ignored, rejected, or treated with anxiety in the 1940s as the ultimate formulation of the good life. After all, rights talk had often been used to hem the state in rather than expand it. There were those who risked a call for "social rights" in the era of the Universal Declaration. But that call took its meaning from the grand revision of the entitlements of citizenship for the sake of sufficiency and equality alike. Even Franklin Roosevelt, offering a "Second Bill of Rights" just as New Deal ambition died in his comparatively libertarian country, reserved the highest rhetoric for not merely adequate provision for the common man but a modicum of material equality through an end of "special privileges for the few."

Although many certainly hoped that those ideals would span the globe, welfare came to be nationally rather than internationally organized when it spread—in stark contrast to the assumptions of both political economy and human rights as they prevail in our time. Everywhere in the world, welfare was both announced and achieved on a national basis. Of course, the Universal Declaration is international in source and form, but essentially as a template for nations—"a high standard of achievement for all peoples and nations," as its own preamble says. Welfare had been national ever since it emerged strongly during the crisis between the world wars. Governance of political economy ascended beyond the nation in the 1940s only for the sake of avoiding catastrophe if individual states failed in their obligation to manage their own national economies, never for the sake of a global floor of protection, let alone a global ceiling on inequality. The original relationship between the Universal Declaration and political economy was thus a minimum set of guarantees for which experiments in national welfare should strive. The United Nations statement of rights coexisted with a more ambitious egalitarian project that it did not mention.

The pursuit of twin campaigns against abjection and for equality succeeded only partially, whether measured by the extent of their generosity or the portion of the world's peoples they benefited. There was, some hoped, the possibility of globalizing welfare so as to seek the floor of protection and ceiling on inequality that some nations had achieved internally. Most visibly, developing nations proposed a "New International Economic Order" (NIEO) that explicitly aimed at global equity, and its set of proposals had a moment of fame when the oil shock of 1973 stoked fears that the developed nations might face extractive prices for all commodities. Instead, the "real new international economic order" of market fundamentalism triumphed. Welfare states were perceived to be in crisis, undermined by their enemies and their own successes, and politicians were elected (or, in Augusto Pinochet's Chile, took power) who set out to destroy the ideological consensus around national welfare. The legacy of the NIEO is that it is now impossible to imagine retreating to a world in which global material unfairness is ethically irrelevant. Otherwise, hopes were dashed and neoliberal dreams of a very different kind of global marketization came true.

After the 1970s, Croesus's world came closer and closer to being a reality, for his ethics became our own. To the extent that a utopia of justice survived, it was global but minimal, allowing for the worst state abuses to be decried. When it came to the distribution of the good things in life, the investment in sufficient provision expanded, but any commitment to policy constraints on material inequality evaporated. Status equality was given a major boost, overcoming the welfare state's biases and exclusions on grounds of gender and race, flaws that have made it not only irretrievable but also undesirable. Women's rights, for example, became human rights, and multifarious subordination was challenged. But material hierarchy was frequently ratified and strengthened.

Whatever its potential in theory, the human rights movement adapted in practice to the new ambiance. For one thing, the idea of human rights followed the transformation of political economy to a global outlook. Further, activists gave priority no longer to the agency of states to launch and manage national welfare, but rather to the rights of individuals to be free from harm and to enjoy a rudimentary government that averts disaster and abjection. In the economic realm, material equality was forsaken as an ideal.

In exchange for its cosmopolitanism, and in spite of some initial uncertainty, the new human rights movement forswore any relationship to postwar egalitarianism in both theory and practice.

Despite the obvious objection that the Universal Declaration—like our generous Croesus—offers guarantees of sufficient provision against the worst miseries of free markets, the apparently tight chronological relationship between human rights and neoliberalism is tantalizing. Could the rise of human rights to the status of moral lingua franca really have nothing to do with the rise of market fundamentalism, or at least the decline of national welfare? The answer requires navigating between those who claim that human rights escape scot-free from the charge that they abet market fundamentalism and those Marxists who reply that human rights amount to little more than an apology for it. Conspiratorial accounts that view human rights as a dastardly accomplice of shifts in the global political economy are unconvincing, but the simple failures and limitations of human rights in the face of material unfairness are no less disturbing for it.

The real trouble about human rights, when historically correlated with market fundamentalism, is not that they promote it but that they are unambitious in theory and ineffectual in practice in the face of market fundamentalism's success. Neoliberalism has changed the world, while the human rights movement has posed no threat to it. The tragedy of human rights is that they have occupied the global imagination but have so far contributed little of note, merely nipping at the heels of the neoliberal giant whose path goes unaltered and unresisted. And the critical reason that human rights have been a powerless companion of market fundamentalism is that they simply have nothing to say about material inequality. The chief worry about human rights is not that they destroy the very distributive protections they set out to afford, let alone that they abet "disaster capitalism." In too many places, those protections never existed. And global capitalism is hardly the only or even the main source of state abuses. Indeed, there is no denying that after the 1970s, mainly thanks to Chinese marketization, more humans were brought out of the most extreme poverty—and thus above a basic threshold of subsistence—than by any prior force in history.

Rather, the problem is the one that Croesus's example illustrates. Low ambitions, as much as the failure to realize them, are what have made human rights the companion of market fundamentalism, both experiencing their greatest strides in the same period. The chief connection between human rights and market fundamentalism is a missed connection. Precisely because the human rights revolution has focused so intently on state abuses and has, at its most ambitious, dedicated itself to establishing a guarantee of sufficient provision, it has failed to respond to—or even recognize— neoliberalism's obliteration of any constraints on inequality. Human rights have been the signature morality of a neoliberal age because they merely call for it to be more humane. Our world has come to resemble Croesus's world more and more.

None of this is to say that human rights activism is irrelevant, any more than it would indict a hammer to say it is useless for turning a screw. The stigmatization of states and communities that fail to protect basic values is—so long as it is not selective and a smokescreen for great power politics—an indubitable contribution. The rise of social rights in the last twenty-five years is certainly significant, however much most advocates and the most powerful states (led by the United States, which has consistently rejected economic and social rights as principles in the international system) prioritize political atrocity and repression for attention. *Even when they are accorded more importance*, however, social rights generally concern a threshold above indigence, not how far the rich tower over the rest.

Croesus understands this, and it is a reason why his overlordship is secure as those who focus on abject human needs work within his rule. Unwittingly, the current human rights movement appears to be helping Croesus live out his plan. One might respond that material equality is someone else's problem to make vivid and organize to solve: it is not the job of one movement to build another. The coexistence of the human rights phenomenon with the death of socialism, however, is a historical fact that needs to be named. And for those activists and lawyers who have inherited the world's stock of idealism in our day, there ought to be some shame in succeeding only amid the ruins of materially egalitarian aspiration at every scale. The human rights movement will even risk looking like an ally of Croesus—it has prospered as his rule has become more powerful—unless it does not engage in open dissidence against him or, at the very least, connive with others who break into open rebellion. If human rights movements today focused even more than they do on social rights, for example, especially in the promotion of labor rights that functioned as mechanisms of collective empowerment, it might make a significant difference to material outcomes.

In the absence of egalitarian pressure, it is clearer than ever that populist rage will explode in nations beset by increasing hierarchy and material stagnation. Similarly, persistent global inequality creates permanent incentives for migration, exacerbating refugee crises and converting penury from a structural evil to a visible spectacle. The response of human rights movements has been to double down on their strengths, indicting the consequences of material inequality when it leads to political catastrophe. But if it does not save itself from its peaceable companionship with neoliberalism, the human rights movement looks more and more like a palliative that accepts the permanence of recurrent evil without facing it more frontally. Populism is only one example of the dynamic of ignoring the disease only to denounce the symptoms.

Could a different form of human rights law or movements correct for their coexistence with a crisis of material inequality? There is reason to doubt that they can do so by changing radically—for example by transforming into socialist movements. There is no contradicting the moral significance and possibly even historical success of human rights when it comes to combating political repression and restraining excessive violence or indeed, although more controversially, in campaigns for economic and social rights. But whenever inequality has been limited, it was never on the sort of individualistic and often antistatist basis that human rights share with their market fundamentalist *Doppelgänger*. And when it comes to mobilizing support for economic fairness, the chief tools of the human rights movement—playing informational politics to stigmatize the repressions of states or the disasters of war—are simply not fit for use. It is in part because the human rights movement is not up to the challenge that it has been condemned to offer no meaningful alternative, and certainly no serious threat, to market fundamentalism. In Herodotus's *Histories*, the philosopher Solon's shaming of Croesus merely took the king down a peg; it was Persian armies that toppled him. The truth is that local and global economic justice requires redesigning markets or at least redistributing from the rich to the rest, something that naming and shaming are never likely to achieve, even when supplemented by novel forms of legal activism.

Not that neoliberalism dispensed with the state—far from it—but from the Jacobins on, a very different kind of state than it has brought about surged in the imagination, in the guise of savior of the people, attracting their devotion and self-sacrifice. Like neoliberalism, human rights movements depend on the state. But even their pursuit of economic and social rights has done nothing to build state capacity for achieving them or stoke the will to do so. In the alternative tradition of welfare combining the aims of sufficiency and equality, from the Jacobins on, a strong state—built with interventionist capacities, funded by high taxes, and able to call forth the zeal of its people—served as the equalizing power. Equality was never achieved by stigmatizing governance but instead by enthusiasm for it and even devotion to it. The movement for global equality, before the New International Economic Order died, was a governmental rather than a nongovernmental one, for the sake of building new institutions rather than only stigmatizing existing ones. Global welfare would require the same emotional commitment to governmental capacity, scaled all the way up from its avatar in national welfare to the world stage. Croesus, like the human rights movement, is correct that there is no way to proceed state-by-state without the whole world in view. It is just that neither adopts equality in distribution as a compelling norm.

But there is a deeper reason than its diffident relation to programmatic thinking and state power to believe that the human rights movement cannot disrupt its companionship with neoliberalism simply by pivoting to equality. More disturbingly, it can be no accident that the era of relative material equality in the mid-twentieth century was also the age of totalitarian regimes and of the Cold War, which exacted an appalling toll on the world. National welfare built a floor of protection and ceiling on inequality only in the presence of frightening internal and external threats—a prominent and well-organized labor movement and a communist menace, however magnified out of proportion. In response to those dangers, change came thanks to what Pierre Rosanvallon has dubbed a "reformism of fear." Governance expanded to secure material equality because the state was viewed as less frightening than the threats only it could stave off. By contrast, the human rights movement at its most inspiring has stigmatized governmental repression and violence, but it has never offered a functional replacement for the sense of fear that led to both protection and redistribution for those left alive by the horrors of the twentieth century.[3]

If a dream of welfare is ever to be brought back from the realm of the ideal, where it is currently exiled, it will need to be championed not only as a program but also by a movement. But it will not look like our human rights movement, which has become prominent as our world has become more like Croesus's. Above all, it will need to take on the task of governance, local and global, and not critique alone. And it will need to be frightening enough to prompt the social bargains that the welfare state supervised to the end of material fairness, while not incurring the tremendous costs of twentieth-century conflict. The age of human rights has involved greater inclusion in national social justice, especially for women, and any new program and movement will need to preserve and extend those gains. Finally, it will need to be global in scale. On moral grounds, the wealthy in the world should want to save themselves from narrow identification with their fellow humans only when their lives are at stake in the most spectacular displacement, penury, and violence. To date, a global welfare structure has only been imagined but never institutionalized. Our job is, therefore, not an easy one. Indeed, it is daunting in the extreme.

But there is no reason to think that material equality necessarily depends on either exclusion or violence, or that a bold program of international fairness is a pipe dream. For a generation, it has been familiar to think that human rights are the essential bulwark against atrocity and misrule. It is time, however, to relearn the older and grander choice between socialism or barbarism, and time to elevate it to the global project it has rarely been but must become. Croesus's world of basic rights and needs fulfilled in the midst of continuing or even escalating inequality is not only still immoral: it has become clearer every day that it is destined to instability and ruin.

Human rights became our highest ideals only as material hierarchy remained endemic or worsened. It was both a breakthrough of conscience and an immense reversal. Human rights emerged as the highest morality of an unequal world, in a neoliberal circumstance its partisans could struggle to humanize, only to find themselves accused of complicity with it. Human rights activists should not desire that companionship, even if they decide that their role is not to argue for equality. More important, their audience should not believe human rights are the only or even the main keys to unlock the portal to the world's future. Human rights will return to their defensible importance only as soon as humanity saves itself from its low ambitions. If it does, for the sake of local and global welfare, sufficiency and equality can again become powerful companions, both in our moral lives and in our political enterprises.

NOTES

ACKNOWLEDGMENTS

INDEX

Notes

Introduction

1. Zdena Tominová, "Human Rights and Socialism," *The Crane Bag* 7, no. 1 (1983): 119.

2. Ibid. For the beating, Jonathan Bolton, *Worlds of Dissent: Charter 77, the Plastic People of the Universe, and Czech Culture under Communism* (Cambridge, Mass., 2012), 180.

3. See below, chap. 7, for the data.

4. On status or "basic" equality, see Siep Stuurman, *The Invention of Humanity: Equality and Cultural Difference in World History* (Cambridge, Mass., 2017), and Jeremy Waldron, *One Another's Equals: The Basis of Human Equality* (Cambridge, Mass., 2017).

5. Thomas Paine, "Agrarian Justice," in *Political Writings*, ed. Bruce Kuklick (Cambridge, 2000), 332.

6. Frankfurt's "sufficientarian" argument (so-called) dates back to the 1980s, and has since been pursued by Roger Crisp and others. Harry Frankfurt, "Equality as a Moral Ideal," *Ethics* 98, no. 1 (1987): 21–43, and most visibly, Frankfurt, *On Inequality* (Princeton, 2015). For one response, see Paula Casal, "Why Sufficiency Is Not Enough," *Ethics* 117, no. 2 (2007): 296–326.

7. The famous demonstration of this achievement and its erosion in selected national settings is Thomas Piketty, *Capital in the Twenty-First Century*, trans. Arthur Goldhammer (Cambridge, Mass., 2013). See also Anthony B. Atkinson, *Inequality: What Can Be Done?* (Cambridge, Mass., 2015). On global inequality, see François Bourguignon, *The Globalization of Inequality* (Princeton, 2015); Branko Milanovic, *The Haves and the Have-Nots: A Brief and Idiosyncratic History of Global Inequality* (New York, 2011); Milanovic, *Global Inequality: A New Approach for the Age of Globalization* (New

York, 2016); and Simon Reid-Henry, *The Political Origins of Inequality: Why a More Equal World Is Better for Us All* (Chicago, 2015).

8. For one among many examples of uncritical nostalgia, see Tony Judt, *Ill Fares the Land* (New York, 2010); compare my "Unfinished Arguments," *New York Times,* January 28, 2015.

1. Jacobin Legacy

1. William Temple, "The State," in *Citizen and Churchman* (London, 1941).

2. R. R. Palmer, *Twelve Who Ruled: The Committee of Public Safety during the Terror* (Princeton, 1941), 311. This chapter suggests reviving a social democratic historiography of the French Revolution and modern history, dissident in relation to successively dominant Marxist and "revisionist" accounts.

3. I have drawn substantially on two (contending) general histories of distributive justice: Christopher Brooke, *Who Gets What? A History of Distributive Political Theory from Rousseau to Rawls* (forthcoming); and Samuel Fleischacker, *A Brief History of Distributive Justice* (Cambridge, Mass., 2004). On the history of egalitarianism, see Pierre Rosanvallon, *The Society of Equals,* trans. Arthur Goldhammer (Cambridge, Mass., 2013). Attempts to synthesize the history of social rights before the twentieth century are essentially nonexistent, but see Wilhelm Brepohl, *Die sozialen Menschenrechte: ihre Geschichte und ihre Begründung* (Wiesbaden, 1950); and Peter Krause, "Die Entwicklung der sozialen Grundrechte," in Gunter Birtsch, ed., *Grund- und Freiheitsrechte im Wandel von Gesellschaft und Geschichte* (Göttingen, 1981).

4. See Paul Veyne, *Bread and Circuses: Historical Sociology and Political Pluralism,* trans. Brian Pearce (London, 1992); Peter Brown, *Poverty and Leadership in the Later Roman Empire* (Hanover, 1992), esp. chap. 1; L. L. Wellborn, " 'That There May Be Equality': The Contexts and Consequences of a Pauline Ideal," *New Testament Studies* 59 (2013): 73–90.

5. The Septuagint rendered the Hebrew *lehem ḥuqqi* as "τὰ δέοντα καὶ τὰ αὐτάρκη" (what is needful and sufficient), presumably the basis for some later Latin translations as *sufficientia.* For the novelty of "sufficiency" in Latin and for *On Riches,* Peter Brown, *Through the Eye of a Needle: Wealth, the Fall of Rome, and the Making of Christianity in the West, 350–550* (Princeton 2012), chap. 19 at 315.

6. I owe much to Julia McClure, "The Deep History of Socio-Economic Rights" (unpublished), which relies on such literature as Gilles Couvreur, *Les pauvres ont-ils des droits? Recherches sur le vol en cas d'extrême nécessité depuis la Concordia de Gratien (1140) jusqu'à Guillaume d'Auxerre* (1231) (Rome, 1961); and Virpi Mäkinen, "The Franciscan Background of Early Modern Rights Discussion: Rights of Property and Subsistence," in Jill Kraye and Risto Saarinen, eds., *Moral Philosophy on the Threshold of Modernity* (Dordrecht, 2005). On the priority of social order in policy regarding dearth and plague, see, for example, Michael Braddick, *State Formation in Early Modern England,*

c. 1550–1700 (Cambridge, 2000), chap. 3. On later French state policies before the revolution such as the *ateliers de charité*, see Olwen H. Hufton, *The Poor of Eighteenth-Century France, 1750–1789* (Oxford, 1974), chap. 6.

7. David Bell, *The Cult of the Nation in France: Inventing Nationalism, 1600–1800* (Cambridge, Mass., 2001), 26, relying on the thinking of Keith Baker and especially Marcel Gauchet.

8. James Scott, *The Moral Economy of the Peasant: Rebellion and Subsistence in Southeast Asia* (New Haven, 1976), 176, 181, 184, 40.

9. See E. P. Thompson, "The Moral Economy of the English Crowd in the Eighteenth Century," *Past & Present* 50 (February 1971): 76–136. Anticipated by Karl Polanyi's portrait of the rise of market society in *The Great Transformation* (London, 1944), Thompson's brilliant reconstruction was connected to an outpouring of related argument. See esp. R. B. Rose, "Eighteenth-Century Price Riots and Public Policy in England," *International Review of Social History* 6, no. 2 (1961): 277–92.

10. Jean-Jacques Rousseau, *The Social Contract and Other Later Political Writings*, ed. Victor Gourevitch (Cambridge, 1997), 78, 54.

11. For context, see Steve Pincus, *The Heart of the Declaration: The Founders' Case for an Activist Government* (New Haven, 2016); Paul Cheney, *Revolutionary Commerce: Globalization and the French Monarchy* (Cambridge, Mass., 2010); and John Shovlin, *The Political Economy of Virtue: Luxury, Patriotism, and the Origins of the French Revolution* (Ithaca, 2007).

12. On Paine and "the moral economy of the American crowd," see Eric Foner, *Tom Paine and Revolutionary America* (New York, 1976), chap. 5. On Condorcet and Paine during the French events, see Gareth Stedman-Jones, *An End to Poverty? A Historical Debate* (New York, 2004), chap. 1, though lacking the distinction between sufficiency and equality. On the 1791 Constitution, see Dan Edelstein, *On the Spirit of Rights* (forthcoming), which emphasizes the role of physiocracy and the early part of the revolution rather than Jacobinism and the later part, in spite of the obvious significance of 1793–1794.

13. R. C. Cobb, *The Police and the People: French Popular Protest, 1989–1820* (Oxford, 1970), 251, 283–84; Albert Soboul, *Les San-culottes parisiens en l'An II: Mouvement populaire et gouvernement révolutionnaire* (Paris, 1958), part 2, chap. 2; compare William H. Sewell, Jr., "The *Sans-Culottes* Rhetoric of Subsistence," in Keith Michael Baker, ed., *The French Revolution and the Creation of Modern Political Culture*, 4 vols. (Oxford, 1987–1994). On price controls, see esp. R. B. Rose, "18th Century Price Riots, the French Revolution, and the Jacobin Maximum," *International Review of Social History* 4, no. 3 (1959): 432–55.

14. Palmer, *Twelve Who Ruled*, 226.

15. Cited in Jean-Pierre Gross, *Fair Shares for All: Jacobin Egalitarianism in Practice* (Cambridge, 1997), 126, which very explicitly associates Jacobin egalitarianism with that of John Rawls in the twentieth century.

16. Harold J. Laski, *The Socialist Tradition in the French Revolution* (London, 1930), 35. See also Alan Forrest, *The French Revolution and the Poor* (Oxford, 1981); Florence Gauthier, "De Mably à Robespierre: un programme économique égalitaire," *Annales historiques de la Révolution française* 57, no. 261 (July 1985): 265–89; P. M. Jones, "The 'Agrarian Law': Schemes for Land Redistribution during the French Revolution," *Past & Present* 133 (November 1991): 96–133; Isser Woloch, *The New Regime: Transformations of the French Civic Order, 1789–1820s* (New York, 1994), chaps. 6–8. On women's struggle to be subjects of welfare policies, see Lisa DiCaprio, *The Origins of the Welfare State: Women, Work, and the French Revolution* (Urbana, 2007).

17. Maurice Dommanget, "Les Égaux et la Constitution de 1793," in Dommanget et al., *Babeuf et les problèmes du babouvisme* (Paris, 1963). For the Jacobin clubs and equality (and their complex relationship to Babeuf), see Isser Woloch, *Jacobin Legacy: The Democratic Movement under the Directory* (Princeton, 1970), esp. 27–28, 32–38.

18. Gracchus Babeuf, "Manifeste des plébéiens," in *Pages choisies de Babeuf*, ed. Maurice Dommanget (Paris, 1935), 261–62; Jean Dautry, "Le péssimisme économique de Babeuf et l'histoire des utopies," *Annales historiques de la Révolution française* 33, no. 164 (April 1961): 215–33; William H. Sewell, Jr., "Beyond 1793: Babeuf, Louis Blanc, and the Genealogy of 'Social Revolution,'" in Baker, ed., *The French Revolution*.

19. Thomas Paine, "Agrarian Justice," in *Political Writings*, ed. Bruce Kuklick (Cambridge, 2000), 332. As Mark Philp writes, Paine most definitely "falls short of the difference principle." Mark Philp, *Paine* (Oxford, 1989), 91. Recent celebrants of Paine, and notably Elizabeth Anderson, both distort his sufficientarianism (which came nowhere near the notion that inequality must redound to the advantage of all) and buy in to old Cold War charges of Babeuf as proto-totalitarian. For all the latter's limits, these charges make it impossible to see the way that the egalitarian argument, owing to Babeuf and coming out of the Jacobin state, proved critical to the welfare state future. See Elizabeth Anderson, "Thomas Paine's *Agrarian Justice* and the Origins of Social Insurance," in Eric Schliesser, ed., *Ten Neglected Classics of Philosophy* (Oxford, 2017), and "Common Property: How Social Insurance Became Confused with Socialism," *Boston Review*, July / August, 2016; see also Robert Lamb, *Thomas Paine and the Idea of Human Rights* (Cambridge, 2015), chap. 4. Touting the virtues of social insurance in a market society, Anderson also ignores that the expansion of such protections was prompted by socialism—much as Paine wrote after Jacobins and their self-appointed heirs prompted him to do so and the liberal welfare state emerged in the presence of the Soviet (and fascist) one.

20. Anton Menger, *The Right to the Whole Produce of Labour: The Origin and Development of the Theory of Labour's Claim to the Whole Product of Industry*, trans. M. E. Tanner (London, 1899).

21. Adam Smith, *An Inquiry into the Causes of the Wealth of Nations*, ed. Edwin Cannan (Chicago, 1976), 88; Thomas Malthus, *An Essay on the Principle of Population*, 2nd ed. (London, 1803), 531. See also Dennis Rasmussen, "Adam Smith on What

Is Wrong with Economic Inequality," *American Political Science Review* 110, no. 2 (2016): 342–52. Compare Holly Case, "The 'Social Question,' 1820–1920," *Modern Intellectual History* 13, no. 3 (2016): 747–75.

22. Menger, *The Right*, 13; Victor Considérant, *Théorie du droit de propriété et du droit au travail* (Paris, 1848); Considérant cited in Beecher, *Victor Considérant and the Rise and Fall of French Romantic Socialism* (Berkeley, 2001), 143; Émile Girardin, ed., *Le droit au travail au Luxembourg et à l'Assemblée Nationale*, 2 vols. (Paris, 1849); Bismarck cited in Friedrich Johannes Haun, *Das Recht auf Arbeit: ein Beitrag zur Geschichte, Theorie, und praktischen Lösung* (Berlin, 1889), 45, which covers the spike in German discussion that Bismarck's "golden words" provoked. For later surveys, see Jacques Bénet, *Le capitalisme libéral et le droit au travail*, 2 vols. (Neuchâtel, 1949); Max Bentele, *Das Recht auf Arbeit in rechtsdogmatischer und ideengeschichtlicher Betrachtung* (Zurich, 1949); and J. M. van de Ven, "The Right to Work as a Human Right," *Howard Law Journal* 11, no. 2 (1965): 397–412.

23. Menger, *The Right*, 160, 9. For Menger, Babeuf could hardly have affirmed equal distributive outcomes: his real principle concerned sufficiency. Ibid., 63–64. "Equality is an objective central to socialism," Steven Lukes once wrote, but "socialists have not, in general, been very explicit about its content or the values on which it rests." Steven Lukes, "Socialism and Equality," in *Essays in Social Theory* (London, 1977), 212–13n.

24. Jean-Jacques Pillot, *Ni Châteaux ni chaumières, ou État de la question sociale en 1840* (Paris, 1840), rpt. in Gian Mario Bravo, ed., *Les socialistes avant Marx*, 3 vols. (Paris, 1980), 2: 247. The same year, he published *Histoire des égaux, ou moyens d'établir l'égalité absolue parmi les hommes* (Paris, 1840), esp. 20–21, for a rejection of any austerity or mere sufficiency.

25. Friedrich Engels and Karl Kautsky, "Juristen-Sozialismus," *Die neue Zeit* 2 (1887): 491–508.

26. Rosanvallon, *The Society of Equals*, chap. 3.

27. R. H. Tawney, *Equality*, 4th ed. (London, 1952), 246; Seebohm Rowntree, *The Human Needs of Labour* (London, 1937); Dana Simmons, *Vital Minimum: Need, Science, and Politics in Modern France* (Chicago, 2015).

28. T. H. Marshall, "Citizenship and Social Class," in *Citizenship and Social Class and Other Essays* (Cambridge, 1950), 26.

29. Michael Stolleis, "Einführung in die Geschichte des Sozialrechts," in Stolleis, ed., *Quellen zur Geschichte des Sozialrechts* (Göttingen, 1976); Stolleis, *History of Social Law in Germany*, trans. Thomas Dunlap (Berlin, 2014); Kevin Repp, *Reformers, Critics, and the Paths of German Modernity: Anti-Politics and the Search for Alternatives, 1890–1914* (Cambridge, Mass., 2000); Larry Frohman, *Poor Relief and Welfare in Germany from the Reformation to World War I* (Cambridge, 2008), chaps. 6–7.

30. Menger, *The Right*, 6, and 177 on his program; J. A. Hobson, *The Social Problem: Life and Work* (London, 1901), 89; compare Morris Ginsberg, "The Growth of Social

Responsibility," in Ginsberg, ed., *Law and Opinion in England in the 20th Century* (London, 1959).

31. There is no general treatment, but see M. C. Curthoys, *Labour, Legislation, and the Law: The Trade Union Legislation of the 1870s* (Oxford, 2004); or Maurice Def-frennes, *La coalition ouvrière et le droit de grève: Étude historique* (Paris, 1903). On public servants of the comparatively large French national state and the right to strike, see H. S. Jones, *The French State in Question: Public Law and Political Argument in the Third Republic* (Cambridge, 1993).

32. Eric J. Hobsbawm, "Labour and Human Rights," in *Workers: Worlds of Labour* (New York, 1984), 312.

33. Beatrice Webb cited in Margaret Cole, *The Story of Fabian Socialism* (Stanford, 1961), 331; R. H. Tawney, *Equality*, rev. ed. (London, 1931), 291, 46. In her study of the minority report, Una McCormack reported that, on Marshall's then-recent account, "the business of the twentieth century . . . has been to claim and security the social rights of the common man. To this I would add that the claim was fully and explicitly announced and canvassed in the first decade of this century." Una Cormack, *The Welfare State: The Royal Commission on the Poor Laws, 1905–1909* (London, 1953), 9. See also the brilliant study of Ben Jackson, *Equality and the British Left: A Study in Progressive Political Thought, 1900–64* (Manchester, 2007).

34. Robert E. Goodin, *Reasons for Welfare: The Political Theory of the Welfare State* (Princeton, 1988), 51. On a modicum of redistributive egalitarianism, see the surveys in Hannu Uusitalo, "Redistribution and Equality in the Welfare State," *European Sociological Review* 1, no. 2 (September 1985): 163–76; and Gøsta Esping-Andersen and Frank Myles, "Economic Inequality and the Welfare State," in Wiemer Salverda et al., eds., *Oxford Handbook of Economic Inequality* (Oxford, 2011).

35. Weimar Constitution (1919), Art. 162; Živojin Perić, "Les dispositions sociales et économiques dans la Constitution yougoslave," *Revue du droit public* 33, no. 3 (1926): 495–94; Boris Mirkine-Guetzévitch, "Les nouvelles tendances du Droit constitutionnel," *Revue du Droit public et de la science politique* 45, no. 1 (1928), 44; A. I. Svōlos, *Le Travail dans les Constitutions contemporaines* (Paris, 1939).

36. In a massive and rich literature, starting points are Peter Baldwin, *The Politics of Social Solidarity: Class Bases of the European Welfare State 1875–1975* (Cambridge, 1990); Asa Briggs, "The Welfare State in Historical Perspective," *European Journal of Sociology* 2, no. 2 (1961): 221–58; François Ewald, *L'État-providence* (Paris, 1986); Gøsta Esping-Andersen, *The Three Worlds of Welfare Capitalism* (Princeton, 1990); Aigun Hu and Patrick Manning, "The Global Social Insurance Movement since the 1880s," *Journal of Global History* 5, no. 1 (2010): 125–48; and Francis Sejersted, *The Age of Social Democracy: Norway and Sweden in the Twentieth Century*, trans. Richard Daly (Princeton, 2011).

37. V. I. Lenin, *State and Revolution* (New York, 1992), 84; Richard Stites, *Revolutionary Dreams: Utopian Vision and Experimental Life in the Russian Revolution* (Oxford, 1989), 124 and chap. 6 generally.

38. Francesco Cassata, *Il fascismo razionale: Corrado Gini fra scienza e politica* (Rome, 2006); Jean-Guy Prévost, *A Total Science: Statistics in Liberal and Fascist Italy* (Montreal, 2009).

39. Joseph Goebbels cited in Karl Dietrich Bracher, *The German Dictatorship*, trans. Jean Steinberg (New York, 1970), 10; Young-Sun Hong, *Welfare, Modernity, and the Weimar State, 1919–1933* (Princeton, 1998); Götz Aly, *Hitler's Beneficiaries: Plunder, Racial War, and the Nazi Welfare State*, trans. Jefferson Chase (New York, 2005), 13 and 30 for the Adolf Hitler citation; on autarky, and more responsibly on welfare finance, compare Adam Tooze, *The Wages of Destruction: The Making and Breaking of the Nazi Economy* (New York, 2006).

40. The exclusionary nature of welfare from place to place, not its unprecedented generosity, has been the main focus of scholarship in recent decades. Some classic starting points include Gunnar Broberg and Nils Roll-Hansen, eds., *Eugenics and the Welfare State: Norway, Sweden, Denmark, and Finland* (East Lansing, 2005); Ira Katznelson, *When Affirmative Action Was White* (New York, 2005); Susan Pedersen, *Family, Dependence, and the Origins of the Welfare State: Britain and France, 1914–1945* (Cambridge, 1993).

41. John Rawls, *A Theory of Justice* (Cambridge, Mass., 1971); Ben Jackson, "Property-Owning Democracy: A Short History," in Martin O'Neill and Thad Williamson, eds., *Property-Owning Democracy: Rawls and Beyond* (Chichester, 2012).

42. Daniel T. Rodgers, *Age of Fracture* (Cambridge, Mass., 2011), esp. 182–90.

43. Frank I. Michelman, "In Pursuit of Constitutional Welfare Rights: One View of Rawls' Theory of Justice," *University of Pennsylvania Law Review* 121, no. 5 (May 1973), 982. For the inception of his broader project, see Michelman, "On Protecting the Poor through the Fourteenth Amendment," *Harvard Law Review* 83, no. 1 (1969): 7–59, esp. 14–15 on Rawls and the importance of sufficiency (at least for constitutional purposes) contrasted with "the magnetism of equality."

2. National Welfare and the Universal Declaration

1. T. H. Marshall, "Citizenship and Social Class," in *Citizenship and Social Class and Other Essays* (Cambridge, 1950), 31–32 (citing Patrick Colquhoun's *A Treatise on Indigence* [London, 1806]), 47–48.

2. See also Julia Moses, "Social Citizenship and Social Rights in the Age of Extremes: T. H. Marshall's Social Philosophy in the *Longue Durée*," *Modern Intellectual History* (forthcoming), which properly emphasizes the culturalist and nationalist premises of Marshall's vision of social citizenship. On the gendering of Marshall's welfare state, see Susan Pedersen's classic *Family, Dependence, and the Origins of the Welfare State: Britain and France, 1914–1945* (Cambridge, 1993), esp. 5–7 and 336–54; compare Laura L. Frader, *Breadwinners and Citizens: Gender and the Making of the French Social Model* (Durham, 2008).

3. In America and perhaps other places, an earlier notion of "social rights" as associative entitlements had been used (and abused), but was displaced as the category was redefined everywhere in the twentieth century in distributive terms. On post–Civil War social rights, see, for example, Richard A. Primus, *The American Language of Rights* (Cambridge, 1999), chap. 4.

4. In this sense, even my own prior account of the Universal Declaration, mainly oriented to upending the internationalist triumphalism that has recently celebrated the document, failed to break adequately with the greatest distortion of the literature it sought to overturn: that the Universal Declaration's primary vocation was the reform of international governance in the first place. See Samuel Moyn, *The Last Utopia: Human Rights in History* (Cambridge, Mass., 2010), chap. 2; and, for an interim corrective, Moyn, "The Universal Declaration of Human Rights in the History of Cosmopolitanism," *Critical Inquiry* 40, no. 4 (2014): 365–84. I am in agreement with Roland Burke's comment that extant literature seeks "the magically transformative international," failing to see—at any rate for the 1940s—that the Universal Declaration of Human Rights was crafted not simply for a world of nations but also for a series of presumptively nationalist projects. Roland Burke, "The Internationalism of Human Rights," in Glenda Sluga and Patricia Clavin, eds., *Internationalisms: A Twentieth-Century History* (Cambridge, 2017), 287.

5. Pedro Ramos Pinto, "Housing and Citizenship: Building Social Rights in Twentieth-Century Portugal," *Contemporary European History* 18, no. 2 (2009): 199–215.

6. In 1945 Austria revived the constitution its famous jurist Hans Kelsen had drafted in 1920, which had and has no list of constitutional rights. Wolfgang Abendroth, "Zum Begriff des demokratischen und sozialen Rechtstaates im Grundgesetz des Bundesrepublik Deutschlands," in Alfred Herrmann, ed., *Aus Politik und Geschichte: Festschrift zum 70. Geburtstag von Ludwig Bergsträsser* (Düsseldorf, 1954); Peter C. Caldwell, "Is a 'Social Rechstaat' Possible? The Weimar Roots of a Bonn Controversy," in Caldwell and William E. Scheuerman, eds., *From Liberal Democracy to Fascism* (Boston, 2000).

7. Boris Mirkine-Guetzévitch, "Quelques problèmes de la mise en oeuvre de la Déclaration universelle des droits de l'homme," *Recueil des cours de l'Académie de droit international* 83 (1953): 284; Jacques Maritain, *Les droits de l'homme et la loi naturelle* (New York, 1942); Emmanuel Mounier, "Faut-il réviser la Déclaration des droits?" *Esprit* 1 and 5–7 (December 1944 and April–June 1945), with final text from the last number reprinted in *Les certitudes difficiles* (Paris, 1951); Léon Blum, *A l'échelle humaine* (Paris, 1945) as cited in Mirkine-Guetzévitch, "Quelques problèmes," 291. Prime in importance for the postwar evolution of the welfare state was the program of action announced by the Conseil National de la Résistance in March 1944, in which social rights were ubiquitous. See Henri Michel and Boris Mirkine-Guetzévitch, eds., *Les Idées politiques et sociales de la Résistance: Documents clandestines (1940–1944)* (Paris, 1954); and Claire Andrieu, *Le Programme commun de la Résistance: Des idées dans la guerre* (Paris, 1984).

8. Marshall, "Citizenship and Social Class," 70. The likeliest explanation for his use of the notion of social rights is that he hoped to insert himself in a local Cambridge tradition by affiliating with famed legal historian F. W. Maitland's earlier account of the progress of prior "rights" in sketching how citizenship had developed since medieval times. "[R]ooted in the intellectual culture of Cambridge[,] Marshall's sociology is, first, an extension of Maitland's view of history." A. H. Halsey, "T. H. Marshall: Past and Present 1893–1981," *Sociology* 18, no. 1 (1984), 4. Marshall's opening was, philosopher Michael Oakeshott pointed out immediately, more a *histoire raisonnée* than a serious history. Michael Oakeshott, review, *Cambridge Journal* 4, no. 10 (1951), 629.

9. Robert A. Feldmesser, "Toward the Classless Society?" in Reinhard Bendix and Seymour Martin Lipset, eds., *Class, Status, and Power: Social Stratification in Comparative Perspective*, 2nd ed. (New York, 1960).

10. In a vast literature, Pitirim Sorokin, *The Basic Trends of Our Times* (New Haven, 1964). On China, see Nara Dillon, *Radical Inequalities: China's Revolutionary Welfare State in Comparative Perspective* (Cambridge, Mass., 2015).

11. Mark Roodhouse, *Black Market Britain: 1939–1955* (Oxford, 2013), 127; William A. Robson, *The Welfare State* (London, 1957), 6; R. H. Tawney, *Equality*, 4th ed. (London, 1951), 252. On Labour in power, see, for example, Elizabeth Durbin, *New Jerusalems: The Labour Party and the Economics of Democratic Socialism* (London, 1985); Martin Francis, *Ideas and Policies under Labour, 1945–1951* (Manchester, 1997); or Jim Tomlinson, *Democratic Socialism and Economic Policy: The Attlee Years, 1945–1951* (Cambridge, 1997), esp. chap. 12.

12. Donald Sassoon, *One Hundred Years of Socialism: The West European Left in the Twentieth Century* (New York, 1997), chaps. 5–6; Pius XI, *Quadragesimo Anno* (1931), §58; James Chappel, *Catholic Modern: The Challenge of Totalitarianism and the Remaking of the Church* (Cambridge, Mass., 2018).

13. Julius Stone, *The Atlantic Charter: New Worlds for Old* (Sydney, 1943), 169, 172.

14. Karl Polanyi, *The Great Transformation* (New York, 1944), 254–56.

15. Georges Gurvitch, *La Déclaration des droits sociaux* (New York, 1944); in English, *The Bill of Social Rights* (New York, 1946).

16. See the chapters on "Rousseau et la Déclaration des droits: L'idée des droits inaliénables dans la doctrine politique de J.-J. Rousseau" (1918) and "L'idée des droits inaliénables de l'homme dans la doctrine politique des XVIIIe at XVIIIe siècles" (1922), in Georges Gurvitch, *Écrits russes*, trans. Cécile Rol and Mikhaïl Antonov (Paris, 2006); Georges Gurvitch, "The Problem of Social Law," *Ethics* 52, no. 1 (1941): 26. For Gurvitch's place in French sociology, see, for example, Georges Balandier, *Gurvitch*, trans. Margaret Thompson (New York, 1975); or Johan Heilbron, *French Sociology* (Ithaca, 2015), 131–35.

17. Gurvitch, *La Déclaration*, 40; in English, 30; Hersch Lauterpacht, *An International Bill of Rights* (1945; new ed., Oxford, 2013), 163.

18. Gurvitch, "The Problem of Social Law," 18. The analysis of social rights in this book is ideological and economic; for a radically different "biopolitical" account in which the socialization of rights implies power over life, see François Ewald, *L'État-providence* (Paris, 1986) and Pheng Cheah, "Second Generation Human Rights as Biopolitical Rights," in Costas Douzinas and Conor Gearty, eds., *The Meaning(s) of Human Rights* (Cambridge, 2014), 215–232.

19. Reflecting on developments thirty years later, Marshall specified that he did not mean welfare as a simple legal entitlement ruling out policymaking discretion. It was an obligation of some sort, but might not even give rise to a claimable right. Citing one welfare commission to the effect that a legalistic approach prompts "a narrower not a broader concept of the 'rights' of claimants, since those rights are or should be social as well as legal," Marshall drily commented, "That blessed word 'social' papers over all the cracks in the argument." T. H. Marshall, "Afterthought on 'The Right to Welfare,'" in *The Right to Welfare and Other Essays* (London, 1980), 96.

20. Gurvitch, *La Déclaration*, 44, 82; *The Bill*, 33, 66. Mark B. Smith, "Social Rights in the Soviet Dictatorship: The Constitutional Right to Welfare from Stalin to Brezhnev," *Humanity* 3, no. 3 (2012): 385–405; Karen M. Tani, "Welfare and Rights before the Revolution: Rights as a Language of the State," *Yale Law Journal* 122, no. 2 (2012): 314–83; and Tani, *States of Dependency: Welfare, Rights, and American Governance, 1935–1972* (Cambridge, 2016).

21. Gurvitch, *La Déclaration*, 87, 106, 94–95; *The Bill*, 70–71, 85, 75.

22. Mirkine-Guetzévitch, "Quelques problèmes," 290. For an analysis with a similar spirit, see Swiss economist François Schaller's *De la charité privée aux droits économiques et sociaux du citoyen* (Neuchâtel, 1950).

23. John Somerville, "Comparison of Soviet and Western Democratic Principles," in UNESCO, *Human Rights: Comments and Interpretation* (New York, 1948), esp. 152.

24. The best of the traditional historiography of the makings of the Universal Declaration remains Johannes Morsink, *The Universal Declaration of Human Rights: Origins, Drafting, and Intent* (Philadelphia, 1999), esp. chaps. 5–6 on social rights.

25. William A. Schabas, ed., *The Universal Declaration of Human Rights: The Travaux Préparatoires*, 3 vols. (Cambridge, 2013), 1: 134, 195; John N. Hazard, "The Soviet Union and a World Bill of Rights," *Columbia Law Review* 47, no. 7 (1947): 1095–1117. The Yugoslav representative Vladislav Ribnikar, the most engaged communist voice in the discussions, critically singled out the AFL's declaration for treating "certain principles as eternal," to which Toni Sender, a prominent German Social Democrat before the war representing the AFL in the sessions, replied that "the idea of individual liberty was not outmoded." Ribnikar presumably had in mind private property, for he himself had argued that "[t]he social ideal lay in the interests of society and of the individual being identical." Schabas, *Universal Declaration*, 1: 174.

26. See Universal Declaration, Arts. 17 and 23(4); the materials in Schabas, ed., *The Universal Declaration of Human Rights*, 1: 969–99 and 1003–6; and Tonia Novitz, *International and European Protection of the Right to Strike* (New York, 2004), esp. chap. 5.

27. Though far more remains to be done, see John Tobin, *The Right to Health in International Law* (Oxford, 2012), chap. 1; Larry Frohman, "The Right to Health and Social Citizenship in Germany, 1848–1918," in Anne Hardy et al., eds., *Health and Citizenship: Political Cultures of Health in Britain, the Netherlands, and Germany* (London, 2014), 123–40; and now Adam Gaffney, *To Heal Humankind: The Right to Health in History* (New York, 2017).

28. Harold J. Laski, "The Crisis in Our Civilization," *Foreign Affairs* 26, no. 1 (1947), 36.

29. UNESCO, *Human Rights*.

30. Emmanuel Levinas, "Existentialisme et antisémitisme," *Les Cahiers de l'Alliance Israélite Universelle* 14–15 (1947): 2–3. For an exemplary statement of the belief that the Universal Declaration and the symposium reflected convergence or "incompletely theorized agreement," see Cass R. Sunstein, "Rights of Passage," *The New Republic*, February 25, 2002. On the symposium, see also Mark Goodale, ed., *Letters to the Contrary: A Curated History of the UNESCO Human Rights Survey*, pref. Samuel Moyn (Stanford, 2018), for Goodale's similar analysis of reservations about rather than convergence around rights among intellectuals.

31. Herbert A. Deane, *The Political Ideas of Harold J. Laski* (New York, 1955), 48–52 on natural rights in the early phase; Harold J. Laski, "Democracy in War Time," in G. D. H. Cole et al., *Victory or Vested Interest?* (London, 1942), 38; Harold J. Laski, "Toward a Universal Declaration of Human Rights," in *Human Rights*, 78.

32. Harold J. Laski, *Reflections on the Revolution of Our Time* (London, 1943), chap. 8, "Freedom in a Planned Democracy"; Harold J. Laski, *Faith, Reason and Civilisation: An Essay in Historical Analysis* (London, 1944), 196, 79; Harold J. Laski, *Liberty in the Modern State*, new ed. (London, 1948), 175–76.

33. John Lewis, "On Human Rights," in UNESCO, *Human Rights*, 56.

34. Laski, "Toward a Universal Declaration," 82.

35. E. H. Carr, "Rights and Obligations," *Times Literary Supplement*, November 11, 1949, also in Carr, *From Napoleon to Stalin, and Other Essays* (London, 1980).

36. Ibid.

37. Ibid; compare E. H. Carr, *The New Society* (London, 1951).

38. Ibid.

39. Marshall, "Citizenship and Social Class," 62, 75; W. G. Runciman, "Why Social Inequalities Are Generated by Social Rights," in Martin Bulmer and Anthony M. Rees, eds., *Citizenship Today: The Contemporary Relevance of T. H. Marshall* (London, 1986).

3. FDR's Second Bill

1. Franklin D. Roosevelt, "State of the Union Message to Congress," January 11, 1944.

2. James T. Sparrow, *Warfare State: World War II Americans and the Age of Big Government* (New York, 2011); Elizabeth Borgwardt, *A New Deal for the World: America's Vision for Human Rights* (Cambridge, Mass., 2007).

3. Cass R. Sunstein, *The Second Bill of Rights: FDR's Unfinished Revolution and Why We Need It More Than Ever* (New York, 2004), 86.

4. Ira Katznelson, *Fear Itself: The New Deal and the Making of Our Time* (New York, 2013); Alice Kessler-Harris, *In Pursuit of Equity: Women, Men, and the Quest for Economic Citizenship in the Twentieth Century* (Oxford, 2001).

5. Emily Zackin argues persuasively that both educational and labor rights featured in some U.S. state constitutions back into the earlier and later nineteenth century respectively. Zackin, *Looking for Rights in All the Wrong Places: Why State Constitutions Contain America's Positive Rights* (Princeton, 2013).

6. Pondering the reasons America lacked enduring socialism is, of course, an old chestnut, starting with Werner Sombart, *Warum gibt es in den Vereinigten Staaten keinen Sozialismus?* (Tübingen, 1906). An otherwise worthwhile recent study that idealizes American origins and abjures international comparison of reform is Ganesh Sitaraman, *The Crisis of the Middle-Class Constitution: Why Economic Inequality Threatens Our Republic* (New York, 2017).

7. Franklin D. Roosevelt, "Commonwealth Club Address," September 23, 1932.

8. See the reflections in Jeffrey A. Engel, ed., *The Four Freedoms: Franklin D. Roosevelt and the Evolution of an American Idea* (New York, 2016).

9. Katznelson, *Fear Itself,* 231; Gary Gerstle, *American Crucible: Race and Nation in the Twentieth Century,* new ed. (Princeton, 2017), chap. 4. For the best-known comparative account, see Wolfgang Schivelbusch, *Three New Deals: Reflections on Roosevelt's America, Mussolini's Italy, and Hitler's Germany, 1933–1939* (New York, 2006); see also, more expansively, Kiran Klaus Patel, *The New Deal: A Global History* (Princeton, 2016).

10. For the claim that planning was already off the table as of the death of NIRA, see Ellis W. Hawley, *The New Deal and the Problem of Monopoly: A Study in Economic Ambivalence* (Princeton, 1966), esp. chap. 9.

11. Barry D. Karl, *The Uneasy State: The United States from 1915 to 1945* (Chicago, 1983), 166. See also the profoundly important work of William E. Forbath, "The New Deal Constitution in Exile," *Duke Law Journal* 51, no. 1 (2001): 165–222; and Forbath with Joseph Fishkin, "The Anti-Oligarchy Constitution," *Boston University Law Journal* 94 (2014): 669–98; and a forthcoming book of the same name canvassed and critiqued in the special issue of the *Texas Law Review* 94, no. 7 (2016). I differ mainly in avoiding talk of constitutions, because constitutions have often been the place to canonize minima (but not broader distributive goals) and in focusing normatively on

the contrast between sufficiency and equality (only the most egregious departures from which Forbath's revival of the New Deal critique of oligarchy targets).

12. John G. Winant, "The Social Security Act," *Vital Speeches of the Day*, May 4, 1936; Winant, "Labor and Economic Security," *Annals of the American Academy of Political and Social Science* 184 (1936), 100; Winant, "The Price of Responsible Citizenship," *American Labor Legislation Review* 31 (1941), 5.

13. Winant, "The Pursuit of Happiness in the Economic and Social World," *International Conciliation* 24, no. 422 (1946), 283.

14. On the rise of the imperative of full employment, see Alan Brinkley, *The End of Reform: New Deal Liberalism in Recession and War* (New York, 1995), chap. 10.

15. Lewis L. Lorwin, *Postwar Plans of the United Nations* (New York, 1943), 292. As a leading recent historian of the New Deal warns, "the NRPB's importance should not be overestimated [for] it did not plan but, rather, called for planning by gathering information and offering proposals." Katznelson, *Fear Itself*, 375. Ben Zdencanovic, "The Man with the Plan: William Beveridge, Transatlantic Postwar Planning, and the Idea of an American Welfare State during World War II," Harvard Graduate Student Conference on International History, March 2016.

16. Brinkley, *The End of Reform*, 247; Barry D. Karl, *Charles E. Merriam and the Study of Politics* (Chicago, 1974); Hawley, *The New Deal*, 169. Brinkley's brilliant study of the late New Deal (precisely when social rights were born), like his unexampled attention to the NRPB, informs my account throughout. See also Brinkley, "The National Resources Planning Board and the Reconstruction of Planning," in Robert Fishman, ed., *The American Planning Tradition* (Washington, DC, 2000).

17. Charles E. Merriam, *The New Democracy and the New Despotism* (New York, 1939), 205.

18. See the paper trail in Charles E. Merriam Papers, Regenstein Library, University of Chicago, Box 238, Folder 7, and Box 220, Folder 6. There is some evidence that a proposal for a second bill dates back even earlier to August 1939; see Patrick Reagan, *Designing a New America: The Origins of New Deal Planning, 1890–1943* (Amherst, 1999), 218–19; and, following him, Sunstein, *The Second Bill of Rights*, 86. Charles E. Merriam, *On the Agenda of Democracy* (Cambridge, Mass., 1941), 99, 101, 107.

19. National Resources Planning Board, *Security, Work, and Relief Policies* (Washington, D.C., 1942), 449, for an especially clear statement of the need for "decent" minima beyond basic survival. NRPB, *National Resources Development Report for 1943* (Washington, D.C., 1942), 3, for the Bill of Rights. For its unfolding reception, see, for example, "New Bill of Rights Is Urged for Peace," *New York Times*, November 15, 1942; "Planning Board Calls for New 'Bill of Rights,'" *New York Herald Tribune*, November 15, 1942; "Congress Gets FDR Social 'Rights' Plan," *Atlanta Constitution*, January 14, 1943.

20. "A New Bill of Rights," *The Nation*, March 20, 1943; Arthur MacMahon in "A New Bill of Rights," *Frontiers of Democracy*, May 15, 1942.

21. Charles E. Merriam, "Physics and Politics" (six Charles R. Walgreen Foundation lectures given at the University of Chicago, April / May 1947), Lecture 5, 8; Merriam, *The New Democracy*, 260–61.

22. "Fatuous," *Wall Street Journal*, January 16, 1942; see also its response to the main report, "A Totalitarian Plan," *Wall Street Journal*, March 12, 1943. "Cradle to Grave to Pigeonhole," *Time*, March 22, 1943; "Promised Land," *Newsweek*, March 22, 1943. On the role of states, see Karen Tani, *States of Dependency: Welfare, Rights, and American Governance, 1935–1972* (Cambridge, 2016).

23. Henry A. Wallace, "Our Second Chance" (address before the Foreign Policy Association, April 8, 1941), rpt. in Wallace, *The Century of the Common Man*, ed. Russell Lord (New York, 1943), 6; and Wallace, *Democracy Reborn*, ed. Lord (New York, 1944), 177. Wallace, "The Price of Free World Victory" (address to the Free World Association, May, 8, 1942), in *The Century of the Common Man*, 18–19, and *Democracy Reborn*, 193. This speech was very far from being "little-noticed." Borgwardt, *A New Deal for the World*, 157.

24. See, for example, "Wallace Denies He Favors U.S. as World Milkman," *Chicago Tribune*, December 11, 1942; John Morton Blum, ed., *The Price of Vision: The Diary of Henry A. Wallace 1942–1946* (Boston, 1973), 363; John C. Culver and John Hyde, *American Dreamer: A Life of Henry A. Wallace* (New York, 2000), 347.

25. Hanne Hagtvedt Vik, "Taming the States: The American Law Institute and the 'Statement of Essential Human Rights,'" *Journal of Global History* 7, no. 3 (2012): 461–82. See also the now large literature dedicated to honorably (but I think rather myopically) proving American or even broader "Western" interest in social rights in the 1940s, starting with Jack Donnelly and Daniel Whelan, "The West, Economic and Social Rights, and the Global Human Rights Regime: Setting the Record Straight," *Human Rights Quarterly* 29, no. 4 (2007): 908–49.

26. Karl, *Charles E. Merriam*, 278–79; Marion Clawson, *New Deal Planning: The National Resources Planning Board* (Baltimore, 1981), 227. For the fate of the Wagner Act's aspirations after the war, see Nelson Liechtenstein, "From Corporatism to Collective Bargaining: Organized Labor and the Eclipse of Social Democracy in the Postwar Era," in Steve Fraser and Gary Gerstle, eds., *The Rise and Fall of the New Deal Order, 1930–1980* (Princeton, 1989); and Reuel Schiller, "From Group Rights to Individual Liberties: Post-War Labor Law, Liberalism, and the Waning of Union Strength," *Berkeley Journal of Employment and Labor Law* 20, no. 1 (1999): 1–73.

27. "Assails End of 'Rights,'" *New York Times*, July 19, 1936. See James Holt, "The New Deal and the American Anti-Statist Tradition," in John Braeman et al., eds., *The New Deal* (Columbus, 1975); Kim Phillips-Fein, *Invisible Hands: The Making of the Conservative Movement from the New Deal to Reagan* (New York, 2009), chaps. 1–2. For the war economy, see Mark R. Wilson, *Destructive Creation: American Business and the Winning of World War II* (Philadelphia, 2016).

28. Karl, *The Uneasy State*, 215; Angus Burgin, *The Great Persuasion: Reinventing Free Markets since the Depression* (Cambridge, Mass., 2012), 87–89; Charles E. Merriam, review of *The Road to Serfdom*, *American Journal of Sociology* 50, no. 3 (1944), 234; transcript of radio discussion with Friedrich Hayek and Charles Merriam, NBC Network, April 22, 1945, Merriam papers, Box 284, Folder 18.

29. On consumerism, see Victoria de Grazia, *Irresistible Empire: America's Advance through Twentieth-Century Europe* (Cambridge, Mass., 2005), esp. chap. 2 on the consumerist implications of the "decent standard of living" rhetoric; as well as Kathleen G. Donohue, *Freedom from Want: American Liberalism and the Idea of the Consumer* (Baltimore, 2003), chaps. 6–7; and James T. Sparrow, "Freedom to Want: The Federal Government and Politicized Consumption in World War II," in Kevin M. Kruse and Stephen Tuck, eds., *Fog of War: The Second World War and the Civil Rights Movement* (New York, 2012).

30. Roosevelt's speechwriter, Sam Rosenman, recognized the service plan as the "controversial core" of the address. Samuel I. Rosenman, *Working with Roosevelt* (New York, 1952), 419, and, for details of how the second bill of rights was resurrected for the speech, 427–28. Congress of Industrial Organizations Political Action Committee, *People's Program for 1944* (New York, 1944); Dwight Macdonald, *Henry Wallace: The Man and the Myth* (New York, 1948), 68.

31. The allusions are to Jefferson Cowie, *The Great Exception: The New Deal and the Limits of American Politics* (Princeton, 2016); and Steve Fraser, *The Age of Acquiescence: The Life and Death of American Resistance to Organized Wealth and Power* (New York, 2015).

4. Globalizing Welfare after Empire

1. Sumner Welles, "A Great Vision," in *The World of the Four Freedoms* (New York, 1943), 72, 74.

2. Harold J. Laski, "The Crisis in Our Civilization," *Foreign Affairs* 26, no. 1 (1947), 43; Silvio Pons, *The Global Revolution: A History of International Communism 1917–1991*, trans. Alan Cameron (Oxford, 2014), chap. 4.

3. Richard Whatmore, "Liberty, War, and Empire: Overcoming the Rich State–Poor State Problem, 1789–1815," in Béla Kapossy et al., eds., *Commerce and Peace in the Enlightenment* (Cambridge, 2017).

4. Thomas Paine, "Address to the People of France" (September 1792), cited in Robert Lamb, *Thomas Paine and the Idea of Human Rights* (Cambridge, 2015), 157; Anacharsis Cloots, speech of April 1793, cited in Sophie Wahnich, *L'impossible citoyen: L'étranger dans le discours de la Révolution française* (Paris, 1997), 194.

5. See the brilliant and neglected ideological account in Franz Borkenau, *Socialism, National or International?* (London, 1942). On more institutional and political matters,

see Pons, *The Global Revolution*, 155–66, 231–43; for the Socialist International's 1951 Frankfurt Declaration of Principles, see Pradib Bose, *Social Democracy in Practice: Socialist International (1951–2001)* (Delhi, 2005), Appendix A; see also Talbot C. Imlay, "Socialist Internationalism after 1914," in Glenda Sluga and Patricia Clavin, eds., *Internationalisms: A Twentieth-Century History* (Cambridge, 2017).

6. Compare Eric Helleiner, "Back to the Future? The Social Protection Floor of Bretton Woods," *Global Social Policy* 14, no. 3 (2013): 298–318; James Robert Martin, "Experts of the World Economy: European Stabilization and the Origins of International Economic Organization, 1916–1951" (Ph.D. diss., Harvard University, 2016), esp. chap. 7.

7. E. H. Carr, *Nationalism and After* (London, 1945), 20, 47–48, 65.

8. Or Rosenboim, *The Emergence of Globalism: Competing Visions of World Order in Britain and the United States, 1939–1950* (Princeton, 2017); Georges Gurvitch, *La Déclaration des droits sociaux* (New York, 1944), esp. 122; in English, *The Declaration of Social Rights* (New York, 1946), 97; and, for his retrospective comment about his priorities, Georges Gurvitch, "Mon itinéraire intellectuel ou l'exclu de la horde," *L'Homme et la société* 1, no. 1 (1966), 8; Charles E. Merriam, "The Content of an International Bill of Rights," *Annals of the American Academy of Political and Social Science* 243 (January 1946): 11–17; and Merriam, "A World Bill of Human Rights," *Social Service Review* 21, no. 4 (1947): 437–45.

9. H. E. Evatt, "Economic Rights in the United Nations Charter," *Annals of the American Academy of Political and Social Science* 243 (January 1946), 5; Herman Finer, *The United Nations Economic and Social Council* (Boston, 1946). Given the country's history of serial intervention in Latin America, it can be tempting to claim that the United States represented an "intervention-individual rights" system of thinking where Latin American and other states after Mexico's example in 1917 coalesced around a "sovereignty-social rights complex." The risk is that this downplays the success of national welfare ideology everywhere—though certainly within limits in the United States—and the failure everywhere of those who hoped to transcend it. Greg Grandin, "The Liberal Tradition in the Americas: Rights, Sovereignty, and the Origins of Liberal Multilateralism," *American Historical Review* 117, no. 1 (2012): 68–91.

10. These paragraphs rely mainly on the factual account in Antony Alcock, *History of the International Labour Organization* (London, 1971), since much recent literature tends to be apologetic or even promotional in nature, even when it takes distance on the "insider's histories" that have always prevailed. Compare Jasmien Van Daele, "Writing ILO Histories: A State of the Art," in Van Daele et al., eds., *ILO Histories: Essays on the International Labour Organization and Its Impact in the Twentieth Century* (Bern, 2007).

11. See Bruno Cabanes, *The Great War and the Origins of Humanitarianism, 1918–1924* (Cambridge, 2014), chap. 2; Guy Fiti Sinclair, *To Reform the World: International Organizations and the Making of Modern States* (Oxford, 2017), part 1; and, for the colonial scene, Susan Zimmerman, " 'Special Circumstances' in Geneva: The ILO and

the World of Non-Metropolitan Labour in the Interwar Years," in Van Daele et al., eds., *ILO Histories;* as well as J. P. Daughton, "ILO Expertise and Colonial Violence in the Interwar Years," in Sandrine Kott and Joëlle Droux, *Globalizing Social Rights: The International Labour Organization and Beyond* (New York, 2013). Sandrine Kott says that the ILO's "alleged lack of influence is the clearest indication of the invisibility of its action," but more plausible is the claim of influences in nations where standard-setting might matter. Kott, "Constructing a European Social Model: The Fight for Social Insurance in the Interwar Period," in Van Daele et al., eds., *ILO Histories*, 174; and Jeremy Seekings, "The ILO and Welfare Reform in South Africa, Latin America, and the Caribbean, 1919–1950," in the same volume.

12. Harold Karan Jacobson, "The USSR and the ILO," *International Organization* 14, no. 3 (1960): 402–28. "[T]he ILO's position was bad. . . . The obvious way to get the ILO going again was to hold a Conference." Alcock, *History of the International Labour Organization*, 161. It held one in 1941 before the Philadelphian event in 1944. Compare Sandrine Kott, "Fighting the War or Preparing for Peace? The ILO during the Second World War," *Journal of Modern European History* 12 (2014): 359–76; and Alain Supiot, *The Spirit of Philadelphia: Social Justice vs. the Total Market*, trans. Saskia Brown (London, 2012).

13. "Roosevelt Hails ILO Declaration," *New York Times*, May 18, 1944. At the earliest the ILO truly committed to pursuing its agenda in human rights terms in the 1960s, but even later the ILO pioneered the basic needs revolution without converting needs into rights. Compare Nicolas Valticos, "The International Labour Organization (ILO)," in Karel Vasak, ed., *The International Dimensions of Human Rights*, 2 vols. (Westport 1982), with Daniel Roger Maul, "The 'Morse Years': The ILO 1948–1970," in Van Daele, et al., eds., *ILO Histories*, noting (391) that "the ILO's transformation into a human rights agency did not come naturally." It is true that English international lawyer and longtime ILO functionary (as well as social rights specialist for the American Law Institute essential rights project and co-drafter of the Philadelphia declaration) C. Wilfred Jenks, who ultimately led the body in the early 1970s, was a continuous spokesman for the status of social rights in international law. See, for example, C. Wilfred Jenks, "The Five Economic and Social Rights," *Annals of the American Academy of Political and Social Science* 243 (January 1946): 40–46, *Human Rights and International Labour Standards* (London, 1960), "The Corpus Juris of Social Justice," in *Law, Freedom and Welfare* (London, 1963), or *Social Justice in the Law of Nations: The ILO Impact after Fifty Years* (Oxford, 1970).

14. Marco Duranti, *The Conservative Human Rights Revolution: European Identity, Transnational Politics, and the Origins of the European Convention* (Oxford, 2016), esp. chap. 8.

15. See D. J. Harris, *The European Social Charter* (Charlottesville, 1984); A. Glenn Mower, Jr., *International Cooperation for Social Justice: Global and Regional Protection of Economic / Social Rights* (Westport, 1986), part 2.

16. *Statement of Policy on Colonial Development and Welfare* (London, 1940); W. K. Hancock, *Empire in a Changing World* (London, 1943), chap. 10; L. P. Mair, *Welfare in the British Colonies* (London, 1944); Andreas Eckert, "Exportschlager Wohlfahrtstaat? Europäische Sozialstaatlichkeit und Kolonialismus in Afrika nach dem Zweiten Weltkrieg," *Geschichte und Gesellschaft* 32 (2006): 467–88.

17. Stuart Ward, "The European Provenance of Decolonization," *Past & Present* 230 (2016): 227–60; Frantz Fanon, *Toward the African Revolution (Political Essays)*, trans. Haakon Chevalier (New York, 1967), 87–88.

18. On labor law and politics, see Frederick Cooper, *Decolonization and African Society: The Labor Question in French and British Africa* (Cambridge, 1986); on federalism, see Samuel Moyn, "Fantasies of Federalism," *Dissent* 62, no. 1 (2015): 145–51.

19. Paul E. Sigmund, *The Political Ideologies of Developing Nations* (New York, 1963), 11; Sugata Bose, "Instruments and Idioms of Colonial and National Development: India's Historical Experience in Comparative Perspective," in Frederick Cooper and Randall Packard, eds., *International Development and the Social Sciences: Essays on the History and Politics of Knowledge* (Berkeley, 1997); Kenneth A. Kaunda, *Humanism in Zambia and a Guide to its Implementation* (Lusaka, 1968), 3.

20. A. Fenner Brockway, *African Socialism: A Background Book* (London, 1963), 64; Julius K. Nyerere, *Man and Development* (London, 1974), 25.

21. Brockway, *African Socialism*, 98–99; Kaunda, *Humanism in Zambia*, 36; Julian Go, "Modeling States and Sovereignty: Postcolonial Constitutions in Asia and Africa," in Christopher J. Lee, ed., *Making a World after Empire: The Bandung Moment and Its Political Alternatives* (Athens, Ohio, 2010), esp. 130. The lack of centrality of rights altogether to thinking about postcolonial constitutionalism can be gauged by their complete omission in B. O. Nwabueze, *Constitutionalism in the Emergent States* (Rutherford, N.J., 1973).

22. Brockway, *African Socialism*, 98; Sigmund, *Political Ideologies*, 226; Léopold Senghor, "African-Style Socialism," in William H. Friedland and Carl G. Rosberg, Jr., eds., *African Socialism* (Stanford, 1964), 264; Rupert Emerson, *From Empire to Nation: The Rise to Self-Assertion of Asian and African Peoples* (Cambridge, Mass., 1960), 184.

23. Julius K. Nyerere, *Nyerere on Socialism* (Dar es Salaam, 1969), 19; Julius K. Nyerere, *Ujamaa: Essays on Socialism* (Dar es Salaam, 1968), 110; Priya Lal, *African Socialism in Postcolonial Tanzania: Between the Village and the World* (Cambridge, 2015), esp. chap. 1; compare James Scott, *Seeing Like a State: How Certain Schemes to Improve the Human Condition Have Failed* (New Haven, 1998), chap. 7.

24. See, for example, Harry G. Johnson, "The Ideology of Economic Policy in the New States," in Johnson ed., *Economic Nationalism in Old and New States* (Chicago, 1967); Mamadou Dia, *The African Nations and World Solidarity*, trans. Mercer Cook (New York, 1961), 13; Léopold Sédar Senghor, *On African Socialism*, trans. Mercer Cook (New York, 1964), 133.

25. Dia, *African Nations*, 27; Daniel Roger Maul, "The International Labour Organization and the Globalization of Rights, 1944–1970," in Stefan-Ludwig Hoffmann, ed., *Human Rights in the Twentieth Century* (Cambridge, 2011); Maul, *Human Rights, Development, and Decolonization: The International Labour Organization (ILO) 1940–1970* (Basingstoke, 2012).

26. The Egypt lectures were Gunnar Myrdal, *Development and Under-Development: A Note on the Mechanism of National and International Economic Equality* (Cairo, 1956); in its original British edition *Rich Lands and Poor* was entitled *Economic Theory and Under-Developed Regions* (London, 1957) but I cite the American, *Rich Lands and Poor: The Road to World Prosperity* (New York, 1958).

27. Gunnar Myrdal, *An International Economy: Problems and Prospects* (New York, 1956), 321. On Myrdal's early commitments, see Nils Gilman, "The Myrdals' Eugenicist Roots," *Humanity* 8, no. 1 (2017): 133–43.

28. Gunnar Myrdal, *Beyond the Welfare State: Economic Planning in the Welfare States and Its International Implications* (New Haven, 1960); Alfred Marshall, *Industry and Trade: A Study of Industrial Technique and Business Organization, and of Their Influences on the Conditions of Various Classes and Nations* (London, 1919), 4–5, cited in Myrdal, *International*, 366n, and Myrdal, *Rich Lands*, 126; Myrdal, *International*, 322.

29. Myrdal wrote a short piece about economic and social rights in the early 1950s, but it did not affect his thought. Alva Myrdal, "A Scientific Approach to International Welfare," in Myrdal et al., *America's Role in International Social Welfare* (New York, 1955), 3, 5; Myrdal, *International*, 323 (emphasis in original).

30. Myrdal, *International*, 324 (emphasis in original).

31. See, for example, Robert Lekachman, "From Welfare State to Welfare World," *New York Herald Tribune*, August 14, 1960; Edwin G. Nourse, "Beyond the Welfare State, Myrdal Sees Welfare World," *Washington Post*, May 29, 1960. Myrdal, *Development*, 18–78, expanded into Myrdal, *Rich Lands*, chaps. 3–8.

32. Compare Jamie Martin, "Gunnar Myrdal and the Failed Promises of the Postwar International Economic Settlement," *Humanity* 8, no. 1 (2017): 167–73.

33. For the first popular treatment north-south divergence, see Barbara Ward, *The Rich Nations and the Poor Nations* (New York, 1962); Gunnar Myrdal, "The Equality Issue in World Development," *Swedish Journal of Economics* 77, no. 4 (December 1975): 413–32. Gunnar Myrdal, *The Challenge of World Poverty: A World Anti-Poverty Program in Outline* (New York, 1970).

34. Myrdal, *Rich Lands*, 125–27, 64, 127, 129, 8; John Kenneth Galbraith, "Unto Everyone that Hath Shall Be Given," *New York Times*, January 26, 1958; Kwame Nkrumah, *Neo-Colonialism: The Last Stage of Imperialism* (New York, 1966), xix; see also Isaac Nakhimovsky, "An International Dilemma: The Postwar Utopianism of Gunnar Myrdal's *Beyond the Welfare State*," *Humanity* 8, no. 1 (2017): 185–94; and Simon Reid-Henry, "From Welfare World to Global Poverty," *Humanity* 8, no. 1 (2017): 207–26.

35. Steven L. B. Jensen, *The Making of International Human Rights: The 1960s, De-colonization, and the Reconstruction of Global Values* (Cambridge, 2015), esp. chaps. 3–4, with the proviso that Jensen makes no attempt to measure the consistency of new state agendas at the United Nations with broader anticolonial ideology or practices either domestically or internationally (especially with respect to distribution), and vastly over-estimates the relevance of the United Nations to the global human rights revolution that followed.

36. This paragraph repeats earlier findings, which I see no reason to take back. See Samuel Moyn, *The Last Utopia: Human Rights in History* (Cambridge, Mass., 2010), chap. 3; and Moyn, "Imperialism, Self-Determination, and the Rise of Human Rights," in Akira Iriye et al., eds., *The Human Rights Revolution: An International History* (Oxford, 2011).

37. For the right to property, which neither of the sister conventions featured, as well as on the bland version in the Universal Declaration itself, see William A. Schabas, "The Omission of the Right to Property in the International Covenants," *Hague Yearbook of International Law* 4 (1991): 135–70. For controversy about whether ILO Convention No. 87 on freedom of association already protected the right to strike, a view almost certainly the result of later interpretation, see Ben Saul et al., *The International Covenant on Economic, Social, and Cultural Rights* (Oxford, 2014), 577. Ruth Ben-Israel, *International Labour Standards: The Case of Freedom to Strike* (Dordrecht, 1986); Craven, *International Covenant*; John Tobin, *The Right to Health in International Law* (Oxford, 2012), chaps. 1, 4.

38. International Covenant for Economic, Social, and Cultural Rights (ICESCR) (1966), Art. 2. Compare Adom Getachew, *Worldmaking after Empire: The Rise and Fall of Self-Determination* (Princeton, forthcoming).

39. Article 11 actually goes further, treating international cooperation as "essential" but implying no greater consensus as to obligation of wealthy toward poor countries, especially since in the end the article conditioned international help on "free consent." Maschood A. Baderin and Robert McCorquodale, "The International Covenant on Economic, Social, and Cultural Rights: Forty Years of Development," in Baderin and McCorquodale, eds., *Economic, Social, and Cultural Rights in Action* (Oxford, 2007), 5–6. The Mexican diplomat is cited in Matthew C. R. Craven, *The International Covenant on Economic, Social, and Cultural Rights: A Perspective on Its Development* (Oxford, 1995), 144n. ICESCR, Arts 11(2) and 1. For stray references in debates around the treaty to international distribution, see Ben Saul, ed., *The International Covenant on Economic, Social, and Cultural Rights: Travaux Préparatoires, 1948–1965*, 2 vols. (Oxford, 2016), 1: 410, 2: 2151, 2185, and esp. 2193 and 2200. Compare Philip Alston and Gerard Quinn, "The Nature and Scope of States Parties' Obligations under the International Covenant on Economic, Social, and Cultural Rights," *Human Rights Quarterly* 9, no. 2 (May 1987): 156–229. For hunger, see Craven, *The International*, 297–301.

40. Roland Burke, "Some Rights Are More Equal Than Others: The Third World and the Transformation of Economic and Social Rights," *Humanity* 3, no. 3 (2012): 427–48.

41. Jeffrey James Byrne, *Mecca of Revolution: Algeria, Decolonization, and the Third World Order* (Oxford, 2016). George McTurnan Kahin, *The Asian-African Conference: Bandung, Indonesia, April 1955* (Ithaca, 1956). For claims of continuity, see Lee, ed., *Making a World after Empire;* Helen E. S. Nesadurai, "Bandung and the Political Economy of North-South Relations: Sowing the Seeds for Re-visioning International Society," in See Seng Tan and Amitav Acharya, eds., *Bandung Revisited: The Legacy of the 1955 Asian-African Conference for International Order* (Singapore, 2008); and Vijay Prashad, *The Darker Nations: A People's History of the Third World* (New York, 2001). For complication, see Robert Vitalis, "The Midnight Ride of Kwame Nkrumah and Other Fables of Bandung (Ban-doong)," *Humanity* 4, no. 2 (2013): 261–88; Jürgen Dinkel, *Die Bewegung Bündnisfreier Staaten: Genese, Organisation und Politik (1927–1992)* (Berlin, 2015); Lorenz M. Lüthi, "Non-Alignment, 1946–1965: Its Establishment and Struggle against Afro-Asianism," *Humanity* 7, no. 2 (2016): 201–23; and Umut Özsu, " 'Let Us First of All Have Unity among Us': Bandung, International Law, and the Empty Politics of Solidarity," in Luis Eslava et al., eds., *Bandung, the Global South, and International Law: Critical Pasts and Pending Futures* (Cambridge, 2017). On the rise of permanent sovereignty over natural resources, Christopher R. W. Dietrich, *Oil Revolution: Anti-Colonial Elites, Sovereign Rights, and the Economic Culture of Decolonization* (Cambridge, 2017).

42. Raúl Prebisch, *Towards a New Trade Policy for Development: Report by the Secretary-General of the United Nations Conference on Trade and Development* (New York, 1964); Edgar J. Dosman, *The Life and Times of Raúl Prebisch, 1901–1986* (Kingston, 2008); Getachew, *Worldmaking after Empire*, chap. 4.

43. Paul VI, Populorum Progressio, March 26, 1967, §§ 3, 8; four years later, the World Synod of Catholic Bishops issued its "Justice in the World" statement; Joseph Gremillion, ed., *The Gospel of Peace and Justice: Catholic Social Teaching since John* (Maryknoll, 1976).

44. *What Now: Another Development (The 1975 Dag Hammerskjöld Report)* (New York, 1975), 6; Charles Alexandrowicz, "The Charter of Economic Rights and Duties of States," *Millennium* 4, no. 1 (1975), 72, rpt. in *The Law of Nations in Global History*, ed. David Armitage and Jennifer Pitts (Oxford, 2017), 411. For background, see Michael Zammit Cutajar, *UNCTAD and the South-North Dialogue* (Oxford, 1985); Branislav Gosovic, *UNCTAD, Conflict and Compromise: The Third World's Quest for an Equitable World Economic Order through the United Nations* (Leiden, 1972); Kathryn Sikkink, "Development Ideas in Latin America: Paradigm Shift and the Economic Commission for Latin America," in Cooper and Packard, eds., *International Development*.

45. On interdependence, see Victor McFarland, "The New International Economic Order, Interdependence, and Globalization," *Humanity* 6, no. 1 (2015): 217–34. The

most full-fledged intellectual presentation was surely Algerian lawyer Mohamed Bedjaoui, *Towards a New International Economic Order* (New York, 1979); compare Umut
Özsu, "'In the Interests of Mankind as a Whole': Mohamed Bedjaoui's New International Economic Order," *Humanity* 6, no. 1 (2015): 129–44.

46. Julius Nyerere cited in Nils Gilman, "The New International Economic Order:
A Reintroduction," *Humanity* 6, no. 1 (2015), 4; B. V. A. Röling, "The History and
the Sociological Approach of the NIEO and the Third World," in *North-South Dialogue: A New International Economic Order* (Thessaloniki, 1982), 194. For one Marxist
critique, see Samir Amin, "Self-Reliance and the New International Economic Order,"
Monthly Review 29, no. 3 (1977): 1–21.

47. Declaration on the Establishment of a New International Economic Order, UN
Gen. Ass. Res. 3201 (S-VI), May 1, 1974; Charter on the Economic Rights and Du-
ties of States, UN Gen. Ass. Res. 3281 (XXIX), December 12, 1974. For the paper
trail, see Karl P. Sauvant, ed., *The Collected Documents of the Group of 77*, 6 vols. (Dobbs
Ferry, 1981–). For various contemporary evaluations, see Branislav Gorovic and John
Gerard Ruggie, "Origins and Evolution of the Concept," *International Social Science
Journal* 28, no. 4 (1976): 639–46; Jagdish N. Bhagwati, ed., *The New International Eco-
nomic Order: The North-South Debate* (Cambridge, Mass., 1977); Karl P. Sauvant and
Hajo Hasenpflug, *The New International Economic Order: Confrontation or Coopera-
tion between North and South?* (Boulder, 1977); and Roger D. Hansen, *Beyond the North-
South Stalemate* (New York, 1979)—the leading edge of a much larger responsive
literature into the next decade. On the ramifications of the Charter, see Roméo Flores
Caballero et al., *Justice économique international: Contributions à l'étude de la Charte
des droits et des devoirs économiques des États* (Paris, 1976); and Robert F. Meagher, *An
International Redistribution of Wealth and Power: A Study of the Charter of Economic Rights
and Duties of States* (New York, 1979). An especially helpful interpretation is Vanessa
Ogle, "State Rights against Private Capital: The 'New International Economic Order'
and the Struggle over Aid, Trade, and Foreign Investment, 1962–1981," *Humanity* 5,
no. 2 (2014): 211–34; compare Stephen Krasner, *Structural Conflict: The Third World
against Global Liberalism* (Berkeley, 1985).

48. Some of the most influential analyses included Raymond Vernon, *Sovereignty
at Bay* (New York, 1971); and Richard J. Barnet and Ronald E. Mueller, *Global Reach:
The Power of the Multinational Corporations* (New York, 1974). For responses, see, for
example, George W. Ball et al., *Global Companies: The Political Economy of World Business* (Englewood Cliffs, 1975).

49. Julius Nyerere, "Third World Negotiating Strategy," *Third World Quarterly* 1,
no. 2 (1979): 22; Antonio Cassese and Edmond Jouvé, eds., *Pour un droit des peoples:
Essais sur la Déclaration d'Alger* (Paris, 1978); Alternative Approaches and Ways and
Means within the United Nations System for Improving the Effective Enjoyment of
Human Rights and Fundamental Freedoms, UN Gen. Ass. Res. 32/130, December 16,
1977.

50. For the phrase, see Mark Mazower, *Governing the World: The History of an Idea* (New York, 2012), chap. 12. On neoliberal opposition, see Jennifer Bair, "Taking Aim at the New International Economic Order," in Philip Mirowski and Dieter Plehwe, eds., *The Road from Mont Pelerin: The Making of the Neoliberal Thought Collective* (Cambridge, Mass., 2009); and Quinn Slobodian, *Globalists: The End of Empire and the Birth of Neoliberalism* (Cambridge, Mass., 2018); for American, Daniel J. Sargent, "North/South: The United States Responds to the New International Economic Order," *Humanity* 6, no. 1 (2015): 201–16; and Sargent, *A Superpower Transformed: The Remaking of American Foreign Relations in the 1970s* (Oxford, 2015); and for European, Giuliano Garavini, *After Empires: European Integration, Decolonization, and the Challenge from the Global South, 1957–1986*, trans. Richard Nybakken (Oxford, 2012).

5. Basic Needs and Human Rights

1. Paul Streeten, "Basic Needs and Human Rights," *World Development* 8, no. 2 (1980), 107; Paul Streeten, "Gunnar Myrdal," *World Development* 18, no. 7 (1990), 1035.

2. This paragraph and the next summarize Samuel Moyn, *The Last Utopia: Human Rights in History* (Cambridge, Mass., 2010).

3. Peter Benenson cited in James Loeffler, *Rooted Cosmopolitans: Jews and Human Rights in the Twentieth Century* (New Haven, 2018), chap. 9.

4. Laura M. Weinrib, *The Taming of Free Speech: America's Civil Liberties Compromise* (Cambridge, Mass., 2016); interview with Aryeh Neier, *Quellen zur Geschichte der Menschenrechte*, www.geschichte-menschenrechte.de/personen/aryeh-neier/; Aryeh Neier, "Economic and Social Rights: A Critique," *Human Rights Brief* 12, no. 2 (2006): 1–3.

5. On Latin America, see Patrick William Kelly, *Sovereign Emergencies: Latin America and the Making of Global Human Rights Politics* (Cambridge, 2018).

6. Salar Mohandesi, "From Anti-Imperialism to Human Rights: The Vietnam War, Internationalism, and the Radical Left in the Long 1960s" (Ph.D. diss., University of Pennsylvania, 2017), chap. 5; Jorge González-Jácome, "The Emergence of Revolutionary and Democratic Human Rights Activism in Colombia between 1974 and 1980," *Human Rights Quarterly*, forthcoming; Mark Engler, "Towards the 'Rights of the Poor': Human Rights in Liberation Theology," *Journal of Religious Ethics* 28, no. 3 (2000): 339–65.

7. Jiří Hájek, "The Human Rights Movement and Social Progress," in Václav Havel et al., *The Power of the Powerless: Citizens against the State in East-Central Europe*, ed. John Keane (London, 1985), 136, 140. On Tominová, see the introduction to this book.

8. *The Book of Lech Wałęsa* (New York, 1982), 88; "The 21 Demands," in Lawrence Weschler, *Solidarity: Poland in the Season of Its Passion* (New York, 1982), 209–11. On Solidarity more broadly, see David Ost, *Solidarity and the Politics of Anti-Politics: Opposition and Reform in Poland since 1968* (Philadelphia, 1990).

9. Orlando Letelier and Michael Moffitt, *The International Economic Order* (Washington, D.C., 1977); and Paul Adler, "'The Basis of a New Internationalism?': The Institute for Policy Studies and North-South Politics from the NIEO to Neoliberalism," *Diplomatic History* 41, no. 4 (2017): 665–93.

10. The historiography of development is now staggeringly large, yet it mostly stops in the early 1970s. For one overview, see Joseph M. Hodge, "Writing the History of Development," *Humanity* 6, no. 3 (2015): 429–63, and 7, no. 1 (2016): 125–74.

11. For responses to the Pearson report, see Barbara Ward et al., eds., *The Widening Gap: Development in the 1970s* (New York, 1971). See also the much noticed Edgar Owens and Robert Shaw, *Development Reconsidered: Bridging the Gap between Government and People* (Lexington, Mass., 1972).

12. Mahbub ul Haq, *The Strategy of Economic Planning: A Case Study of Pakistan* (Cambridge, 1963); Mahbub ul Haq, "System Is to Blame for the 22 Wealthy Families," *Times* (London), March 22, 1973; Peter Hazelhurst, "The Funny Coincidence of Mrs. Gandhi and a Pakistani Economist," *Times* (London), April 12, 1972; Mahbub ul Haq, "Mrs. Gandhi's Speech," *Times* (London), April 26, 1972.

13. Mahbub ul Haq, "Employment in the 1970's: A New Perspective," *International Development Review* 4 (1971), rpt. in *The Poverty Curtain: Choices for the Third World* (New York, 1976), 35.

14. Mahbub ul Haq, "The Third World Crisis," *Washington Post*, April 30, 1972, rpt. "Crisis in Development Strategies," *World Development* 1, no. 7 (1973): 29, as well as in *The Poverty Curtain*, 40.

15. Haq, "Crisis," 30, in *Poverty Curtain*, 43, as well as chap. 4 and 74–75 on international efforts. On the prominence of GNP, see Dirk Philipsen, *The Little Big Number: How GDP Came to Rule the World and What to Do about It* (Princeton, 2015).

16. Seebohm Rowntree, *The Human Needs of Labour* (London, 1937). See, for example, Agnes Heller, *The Theory of Need in Marx* (New York, 1976); Michael Ignatieff, *The Needs of Strangers* (New York, 1984). On Pant, see A. Vaidyanathan, C. R. Rao, T. N. Srinivasan and J. N. Bhagwati, "Pitambar Pant: An Appreciation," *Economic and Political Weekly*, April 28, 1973, and "Pitambar Pant," in T. N. Srinivasan and P. K. Bardhan, eds., *Poverty and Income Distribution in India* (Calcutta, 1974).

17. R. H. Green, "Basic Human Needs: Concept or Slogan, Synthesis or Smokescreen?" *Institute for Development Studies Bulletin* 9, no. 4 (1978): 7–11; Mahbub ul Haq, "Foreword," in Paul Streeten et al., *First Things First: Meeting Basic Human Needs in the Developing Countries* (Oxford, 1981), ix. For the move from late empire to the 1960s, see Daniel Roger Maul, *Human Rights, Development and Decolonization: The International Labour Organization, 1940–70* (New York, 2012), chap. 7; or Sandrine Kott, "The Forced Labor Issue between Human and Social Rights, 1947–1957," *Humanity* 3, no. 3 (2012): 321–35.

18. See Tripartite World Conference on Employment, Income Distribution and Social Progress and the International Division of Labour, *Employment, Growth, and Basic*

Needs: A One-World Problem (Geneva, 1976), 33. For various assignments of credit for the ILO "breakthrough," see Thomas G. Weiss et al., eds., *UN Voices: The Struggle for Development and Social Justice* (Bloomington, 2005), 239–45.

19. "Declaration of Cocoyoc," *International Organization* 29, no. 3 (1975), 896; Amílcar Herrera, *Catastrophe or New Society? A Latin American World Model* (Ottawa, 1976), esp. 103. The Bariloche ideas were especially associated with the United Nations Institute for Training and Research (UNITAR) and the Argentine-turned-Ivy-League economist Graciela Chichilnisky. See the survey in D. P. Ghai, "What Is a Basic Needs Approach All About?" in Ghai et al., *The Basic Needs Approach to Development: Some Issues Regarding Concepts and Methodology* (Geneva, 1977); and more recently in Gilbert Rist, *The History of Development: From Western Origins to Global Faith*, 3rd ed. (London, 2008), 162–69; for Chichilnisky, see her "Development Patterns and the International Order," *Journal of International Affairs* 31, no. 1 (1977): 275–304 and Sybille Duhautois' forthcoming dissertation on UNITAR and futurism.

20. See the internal history Devesh Kapur et al., *The World Bank: Its First Half Century*, vol. 1, *History* (Washington, D.C., 1997), chaps. 5–6; and Patrick Allan Sharma, *Robert McNamara's Other War: The World Bank and International Development* (Philadelphia, 2017), chap. 3, esp. 67.

21. Robert S. McNamara, *The McNamara Years at the World Bank: Major Policy Addresses, 1968–81* (Baltimore, 1981), 277, 445–46, 472.

22. Ibid., 177, 165, 240.

23. Rob Konkel, "The Monetization of Global Poverty: The Concept of Poverty in World Bank History, 1944–90," *Journal of Global History* 9, no. 2 (2014): 276–300; Sharma, *McNamara's Other War*, chaps. 7–8.

24. Philip Alston, "Human Rights and Basic Needs: A Critical Assessment," *Revue des droits de l'homme* 12, no. 1–2 (1979): 23. As late as 1976, a leading international lawyer could affirm "the idea of need as a basis for entitlement" but not mention human rights. See Oscar Schachter, "The Evolving International Law of Development," *Columbia Journal of Transnational Law* 15 (1976), 10.

25. Paul Streeten and Shahid Javed Burki, "Basic Needs: Some Issues," *World Development Review* 6, no. 3 (1978), 413; Paul Streeten, "Basic Needs: Some Unsettled Questions," *World Development* 12, no. 9 (1984), 978. See also Paul Streeten, "Economic and Social Rights in the Developing Countries," *Revue européene des sciences sociales* 10, no. 26 (1972): 21–38, rpt. in Streeten, *The Frontiers of Development Studies* (New York, 1972); Paul Streeten, "The Distinctive Features of a Basic Needs Approach to Development," *International Development Review* 19, no. 3 (1977): 8–16; Paul Streeten, "Basic Needs: Premises and Problems," *Journal of Policy Modeling* 1 (1979): 136–46. His various papers from this period, from which I have cited the originals, are collected a World Bank publication as Streeten et al., *First Things First*.

26. Streeten, "Basic Needs and Human Rights," 111; Frances Stewart, "Basic Needs Strategies, Human Rights, and the Right to Development," *Human Rights Quarterly* 11,

no. 3 (1989): 350; R. H. Green, "Basic Human Rights/Needs: Some Problems of Categorical Translation and Unification," *International Commission of Jurists Review* 27 (1981), 58. See also Stewart's post-Bank work, *Basic Needs in Developing Countries* (Baltimore, 1985).

27. Alston, "Human Rights and Basic Needs," 28–29, 43, 39; Johan Galtung and Anders Helge Wirak, "Human Rights, Human Rights, and Theories of Development," in Galtung and R. G. Cant, eds., *Indicators of Social and Economic Change and Their Applications* (Paris, 1976); and Galtung and Wirak, "Human Needs and Human Rights—A Theoretical Approach," *Bulletin of Peace Proposals* 8 (1977): 251–58.

28. Amartya Sen, *Choice of Techniques: An Aspect of the Theory of Planned Economic Development* (London, 1960); Amartya Sen, *On Economic Inequality* (Oxford, 1973), chap. 4; Timothy Shenk, *Maurice Dobb: Political Economist* (New York, 2013), 172–74, 180.

29. Amartya Sen, *Poverty and Famines: An Essay on Entitlement and Deprivation* (Cambridge, 1981), 7, 13n. For his first introduction of an entitlement approach, see Amartya Sen, "Famines as Failures of Exchange Entitlements," *Economic and Political Weekly* 11, no. 31/33 (1976): 1273–80. For his other ILO study, see Amartya Sen, *Employment, Technology, and Development* (Oxford, 1975).

30. Sen, *Poverty and Famines*, 10 and 14–17, on the analytical distinction between poverty (or sufficiency generally) and inequality; Richard Cooper cited in Amartya Sen, "Ethical Issues in Income Distribution: National and International," in Sven Grassman and Erik Lundberg, eds., *The World Economic Order: Past and Prospects* (New York, 1981), 477. For his earlier consolidation of poverty and inequality, besides *On Economic Inequality*, see Amartya Sen, "Poverty, Inequality, and Unemployment: Some Conceptual Issues in Measurement," *Economic and Political Weekly* 8, no. 31/33 (1973): 1457–64, rpt. in augmented form in Srinivasan and Bardhan, eds., *Poverty and Income Distribution in India*.

31. Deepak Lal, "Distribution and Development: A Review Article," *World Development* 4, no. 9 (1976): 727, 736; compare 732.

32. Aspen Institute Program on International Affairs, *The Planetary Bargain: Proposals for a New International Economic Order to Meet Human Needs* (New York, 1975), 16–17.

33. Declaration of the Conference of Ministers for Foreign Affairs, Belgrade, July 25–30, 1978, in *The Collected Documents of the Non-Aligned Movement, 1961–1982* (Baghdad, 1982), 321; Commission on Human Rights, Summary Record of the 1489th Meeting, February 21, 1979, UN Doc. E/CN.4/A/SR.1489, para. 29 for the first citation; and Alston, "Human Rights and Basic Needs," 26–27 for the second; Altaf Gauhar, "What Is Wrong with Basic Needs?" *Third World Quarterly* 4, no. 3 (1982), xxii.

34. UNESCO, Expert Meeting on Human Rights, Basic Needs, and the Establishment of a New International Economic Order, Paris, June 19–23, 1978, UN Doc. SS.78/

Conf.630/12; Johan Galtung, "The New International Economic Order and the Basic Needs Approach," *Alternatives* 4 (1978–79), 462–63.

35. Mahbub ul Haq, "Inequities of the Old Economic Order," Overseas Development Council Development Paper No. 22 (1976), rpt. in Charles K. Wilber, ed., *The Political Economy of Development and Underdevelopment*, 2nd ed. (New York, 1979), 184; Mahbub ul Haq, "Development and Independence," *Development Dialogue* 1 (1974), 7; Stephen S. Rosenfeld, "On Inequality among Nations," *Washington Post*, October 22, 1976.

36. Mahbub ul Haq, "Towards a New Planetary Bargain," remarks in Richard N. Gardner, ed., *New Structures for Economic Interdependence* (Rensselaerville, 1975), 20; Mahbub ul Haq, "Basic Needs and the New International Economic Order," in Khadija Haq, ed., *Dialogue for a New Order* (New York, 1980), 235–36.

37. Haq, *Poverty Curtain*, 149, 184–85; Third World Forum, *Proposals for a New International Economic Order* (Mexico City, 1975); Mahbub ul Haq, "The Third World Forum: Intellectual Self-Reliance," *International Development Review* 1 (1975): 8–11; Streeten, "Basic Needs: Premises and Promises," 143. For rueful conclusions that postcolonial states were on their own, Mahbub ul Haq, "Beyond the Slogan of South-South Cooperation," *World Development* 8, no. 10 (1980): 743–51; and, for similar conclusions about the need for the south not to wait around for the north to change, see the influential Eliot Janeway lectures at Princeton by Jamaican economist W. Arthur Lewis, *The Evolution of the International Economic Order* (Princeton, 1978). For conciliatory positions see also R. H. Green and Hans W. Singer, "Toward a Rational and Equitable New International Economic Order: A Case for Negotiated Structural Changes," *World Development* 3, no. 6 (1975): 427–44; and Paul Streeten, "The Dynamics of the New Poor Power," in G. K. Helleiner, *A World Divided: The Less Developed Countries in the International Economy* (Cambridge, 1976). This was a permanent concern of Streeten's; see Paul Streeten, "Basic Needs and the New International Economic Order," in T. E. Barker et al., eds., *Perspectives on Economic Development: Essays in the Honour of W. Arthur Lewis* (Lanham, Md., 1982); and Paul Streeten, "Approaches to a New International Economic Order," *World Development* 10, no. 1 (1982): 1–17. And Haq still defended the NIEO agenda into the 1980s, for example in the University of Texas colloquy with Walt Rostow recorded in Roger D. Hansen, ed., *The "Global Negotiation" and Beyond: Toward North-South Accommodation in the 1980s* (Austin, 1981), esp. 53–56.

38. Daniel Patrick Moynihan, "The United States in Opposition," *Commentary*, March 1975. Upendra Baxi, "The New International Economic Order, Basic Needs, and Rights: Notes toward Development of the Right to Development," *Indian Journal of International Law* 23, no. 2 (1983): 25–45; Alston, "Basic Needs and Human Rights," 51.

39. See Daniel J. Sargent, *A Superpower Transformed: The Remaking of American Foreign Policy in the 1970s* (Oxford, 2016), chap. 6, esp. 178–79; Danny M. Leipziger, "The Basic Human Needs Approach and North-South Relations," in Edwin P. Reubens, ed., *The Challenge of the New International Economic Order* (Boulder, 1981), 260.

40. Rolf H. Sartorius and Vernon W. Ruttan, "The Sources of the Basic Human Needs Mandate," *Journal of Developing Areas* 23, no. 3 (1989), 351; Jimmy Carter, "Commencement Address at the University of Notre Dame," *Public Papers of the Presidents of the United States: Jimmy Carter (1977)*, 2 vols. (Washington, D.C., 1977), 1: 961; Cyrus R. Vance, "Human Rights Policy (April 30, 1977)," *Department of State Bulletin* 77, no. 1978 (May 23, 1977), 505; Warren Christopher, "Human Rights: Principle and Realism," *Department of State Bulletin* 77, no. 1992 (August 29, 1977), 269; "Secretary Vance Attends Ministerial Conference of the Organization for Economic Cooperation and Development," *Department of State Bulletin* 77, no. 1987 (July 25, 1977): 105–109; Sandy Vogelgesang, *American Dream, Global Nightmare: The Dilemma of U.S. Human Rights Policy* (New York, 1980), 184.

41. Patricia Weiss Fagen, *The Links between Human Rights and Basic Needs* (Washington, D.C., 1978) 4; Peter Weiss, "Human Rights and Vital Needs," in John S. Friedman, ed., *First Harvest: The Institute for Policy Studies, 1963–1983* (New York, 1983), 37; Richard A. Falk, "Responding to Severe Violations," in Jorge I. Domínguez et al., *Enhancing Global Human Rights* (New York, 1979), 225.

42. "Secretary Vance Attends," 108; Jimmy Carter, "Ask President Carter," in *Public Papers*, 1: 313, cited in Michael Franczak, "American Foreign Policy in the North-South Dialogue, 1971–1982" (Ph.D. diss., Boston College, 2018), chap. 5. See also Robert K. Olson, *U.S. Foreign Policy and the New International Economic Order: Negotiating Global Problems, 1974–1981* (Boulder, 1981).

43. Jan Tinbergen, ed., *Reshaping the International Economic Order: A Report to the Club of Rome* (New York, 1976); Willy Brandt et al., *North / South: A Programme of Survival* (London, 1980); Giuliano Garavini, *After Empires: European Integration, Decolonization, and the Challenge from the Global South 1957–1986* (Oxford, 2012), 235–40; Cranford Pratt, "From Pearson to Brandt: Evolving Conceptions Concerning International Development," *International Journal* 35, no. 4 (1980): 623–45; R. H. Green, "Brandt on an End to Poverty and Hunger," *Third World Quarterly* 3, no. 1 (1981): 96–103; Susan Strange, "Reactions to Brandt: Popular Acclaim and Academic Attack," *International Studies Quarterly* 25, no. 2 (1981): 328–42; Nigel Harris, *The End of the Third World: Newly Industrializing Countries and the End of an Ideology* (London, 1986), 7. Note that Haq participated in Tinbergen's report but made clear in a personal statement that "the economic liberation of man" meant a priority to "elimination of the worst forms of poverty" (321).

6. Global Ethics from Equality to Subsistence

1. Robert Amdur, "Global Distributive Justice: A Review Essay," *Journal of International Affairs* 31, no. 1 (1977), 81.

2. See John Rawls, *A Theory of Justice* (Cambridge, Mass., 1971), 7–8, 115, 336, 378–79. Rawls relied essentially on James Brierly's international law textbook for his

thinking, but that book, sadly, is absent from Harvard University's archivally preserved selection from his library.

3. Onora O'Neill, "In a Starving World, What's the Moral Minimum?" *Hastings Center Report* 11, no. 6 (1981), 42. Papers of John Rawls, Harvard University Archives, Box 34, Folders 5–14, Lectures on the Law of Nations, 1967–69. For brilliant detail on the relevance of conscientious objection in particular, see Katrina Forrester, "Citizenship, War, and the Origins of International Ethics in American Political Philosophy, 1960–1975," *Historical Journal* 57, no. 3 (2014): 773–801. Brian Barry, "The Strange Death of Political Philosophy," *Government and Opposition* 15 (1980): 284–85. For far more see the relevant chapter of Katrina Forrester, *Reinventing Morality: A History of American Political Thought since the 1950s* (Princeton, forthcoming).

4. Peter Singer, "Famine, Affluence, and Morality," *Philosophy and Public Affairs* 1, no. 3 (1972), 231.

5. On nineteenth-century utilitarianism, see, for example, Eric Stokes, *The English Utilitarians and India* (Oxford, 1959). On the philanthropic context for Singer, see Tehila Sasson, *We Are the World: The End of Empire and the Turn to Market Humanitarianism* (forthcoming); as well as Sasson and James Vernon, "Practicing the British Way of Famine: Technologies of Relief, 1770–1985," *European History Review* 22, no. 6 (2015): 860–72.

6. Singer, "Famine," 243.

7. I follow the excellent research of Christian Gerlach, "Die Welternährungskrise 1972–1975," *Geschichte und Gesellschaft* 31, no. 4 (2005): 546–85; see also Gerlach, "Famine Responses in the World Food Crisis 1972–5 and the World Food Conference of 1974," *European Review of History* 22, no. 6 (2015): 929–39. For some indication of contemporary discussion, see Geoffrey Barraclough, "The Great World Crisis," *New York Review of Books*, January 23, 1975; Herbert Marx, ed., *The World Food Crisis* (New York, 1975); and Sayed Marei, ed., *The World Food Crisis* (London, 1976, 1978).

8. Paul Ehrlich, *The Population Bomb* (New York, 1968). O'Neill's Marx piece was coauthored with her then husband, economist Edward Nell. See Edward and Onora Nell, "On Justice under Socialism," *Dissent* 19, no. 3 (1972): 483–91.

9. Onora Nell, "Lifeboat Earth," *Philosophy and Public Affairs* 4, no. 3 (1975), 273, and 279n on Singer and the claim that obligation is "a corollary of any nonbizarre ethical theory which has any room for a notion of rights," as well as 283n for citations to Marxist dependency literature. For far more, stressing the population control dimensions of the earliest work, see the brilliant work of Hester van Hensbergen, "Famine, Morality, and Modern Moral Philosophy, c. 1967–1980" (forthcoming). Shue's work, discussed below, is good evidence of eventual skepticism about claims about population explosion and management.

10. Henry Shue, "Food, Population, and Wealth: Toward Principles of Global Justice" (paper presented at the annual meeting of the American Political Science

Association, September 1976); Thomas Nagel, "Poverty and Food: Why Charity Is Not Enough," in Peter G. Brown and Henry Shue, eds., *Food Policy: The Responsibility of the United States in the Life and Death Choices* (New York, 1977), 54.

11. Charles R. Beitz, "Justice and International Relations," *Philosophy and Public Affairs* 4, no. 4 (1975): 360–89; Beitz, *Political Theory and International Relations* (Princeton, 1979). For Beitz's own remarks on the genesis of the book, see "Reflections," *Review of International Studies* 41 (2005): 409–23. Samuel Scheffler, "The Idea of Global Justice: A Progress Report," *Harvard Review of Philosophy* 20 (2014), 18. For the houses, Anthony Simon Laden, "The House That Jack Built: Thirty Years of Reading Rawls," *Ethics* 113, no. 2 (2003): 367–90; and Chris Brown, "The House That Chuck Built: Twenty-Five Years of Reading Charles Beitz," *Review of International Studies* 31, no. 2 (2005), 371–79. Henry Shue, "The Geography of Justice: Beitz's Critique of Skepticism and Statism," *Ethics* 92, no. 4 (1982), 710.

12. Charles R. Beitz, "Hail Hunt Terrell," *The Colgate Scene* 27, no. 1 (1998); Charles R. Beitz and Theodore Herman, eds., *Peace and War* (San Francisco, 1973); Charles R. Beitz and Michael Washburn, *Creating the Future: A Guide to Living and Working for Social Change* (New York, 1974), 392–95, 408.

13. Beitz and Washburn, *Creating*, 3; Beitz and Herman, eds., *Peace and War*, xi; Beitz, "Justice," 362. Falk immediately claimed Beitz's venture as a "criticism of the Rawlsian framework from [Falk's own] world order perspective." Richard A. Falk, "The Domains of Law and Justice," *International Journal* 33, no. 1 (Winter 1975 / 1976), 12n.

14. Barbara Ward, "The Fat Years and the Lean," *The Economist*, November 2, 1974. Her most widely read book was *The Rich Nations and the Poor Nations* (New York, 1962); on her role in the origins of sustainability, see Stephen Macekura, *Of Limits and Growth: The Rise of Global Sustainable Development in the Twentieth Century* (Cambridge, 2015).

15. There are four responses of which I am aware, but all were in the nature of passing comments or brief discussions: Brian Barry, *The Liberal Theory of Justice: A Critical Examination of the Principal Doctrines in "A Theory of Justice" by John Rawls* (Oxford, 1973), 128–33; Seyom Brown, *New Forces in World Politics* (Washington, 1974), 206; Peter Danielson, "Theories, Intuitions, and the Problem of World-Wide Distributive Justice," *Philosophy of the Social Sciences* 3 (1973): 331–40; and Thomas M. Scanlon, Jr., "Rawls' Theory of Justice," *University of Pennsylvania Law Review* 121, no. 5 (1973): 1020–69 at 1066–67. See also the papers in Lars O. Ericsson et al., eds., *Justice, Social and Global* (Stockholm, 1980).

16. Beitz, "Justice," 376, 383. Rawls's "theory of international justice bears a striking resemblance to that proposed in the Definitive Articles of Kant's *Perpetual Peace*," Beitz wrote, before moving on to criticize that theory. Ibid., 366.

17. Beitz, "Reflections," 417; *Collected Documents of the Non-Aligned Countries 1961–1982* (Baghdad, 1982), 152; Robert W. Tucker, "A New International Order?" *Commentary*, February 1975; and "Egalitarianism and International Politics," *Commentary*,

September 1975, rpt. in the much noticed book that followed, Tucker, *The Inequality of Nations* (New York, 1977), 52–53, 56; Henry Steele Commager, "Declaration of Interdependence," rpt. in Harlan Cleveland, *The Third Try at World Order* (New York, 1976), 107–109; Henry Kissinger, "The Challenge of Interdependence," *Department of State Bulletin*, May 6, 1974. The best treatment of "interdependence" is Victor Mc-Farland, "The New International Economic Order, Interdependence, and Globalization," *Humanity* 6, no. 1 (2015): 217–33. Interdependence also became a central principle of a new movement in international relations, first stimulated by Richard Cooper but brought to fruition by Robert Keohane and Joseph Nye, which gave a much more fundamental place to economic interrelations than in classic realist accounts of world order. These academic developments were likewise central to Beitz's intervention. In political science, the classic texts are Richard N. Cooper, *The Economics of Interdependence: Economic Policy in the Atlantic Community* (New York, 1968), which he broadened to the globe in "Economic Interdependence and Foreign Policy in the Seventies," *World Politics* 24, no. 2 (1972): 159–81; and then Robert O. Keohane and Joseph S. Nye, Jr., eds., *Transnational Relations and World Politics* (Cambridge, Mass., 1972); and Keohane and Nye, *Power and Interdependence: World Politics in Transition* (Boston, 1977), with its famous first sentence: "We live in an era of interdependence" (3). Beitz later flirted with abandoning the route to a global social contract that relied on the existence or intensity of relations since, if such relations were feasible, a global bargain might be mandated simply by virtue of the moral powers of its hypothetical parties. Compare Charles R. Beitz, "Cosmopolitan Ideals and National Sentiment," *Journal of Philosophy* 80, no. 10 (1983), 595; and Beitz, "Reflections," 421.

18. Beitz, "Justice," 371 and n.

19. Ibid., 373, 375 and n. (citing dependency theory), and 385. For the comment on Singer, see Charles R. Beitz, "Bounded Morality: Justice and the State in World Politics," *International Organization* 33, no. 3 (1979), 418.

20. Beitz, "Justice," 360; Beitz, *Political Theory*, 126. In effect this chapter builds massively on a brief and prior account of the relation of philosophy to the human rights revolution in Moyn, *The Last Utopia: Human Rights and History* (Cambridge, Mass., 2010), 214–16.

21. Beitz, "Justice," 387.

22. Beitz, *Political Theory*, 99, 64, 104, 102. By comparison, Richard Falk, for whose seminar Beitz had first embarked on his project, signed on enthusiastically to the self-determination claims climaxing in the NIEO of the era. See, for example, Falk, "La Déclaration d'Alger et la lutte pour les droits de l'homme," in Antonio Cassese and Edmond Jouvé, eds., *Pour un droit des peuples* (Paris, 1978).

23. Arthur Schlesinger, Jr., "Human Rights: How Far, How Fast?" *Wall Street Journal*, March 4, 1977. For good and more explicit evidence of "egalitarianism" as a theoretical framework intended as an alternative to "dependency," see Beitz's more popular essay, "Global Egalitarianism," *Dissent* 26, no. 1 (1979): 61–64.

24. Beitz, *Political Theory*, 119, 120. For radical economics, compare the subtle differences between Beitz, "Justice," 375n, and Beitz, *Political Theory*, 150n; compare 116–19. On corporations, compare Beitz, "Justice," 373 and n, with Beitz, *Political Theory*, 145 and esp. nn. More generously, Henry Shue interpreted Beitz's case (without noting that it was a revision in its empirical basis) as a "minimalist" one, strategically avoiding reliance on leftist "world-systems theories, *dependencia* theories, or any of a number of other kinds of reasonably well-supported theories according to which the economic ties among nations are considerably stronger (and more vicious) than Beitz claims—he relies mostly upon the work of mainstream U.S. academics." Shue, "The Geography of Justice," 717–18.

25. Tucker, *The Inequality of Nations*, 139.

26. Ibid., 64, 117; Beitz, "Bounded Morality," 409.

27. Beitz, "Bounded Morality," 409; and Beitz, *Political Theory*, 182–83.

28. Beitz, "Global Egalitarianism," 68 and 64–67, for a rich and balanced discussion of the whole situation. Like many others, such as Mahbub ul Haq, Beitz concluded indigenous change in postcolonial states was the sole hope. Beitz, *Political Theory*, 172–75, and "Bounded Morality," 423, 419, strongly influenced by W. Arthur Lewis, *The Evolution of the International Economic Order* (Princeton, 1978).

29. Charles R. Beitz and Robert E. Goodin, "Introduction: *Basic Rights* and Beyond," in Beitz and Goodin, eds., *Global Basic Rights* (New York, 2009), 1; Henry Shue, *Basic Rights: Subsistence, Affluence, and U.S. Foreign Policy* (Princeton, 1980).

30. Henry Shue, "Preface," in *Fighting Hurt: Rule and Exception in Torture and War* (Oxford, 2016), vi, where he also recalls that he was inspired to enter political theory by watching a then-untenured Michael Walzer stand down senior colleagues at war teach-ins. Brown and Shue, eds., *Food Policy*; Brown and Douglas MacLean, eds., *Human Rights and U.S. Foreign Policy: Principles and Applications* (Lexington, Mass., 1979). On the Academy, see Mary McGarry, "Center to Help Solve Issues," *Columbus Dispatch*, February 10, 1974, and, on Brown's appointment, "Academy Appoints Nine Fellows," *Columbus Courier-Journal*, January 29, 1976.

31. For the Center's founding, see "Notes and News," *Journal of Philosophy* 73, no. 19 (1976): 768; Patricia Weiss Fagen, *The Links between Human Rights and Basic Needs* (Washington, D.C., 1978): 1–11; and personal communication.

32. Henry Shue, "Liberty and Self-Respect," *Ethics* 85, no. 3 (1975): 195–203; and Shue, "Justice, Rationality, and Desire: On the Logical Structure of Justice as Fairness," *Southern Journal of Philosophy* 13 (1975–76): 89–97.

33. Albert Camus, *The Plague*, trans. Stuart Gilbert (New York, 1948), 308. Shue, *Basic Rights*, xi (and v and 173–74 for the Camus citations).

34. Shue, *Basic Rights*, chap. 2, as well as Shue, "Rights in the Light of Duties," in Brown and MacLean, eds., *Human Rights and U.S. Foreign Policy*.

35. Shue, *Basic Rights*, 25 and 192n; and Shue, "Torture," *Philosophy and Public Affairs* 7, no. 2 (1978): 124–43; Onora O'Neill, *Faces of Hunger: An Essay on Poverty*,

Justice, and Development (London, 1986), 114–15 (this book is O'Neill's considered response to the debates of the prior decade). In the prior era, few had risen to defend the priority of civil and political rights within human rights explicitly, with the (for Beitz, Shue, and others, glaring) exception of Maurice Cranston, *Human Rights To-day* (London, 1955, 1962), published in the United States as *What Are Human Rights?* (New York, 1963) and later revised heavily under the latter title (London, 1973); echoed by Columbia University philosopher Charles Frankel in the midst of the human rights revolution in Frankel, *Human Rights and Foreign Policy* (New York, 1978), 36–49. But it is true that such prioritization fit well with liberal sensibility that Rawls had defended in his own terms. Shue's revolt against the priority of liberty in 1980 should be compared to his respectful reconstruction of it in his 1975 *Ethics* essay cited earlier. For the proviso concerning the allowable prioritization of development in certain cases (he clearly had postcolonial states in mind), see Rawls, *A Theory of Justice*, 247–48; see also 62–63.

36. Shue, *Basic Rights*, ix.

37. Henry Shue, "Lukács: Notes on His Originality," *Journal of the History of Ideas* 34, no. 4 (1973): 645–50. James Scott, *The Moral Economy of the Peasant: Rebellion and Subsistence in Southeast Asia* (New Haven, 1976), 40, cited by Shue, *Basic Rights*, 28, 207–8n (emphasis added); and Scott, *Moral Economy*, 184, for social rights; Shue's partner Vivienne Shue, a China specialist who taught alongside Scott in the Yale political science department, made the connection. The philosopher also registered the importance of Benedict J. Kerkvliet, *The Huk Rebellion: A Study of Peasant Revolt in the Philippines* (Berkeley, 1977), 252–55, a passage Shue cited for proving the "deep belief in a right of subsistence" of peasants (*Basic Rights*, 184n); the point of interest is what Shue found compelling in an examination of the communist revolutionary bid brutally put down in the 1940s with large U.S. assistance. Similarly to Beitz, Shue was also completely aware of an emerging literature on the deleterious effects of multinational corporations (*Basic Rights*, 188n).

38. Shue, "Food, Population, and Wealth," 14, 7. Charles R. Beitz, "Human Rights and Social Justice," in Peter G. Brown and Douglas MacLean, eds., *Human Rights and U.S. Foreign Policy* (Lexington, Mass., 1979).

39. Shue, *Basic Rights*, 128; Shue, "The Geography of Justice," 719. The image of people who would drown without a basic minimum came, this time unacknowledged, from Scott, who in turn owed it to R. H. Tawney, *Land and Labor in China* (1932; Boston, 1966), 77. Shue surmised from these considerations that people might well reserve the right to take the means of their subsistence violently rather than enter any social contract (local or global) that did not provide them with it. "Is it clearly more rational," Shue wondered, "to agree that one's fortunes may permissibly be indefinitely low, provided only that when those who are already better-off than oneself become still better-off, one's own fortunes must improve at least slightly, rather than trying, at least where there is some prospect of success, to mobilize effective opposition to any system

of institutions that does not redistribute available wealth until everyone has an adequate minimum?" (129). The answer was not obvious: you might well bargain for your own subsistence—and equal social relations only past that threshold—and enter no agreement without it.

40. Shue, *Basic Rights*, chap. 6 and 174. On the need for limits, see James S. Fishkin, *The Limits of Obligation* (New Haven, 1982); Fishkin, "The Boundaries of Justice," *Journal of Conflict Resolution* 27, no. 2 (1983): 355–75; and Shue, "The Burdens of Justice," *Journal of Philosophy* 80, no. 10 (1983): 600–608.

41. Shue, *Basic Rights*, chap. 7.

42. James W. Nickel and Lizbeth L. Hasse, "Book Review," *California Law Review* 69 (1981): 1569–86. For Shue's orientation to the United States government into the 1980s, see, for example, United States Senate, Committee on Foreign Relations, *Perceptions: Relations between the United States and the Soviet Union* (Washington, D.C., 1979), 410–13; or Shue, "In the American Tradition, Rights Remain Unalienable," *The Center Magazine* 17, no. 4 (January 1984): 6–34.

43. Shue, *Basic Rights*, 63–64, 192n.

44. Beitz, "Justice," 389.

7. Human Rights in the Neoliberal Maelstrom

1. Orlando Letelier, "The Chicago Boys in Chile: Economic Freedom's Awful Role," *The Nation*, August 28, 1976.

2. Naomi Klein, "Forty Years Ago, This Chilean Exile Warned Us About the Shock Doctrine, Then He Was Assassinated," *The Nation*, October 10, 2016; Naomi Klein, *The Shock Doctrine: The Rise of Disaster Capitalism* (New York, 2007), 146–47; Susan Marks, "Four Human Rights Myths," in David Kinley et al., eds., *Human Rights: Old Problems, New Possibilities* (Cheltenham, 2013), 226.

3. Compare Joe Wills, "The World Turned Upside Down? Neo-Liberalism, Socioeconomic Rights, and Hegemony," *Leiden Journal of International Law* 27, no. 1 (2014): 11–35; and Jessica Whyte, "Human Rights and the Collateral Damage of Neoliberalism," *Theory & Event* 20, no. 1 (2017): 137–57. I should note that I do not dwell on neoliberalism as a form of life and especially a mode of individual self-creation in the spirit of Michel Foucault or Marcel Gauchet, preferring to substantiate the argument on the relationship between human rights as a new political movement and legal project, on one hand, and distributive aspirations and outcomes, on the other. Even then, it is a promissory note. But see Marcel Gauchet, *L'avènement de la démocratie*, vol. 4, *Le nouveau monde* (Paris, 2017), esp. chap. 9, for a causal-structural but non-Marxist approach to the relationship between human rights and neoliberalism since the 1970s disruption. See also Zachary Manfredi, "An Unlikely Resonance? Subjects of Human Rights and Subjects of Human Capital Reconsidered," in Ben Golder and Daniel McLoughlin, eds., *The Politics of Legality in a Neoliberal Age* (New York, 2018).

4. F. A. Hayek, *The Road to Serfdom* (New York, 2001), 124–25, 89. I follow Angus Burgin, *The Great Persuasion: Reinventing Free Markets since the Great Depression* (Cambridge, Mass., 2012), esp. chaps. 2–3. See also Serge Audier, *Néo-libéralismes: une archéologie intellectuelle* (Paris, 2012); and, for two especially helpful analyses, Raymond Plant, *The Neo-liberal State* (Oxford, 2009); and David Kotz, *The Rise and Fall of Neoliberal Capitalism* (Cambridge, Mass., 2015).

5. Carl J. Friedrich, "The Political Thought of Neo-liberalism," *American Political Science Review* 49, no. 2 (1955): 509–25; Ralf Ptak, *Vom Ordoliberalismus zur Sozialen Marktwirtschaft: Stationenen des Neoliberalismus in Deutschland* (Opladen, 2004), esp. chap. 4; Michael Moffitt, "Chicago Economics in Chile," *Challenge* 20, no. 4 (1977): 34–43; Glen Biglaiser, "The Internationalization of Chicago's Economics in Latin America," *Economic Development and Social Change* 50, no. 2 (2002): 269–86.

6. Mary Nolan, "Human Rights and Market Fundamentalism in the Long 1970s," in Norbert Frei and Annette Weinke, eds., *Toward a New Moral World Order? Menschenrechtspolitik und Völkerrecht seit 1945* (Göttingen, 2013), 172; Robert Chitester, interview with Friedrich A. Hayek, at the University of California-Los Angeles (1978), www.hayek.ufm.edu/index.php?title=Bob_Chitester_part_I&p=video1&b=930&e =1037.

7. Judith A. Teichman, *The Politics of Freeing Markets in Latin America: Chile, Argentina, and Mexico* (Chapel Hill, 2001).

8. East Germany went especially far in seeking domestic and international legitimation through social rights rhetoric, in part because it had adopted it early in the regime's history. See Paul Betts, "Socialism, Social Rights, and Human Rights: The Case of East Germany," *Humanity* 3, no. 3 (2012): 407–26; and Ned Richardson-Little, "Dictatorship and Dissent: Human Rights in East Germany in the 1970s," in Jan Eckel and Samuel Moyn, eds., *The Breakthrough: Human Rights in the 1970s* (Philadelphia, 2014).

9. Compare Benjamin Nathans, "The Disenchantment of Socialism: Soviet Dissidents, Human Rights, and the New Global Morality," in Eckel and Moyn, eds., *The Breakthrough*. The ideological transition is the really significant one even if one wants to stress, like Johanna Bockman, that socialists in power devised neoliberal policies themselves. Johanna Bockman, *Markets in the Name of Socialism: The Left-Wing Origins of Neoliberalism* (Stanford, 2011).

10. Václav Havel, "Power of the Powerless," in *Open Letters: Selected Writings, 1965–1990*, trans. Paul Wilson (New York, 1991), 161.

11. Jean-Yves Potel, *Scènes de grèves en Pologne* (Paris, 1981), chap. 6; on Michnik, David Ost, *The Defeat of Solidarity: Anger and Politics in Postcommunist Europe* (Ithaca, 1985), 41.

12. James Krapfl, *Revolution with a Human Face: Politics, Culture, and Community in Czechoslovakia, 1989–1992* (Ithaca, 2013), 97.

13. Robert Brier, *A Contested Icon: Poland's Solidarity Movement and the Global Politics of Human Rights* (forthcoming), though Ost's brilliant book on the spurned working

class deserves much attention. On trade unions across the region, see Stephen Crowley and David Ost, eds., *Workers after Workers' States: Labor and Politics in Postcommunist Eastern Europe* (Lanham, Md., 2001).

14. Paul Dragos Aligica and Anthony J. Evans, eds., *The Neoliberal Revolution in Eastern Europe* (Cheltenham, 2009); Bojan Bugarič, "Neoliberalism, Post-communism, and the Law," *Annual Review of Law and Social Science* 12 (2016): 313–26; and Venelin I. Ganev, "The 'Triumph of Neoliberalism' Reconsidered: Critical Remarks on Ideas-Centered Analyses of Political and Economic Change in Post-Communism," *East European Politics and Society* 19, no. 3 (2005): 343–78.

15. Philipp Ther, *Europe since 1989: A History*, trans. Charlotte Hughes-Kreutzmüller (Princeton, 2016), chap. 5. The African continent's much later (1981) regional human rights charter highlighted distribution more thoroughly, in calling for both rights to basic provision and a just international order, including the popular right to development.

16. Nicholas Ellison, *Egalitarian Thought and Labour Politics: Retreating Visions* (London, 1994); C. A. R. Crosland, *The Future of Socialism*, new ed. (New York, 1963), 78.

17. Cornel Ban, *Ruling Ideas: How Global Neoliberalism Goes Local* (Oxford, 2016), contrasting Bulgaria and Spain; Mark Dawson, *The Governance of EU Fundamental Rights* (Cambridge, 2017), chap. 5; Margot E. Salomon, "Of Austerity, Human Rights, and International Institutions," *European Law Journal* 21, no. 4 (2015): 521–45. By contrast, the European Social Charter of 1961, intended to complement the European Convention on Human Rights under the auspices of the Council of Europe, never attained much significance, though it is only fair to note that the European Committee on Social Rights overseeing the charter found violations of its principles in the austerity era, albeit without serious consequence. See Colm O'Cinneide, "Austerity and the Faded Dream of a Social Europe," in Aoife Nolan, ed., *Economic and Social Rights after the Global Financial Crisis* (Cambridge, 2014).

18. Devesh Kapur et al., *The World Bank: Its First Half Century*, vol. 1, *History* (Washington, D.C., 1997), chap. 7, esp. 333–39; James Gathii, "Human Rights, the World Bank, and the Washington Consensus, 1949–1999," *Proceedings of the Annual Meeting of the American Society of International Law* 94 (2000): 144–46; Mac Darrow, *Between Light and Shadow: The World Bank, the International Monetary Fund, and International Human Rights Law* (Portland, 2003); Sara Joseph, *Blame It on the WTO?: A Human Rights Critique* (Oxford, 2011); Andrew Lang, *World Trade Law after Neoliberalism: Reimagining the Global Economic Order* (Oxford, 2011).

19. On the origins of the human development index, see Craig N. Murphy, *The United Nations Development Programme: A Better Way?* (Cambridge, 2006), chap. 9. On the development goals, see the influential account of Philip Alston, "Ships Passing in the Night: The Current State of the Human Rights and Development Debate Seen through the Lens of the Millennium Development Goals," *Human Rights Quarterly* 7,

no. 3 (2005): 755–829. Sustainable Development Goal 10 does call for "reducing inequalities within and between countries," but then it was by and large a wish list accommodating every aspiration, which did not mean each item would receive comparable attention. See Edward Anderson, "Equality as a Global Goal," *Ethics and International Affairs* 30, no. 2 (2016): 189–200; Center for Economic and Social Rights, *From Disparity to Dignity: Tackling Economic Inequality through the Sustainable Development Goals* (New York, 2016); Kate Donald, "Tackling Inequality: The Potential of the Sustainable Development Goals," *Open Global Rights*, March 2, 2017.

20. Ernst-Ulrich Petersmann, "Time for a United Nations 'Global Compact' for Integrating Human Rights in the Law of Worldwide Organizations: Lessons from European Integration," *European Journal of International Law* 13, no. 2 (2002), 629; see also Petersmann, "Human Rights and International Trade Law: Defining and Connecting the Two Fields," in Thomas Cottier et al., eds., *Human Rights and International Trade* (Oxford, 2006). Alston famously alleged that Petersmann's goal was "to hijack, or more appropriately to Hayek, international human rights." Alston, "Resisting the Merger and Acquisition of Human Rights by Trade Law: A Reply to Petersmann," *European Journal of International Law* 13, no. 4 (2002), 816. World Bank, *Development and Human Rights: The Role of the World Bank* (Washington, D.C., 1999).

21. Philip Alston, "Human Rights and the New International Development Strategy," *Bulletin of Peace Proposals* 3 (1979): 281–90; Amartya Sen, *Development as Freedom* (New York, 1999); Pascal Lamy, Director-General, World Trade Organization, "Humanising Globalisation" (address in Santiago, Chile, Jan. 30, 2006), www.wto.org /english/news_e/sppl_e/sppl16_e.htm; Report of the Special Rapporteur on Extreme Poverty and Human Rights on the World Bank and Human Rights, UN Doc. A/70/274, August 4, 2015. See also Alston and Mary Robinson, eds., *Human Rights and Development: Towards Mutual Reinforcement* (Oxford, 2005); and Galit Sarfaty, *Values in in Translation: Human Rights in the Culture of the World Bank* (Stanford, 2012). Under Barack Obama, Michael Posner, the assistant secretary of state for democracy, human rights, and labor, offered what some took as a recommitment to economic and social rights. Michael Posner, "The Four Freedoms Turns Seventy," address at the American Society for International Law, March 24, 2011, www.humanrights.gov/assistant-secretary -michael-h.-posner-the-four-freedoms-turn-70.

22. Daniel J. Whelan, *Indivisible Human Rights: A History* (Philadelphia, 2010). Compare Rhoda E. Howard, "The Full-Belly Thesis: Should Economic Rights Take Priority over Civil and Political Rights? (Evidence from Sub-Saharan Africa)," *Human Rights Quarterly* 5, no. 4 (1983): 467–90. The surge of attention to economic and social rights (though not other themes) vindicates Stefan-Ludwig Hoffmann's contention that there was no such thing as human rights politics until the 1990s: Hoffmann, "Human Rights and History," *Past & Present* 232 (2016): 279–310. Manfred Nowak, *Human Rights or Global Capitalism: The Limits of Privatization* (Philadelphia, 2017).

23. Pascal McDougall, "Keynes, Sen, and Hayek: Competing Approaches to International Labor Law in the ILO and the WTO, 1994–2008," *Northwestern Journal of Human Rights* 16, no. 1 (2017): 32–90.

24. Jennifer Bair, "Corporations at the United Nations: Echoes of the New International Economic Order?" *Humanity* 6, no. 1 (2015): 159–71; Guiding Principles on Business and Human Rights, Human Rights Council Res. 17/4, June 16, 2011; John Gerard Ruggie, *Just Business: Multinational Corporations and Human Rights* (New York, 2013).

25. David Kinley, *Civilising Globalisation: Human Rights and the Global Economy* (Cambridge, 2009); Eduardo Silva, *Challenging Neoliberalism in Latin America* (Cambridge, 2009); Tomer Broude, "From Seattle to Occupy: The Shifting Focus of Global Protest," in Daniel Drache and Lesley A. Jacobs, eds., *Linking Trade and Human Rights: New Policy Space in Hard Economic Times* (Cambridge, 2014).

26. Irene Khan, *The Unheard Truth: Poverty and Human Rights* (New York, 2009); Kenneth Roth, "Defending Economic, Social, and Cultural Rights: Practical Issues Faced by an International Human Rights Organization," *Human Rights Quarterly* 26, no. 1 (2004): 63–73: Daniel P. L. Chong, *Freedom from Poverty: NGOs and Human Rights Praxis* (Philadelphia, 2010).

27. Committee for Economic, Social, and Cultural Rights, General Comment No. 3: The Nature of States Parties' Obligations (1990), para. 14; Catarina de Albuquerque, "Chronicle of an Announced Birth: The Coming into Life of the Optional Protocol to the International Covenant on Economic, Social, and Cultural Rights," *Human Rights Quarterly* 32, no. 1 (2010): 144–78; Margot E. Salomon and Ian Seiderman, "Human Rights Norms for a Globalized World: The Maastricht Principles on Extraterritorial Obligations of States in the Area of Economic, Social, and Cultural Rights," *Global Policy* 3, no. 4 (2012): 458–62; International Committee on Human Rights, *Duties Sans Frontières: Human Rights and Global Social Justice* (Versoix, 2003); Mark Gibney, "Establishing a Social and Economic Order for the Realization of Human Rights," in Minkler, ed., *The State*; Malcolm Langford et al., eds., *Global Justice, State Duties: The Extraterritorial Scope of Economic, Social, and Cultural Rights in International Law* (Cambridge, 2013).

28. Philip Alston and Katarina Tomaševski, eds., *The Right to Food* (Utrecht, 1984); Susan Randolph and Shareen Hertel, "The Right to Food: A Global Perspective," in Lanse Minkler, ed., *The State of Economic and Social Human Rights: A Global Overview* (Cambridge, 2013).

29. Jonathan Mann et al., "Health and Human Rights," *Health and Human Rights* 1, no. 1 (1994): 6–23; Audrey Chapman, *Global Health, Human Rights, and the Challenge of Neoliberal Policies* (Cambridge, 2016); Audrey Chapman and Salil Benegal, "Globalization and the Right to Health," in Minkler, ed., *The State*; Amy Kapczynski, "The Right to Medicine in an Age of Neoliberalism," *Humanity* (forthcoming); Paul Farmer, *Pathologies of Power: Health, Human Rights, and the New War on the Poor* (Berkeley,

2003), esp. chap. 9; Farmer, "Rich World, Poor World: Medical Ethics and Global Inequality," in Farmer, *Partner to the Poor: A Paul Farmer Reader*, ed. Haun Saussy (Berkeley, 2010); Alicia Ely Yamin, *Power, Suffering, and the Struggle for Dignity: Human Rights Frameworks for Health and Why They Matter* (Philadelphia, 2016).

30. Cass R. Sunstein, "Against Positive Rights," *East European Constitutional Review* 2 (1993): 35–38; Ran Hirschl, *Towards Juristocracy: The Origins and Consequences of the New Constitutionalism* (Cambridge, Mass., 2004).

31. Ralph K. Winter, Jr., "Poverty, Economic Equality, and the Equal Protection Clause," *Supreme Court Review* 1972 (1972): 41–102; William E. Forbath, "Not So Simple Justice: Frank Michelman on Social Rights, 1969–Present," *Tulsa Law Review* 39 (2004): 597–639. On South Africa, see Mohsen al Attar and Ciaron Murnane, "The Place of Capitalism in Pursuit of Human Rights in Globalized Relationships of States," in Jeffery F. Addicott et al., eds., *Globalization, International Law, and Human Rights* (Oxford, 2011), esp. 218–20.

32. The literature on the judicial enforcement of social rights quickly became a cottage industry, and work from the scholars Daniel Brinks, Sandra Fredman, César Rodríguez Garavito, Varun Gauri, Jeff King, Paul O'Connell, Brian Ray, and Katharine Young has been especially valuable.

33. Ingrid Leijten, "The German Right to an *Existenzminimum*, Human Dignity, and the Possibility of Minimum Core Socioeconomic Rights Protection," *German Law Journal* 16, no. 1 (2015): 23–38; András Sájo, "How the Rule of Law Killed Hungarian Welfare Reform," *East European Constitutional Review* 5, no. 1 (1996): 31–40; Wojciech Sadurski, *Rights before Courts: A Study of Constitutional Courts in Postcommunist States of Eastern Europe*, 2nd ed. (Dordrecht, 2008), chap. 7, esp. 274–81 on the right to work; Paul O'Connell, "Let Them Eat Cake? Socio-Economic Rights in an Age of Austerity," in Aoife Nolan et al., eds., *Human Rights and Public Finance: Budgets and the Promotion of Economic and Social Rights* (Oxford, 2013); Nolan, ed., *Economic and Social Rights*; Aoife Nolan, "Not Fit for Purpose? Human Rights in Times of Financial and Economic Crisis," *European Human Rights Law Review* 2015, no. 4 (2015): 358–69.

34. David Landau, "The Reality of Social Rights Enforcement," *Harvard International Law Journal* 53, no. 1 (2012): 401–59; see also Helena Alviar García, "Distribution of Resources Led by Courts: A Few Words of Caution," in Alviar et al., eds., *Social and Economic Rights in Theory and Practice* (New York, 2015). As Landau records, the centrality of the assumption that economic rights once awarded were not subject to "retrogression" set up the tilt to middle-class benefit. The most optimistic accounts of social rights in the global south in general are Javier A. Couso, "The Changing Role of Law and Courts in Latin America: From an Obstacle to Social Change to a Tool of Social Equity," in Roberto Gargarella et al., eds., *Courts and Social Transformation in New Democracies: An Institutional Voice for the Poor?* (New York, 2006); Lucie E. White and Jeremy Perelman, eds., *Stones of Hope: How African Activists Reclaim Human Rights*

to Challenge Global Poverty (Stanford, 2011); and Sakiko Fukuda Parr et al., *Fulfilling Social and Economic Rights* (Oxford, 2015).

35. For a political reclamation of economic rights for the left, see Ellen Meiskins Wood, "Getting What's Coming to Us: Capitalism and Human Rights," *Against the Current* 24, no. 2 (2009): 28–32; for a judicial one, Paul O'Connell, "The Death of Socioeconomic Rights," *Modern Law Review* 74, no. 4 (2011): 532–54.

36. Nancy MacLean, *Freedom Is Not Enough: The Opening of the American Workplace* (Cambridge, Mass., 2008); Nancy Fraser, *Fortunes of Feminism: From State-Managed Capitalism to Neoliberal Crisis* (New York, 2013); and Melinda Cooper, *Family Values: Between Neoliberalism and the New Social Conservatism* (New York, 2017). Yascha Mounk, *The Age of Responsibility: Luck, Choice, and the Welfare State* (Cambridge, Mass., 2017), does not address women but is highly relevant. In recent years, a few voices have called for a vision of human rights that would change tax policy, but to no avail. See Radhika Balakrishnan et al., *Maximum Available Resources and Human Rights* (New Brunswick, N.J., 2011), esp. 3–4 or Paul Beckett, *Tax Havens and Human Rights* (New York, 2017).

37. For one long-term narrative, see Arvonne S. Fraser, "Becoming Human: The Origins and Development of Women's Human Rights," in Marjorie Agosín, ed., *Women, Gender, and Human Rights: A Global Perspective* (New Brunswick, N.J., 2002). Betty Friedan is cited in Jocelyn Olcutt, "Globalizing Sisterhood: International Women's Year and the Politics of Representation," in Niall Ferguson et al., eds., *The Shock of the Global: The 1970s in Perspective* (Cambridge, Mass., 2010), 281–82. See also Roland Burke, "Competing for the Last Utopia? The NIEO, Human Rights, and the World Conference for the International Women's Year, Mexico City, June 1975," *Humanity* 6, no. 1 (2015): 47–61; Jocelyn Olcutt, *International Women's Year: The Greatest Consciousness-Raising Event in History* (Oxford, 2017); and, for the communist answer to Mexico City, Celia Donert, "Whose Utopia? Gender, Ideology, and Human Rights at the 1975 World Congress of Women in East Berlin," in Eckel and Moyn, eds., *The Breakthrough*.

38. Jean H. Quataert, "The Gendering of Human Rights in the International Systems of Law in the Twentieth Century," in Michael Adas, ed., *Essays on Global and Comparative History* (Washington, D.C., 2006); Convention for the Elimination of All Forms of Discrimination against Women (1978), art. 2(f).

39. Elora Halim Chowdhury, *Transnationalism Reversed: Women Organizing against Gendered Violence in Bangladesh* (Albany, 2011); Catharine A. MacKinnon, *Are Women Human? And Other International Dialogues* (Cambridge, Mass., 2006).

40. Alice M. Miller, "Sexuality, Violence against Women, and Human Rights: Women Make Demands and Ladies Get Protection," *Health and Human Rights* 7, no. 2 (2004): 16–47; Elizabeth Bernstein, "The Sexual Politics of the 'New Abolitionism,'" *Differences* 18, no. 3 (2007): 128–51; Felicity Schaeffer-Grabiel, "Sex Trafficking as the 'New Slave Trade'?" *Sexualities* 13, no. 2 (2010): 153–60.

41. Ester Boserup, *Woman's Role in Economic Development* (New York, 1970); Devaki Jain, *Women, Development, and the UN: A Sixty Year Quest for Equality and Justice* (Bloomington, 2005); Joanne Meyerowitz, *From Modernization to Microcredit: How Women Became the Deserving Poor* (forthcoming), chap. 3.

42. Miller, "Sexuality," 40–41.

43. For the label, David Harvey, *A Brief History of Neoliberalism* (Oxford, 2005), chap. 5. For the influence in China of neoliberals coming out of East European socialism, see Julian Gewirtz, *Unlikely Partners: Chinese Reformers, Western Economists, and the Making of Global China* (Cambridge, Mass., 2017). For Africa under neoliberalism, see James Ferguson, *Global Shadows: Africa in the Neoliberal World Order* (Durham, N.C., 2006).

44. For skepticism about Chinese numbers, both empirical and normative, see Margot E. Salomon, "Why Should It Matter That Others Have More? Poverty, Inequality, and the Potential of International Human Rights Law," *Review of International Studies* 37, no. 5 (2011): 2137–55.

45. Theo van Boven is cited in Jean Quataert, *Advocating Dignity: Human Rights Mobilizations in Global Politics* (Philadelphia, 2009), 188.

46. Jack Donnelly, "The 'Right to Development': How Not to Link Human Rights and Development," in Claude E. Welch, Jr. and Ronald I. Meltzer, eds., *Human Rights and Development in Africa* (Albany, 1984), 268. For origins, see Daniel J. Whelan, " 'Under the Aegis of Man': The Right to Development and the Origins of the New International Economic Order," *Humanity* 6, no. 1 (2015): 93–108. For a more positive reading, see Margot E. Salomon, "From the NIEO to Now and the Unfinishable Story of Economic Justice," *International and Comparative Law Quarterly* 13, no. 1 (2013): 31–54.

47. Preliminary Report on the Realization of Economic, Social and Cultural Rights (titled "The New International Order and the Promotion of Human Rights"); UN Doc. E/CN.4/Sub.2/1989/19, June 28, 1989 and Final Report, UN Doc. E/CN.4/Sub.2/1992/16; Julia Dehm, "Righting Inequality: Human Rights Responses to Economic Inequality within the United Nations" (forthcoming).

48. Report of the Special Rapporteur on Extreme Poverty and Human Rights, UN Doc. A/HRC/29/31, May 27, 2015. In 2017, Alston devoted his report to the suddenly fashionable ideal of a universal basic income.

49. Ibid., paras. 2, 12, 54. Very similar mainstream thinking is to be found in Manfred Nowak, *Menschenrechte: Eine Antwort auf die wachsende ökonomische Ungleichheit* (Vienna, 2015). See also the *Open Global Rights* forum on economic inequality and human rights, in which Alston and others (including myself) participated. For the claim that it is imperative to coax a more ambitious right to distributive equality from extant sources, see Gillian MacNaughton, "Beyond a Minimum Threshold: The Right to Social Equality," in Minkler, ed., *The State*.

50. Angus Deaton, *The Great Escape: Health, Wealth, and the Origins of Inequality* (Princeton, 2013), chap. 6; Branko Milanovic, *Global Inequality: A New Approach for the Age of Globalization* (New York, 2016).

51. Dani Rodrik, "Is Global Inequality the Enemy of National Inequality?" (January 2017), https://drodrik.scholar.harvard.edu/publications/global-equality-enemy-national-equality.

Conclusion

1. Herodotus, *Histories*, Book I.

2. Derek Parfit, "Equality or Priority?" in Matthew Clayton and Andrew Williams, eds., *The Ideal of Equality* (London, 2000).

3. Pierre Rosanvallon, *The Society of Equals*, trans. Arthur Goldhammer (Cambridge, Mass., 2013), 174.

Acknowledgments

For a study that, though quickly written, has taken a long time to conceive, this book's thanks are not enough to make good on the debts I owe to so many who provided help along the way. Danielle Allen offered up a cherished spot and a wonderful experience at Harvard University's Edmond J. Safra Center for Ethics during the sabbatical in 2016–17 when I drafted this manuscript. The Berggruen Institute and the Weatherhead Center for International Affairs funded my stay; deep gratitude, therefore, is due to Nicholas Berggruen, Craig Calhoun, Theodore Gilman, and Michèle Lamont for this break from teaching. The university's Anne and Jim Rothenberg Fund for Arts and Humanities also provided some monies. But I appreciate most the generosity of former Dean Martha Minow of Harvard Law School for allowing me to take leave for a term and, for that matter, supporting my scholarship in a myriad of ways—not to mention for inviting me for a fortunate spell on her faculty in the first place.

Since this book is largely a product of that time at Harvard, it makes sense to seize this opportunity to thank all those who showed me kindness there (or at least tolerated my idiosyncrasy), especially my law school colleagues Gabriella Blum, John Goldberg, Jack Goldsmith, David Kennedy, Duncan Kennedy, and Benjamin Sachs. Carol Steiker provided some final valued pointers thanks to the press. A generous colleague in human rights, Gerald Neuman, not only provided indispensable collegiality but also vetted a chapter with his hallmark care. Frank Michelman afforded always egalitarian attention to my worries about sufficiency, and did not overreact to being treated as a historical protagonist, even as he has always been and will always remain a present exemplar for so many ordinary sorts like me. On the topic of extraordinary intellectuals, it was a humbling privilege to consort and coteach with my former mentor Roberto Mangabeira Unger at the school. He will be unhappy that I work in this book with a distinction between sufficiency and equality rather than one between deep equality and deep freedom, but he will also forgive the fact that some think it best to engage the debates of one's time as a means of instigating future possibilities. The human rights dream team at the university, and most notably Michael Ignatieff, Mathias Risse, Kathryn Sikkink, and Beth Simmons, took me seriously. And I would like to single out Homi Bhabha and Richard Tuck for their extraordinarily gracious welcome to campus.

Numerous Harvard students consulted and conspired with me on this project in different capacities, and the Faculty of Arts and Sciences SHARP program provided summer funding to two of them. Special thanks for exceptional work to Lev Asimov, Luca Martino Levi, Michelle Melton, Kári Ragnarsson, Fran Swanson, and Dan Traficonte, as well as Sandy Diehl (also now a Harvard student) for helping with my initial research on global justice at Columbia University, our common former institution. Melinda Eakin and Thompson Potter offered precious assistance on matters large and small, and the amazing library staff brought me whatever I asked.

I also had a great deal of help beyond Harvard. Years ago, an invitation to revisit the Universal Declaration of Human Rights as part of a University of Chicago lecture series and a special issue of *Critical Inquiry* prompted initial thinking. As I wrote them more recently, the different chapters largely engaged different communities of contacts, and I am grateful to them all: Christopher Brooke, Andrew Jainchill, Darrin McMahon, and Azzan Yadin-Israel for Chapter 1, as well as my old colleague Isser Woloch for inspiring my reclamation of the Jacobin legacy for welfare even today; Charles Walton and others at a conference he organized where I had the opportunity to present a version of Chapter 2; William Forbath and Jeremy Kessler for advice on Chapter 3, along with Anna di Robilant and her colleagues at the Elizabeth Battelle Clark Legal History Series at Boston University where I presented a form of it; Antony Anghie for inspiration for Chapter 4, *Humanity* associates and colleagues for collaborative projects on the New International Economic Order and Gunnar Myrdal that flowed directly into it, Nils Gilman for co-organization and comments, and Adom Getachew for the privilege of early access to a forthcoming book so relevant to touching mine up; Patricia Weiss Fagen for correspondence and Amartya Sen for lunch to reminisce about the era covered in Chapter 5, as well as Paul Adler, Sibylle Duhautois, and Michael Franczak for readings of their relevant ongoing writing; and—since my work on the theme dates back longest—a large number of people when it comes to the global justice materials in Chapter 6, whether the principals Charles Beitz and Henry Shue for providing consultation on their youthful interventions (and making such admirable breakthroughs in the first place), Katrina Forrester and Tehila Sasson for sharing their kindred writing on the topic, Jeffrey Flynn for a brilliant response to mine, or Rob Tempio for some sales figures.

As for Chapter 7, it was written last, but the entire book was inspired by the debate canvassed there. For that reason, I cannot get away without gratitude to Susan Marks for sparking the project—however unintentionally—as well as Quinn Slobodian for some provocative comments on a former book that eventually sent me in the direction of this one. My friends David Grewal and Jedediah Purdy commissioned my earliest conceptualization of the book's argument and deserve credit for introducing reflection on neoliberalism in American legal scholarship, of which this book is a small example. At the University of Connecticut-Storrs Human Rights Institute, the foremost center of expertise I know on economic and social rights, I had the privilege to serve as Marsha Lilien Gladstein Visiting Professor for two weeks and learned a great deal. I owe Julia Dehm for valuable correspondence and draft work on United Nations processes, Amy Kapczynski for help with the right to health and thoughts on the broader argument, Joanne Meyerowitz and Molly Nolan for wonderful counsel and fellow-traveling scholarship, and Margot Salomon for deep inspiration as a thinker and generous support as a colleague. Karen Engle and Ben Golder provided early fora to present my emergent views as talks, and the *Chronicle of Higher Education* opened its pages to a written summation of them, just as the Amnesty International Netherlands research bureau and the Open Global Rights site did later. A special word of thanks to Kári Ragnarsson, who not only did some research on Chapter 4 for me but also read Chapter 7 and the rest of manuscript with care and expertise, surveying the underlying materials and tutoring me on them—even as I purported to be supervising his field on them.

A slew of people on five continents invited presentations of the work, and I was especially glad to give the annual Cyril Foster Lecture in International Relations at the University of Oxford when my thinking on the topic was in an early phase, and the Katholieke Universiteit Leuven Politeia

Lecture and the Tel Aviv University Minerva Lecture in Human Rights somewhat later. Commentary and questions at the various events made all the difference, and I cannot thank the organizers enough. I was also lucky to present some of my thinking at an Open Society Foundation event, with thanks to Leonard Benardo and Alexander Soros. Colleagues and friends in the new human rights history, cited and uncited, have provided constant stimulus, and I should especially single out Mark Bradley, Roland Burke, Christian Christiansen, Marco Duranti, Jan Eckel, Dan Edelstein, Mark Goodale, Stefan-Ludwig Hoffmann, Jorge González Jácome, Steven L. B. Jensen, Patrick Kelly, Barbara Keys, Linde Lindkvist, James Loeffler, Salar Mohandesi, and Umut Özsu. Paul Kahn has done so much on my behalf that his insistence that I drop my original introduction seems almost not worth mentioning, especially since I have rehabilitated it as my conclusion.

Joyce Seltzer commissioned this book long ago, before she or I knew what it was really going to be about, and I owe her once again for superintending it from (mis)conception through execution to publication. James Chappel's insightful comments on the whole manuscript, both substantive and writerly, exposed me to the risk of double embarrassment for my self-imposed shortcomings in the first place and my failure to accept every bit of his extraordinary assistance in saving myself from them in the time allowed. Paul Hanebrink and Mark Mazower furnished pivotally important advice, especially at a critical moment when I was trying to figure out how to bring the manuscript in for a landing, and they have my deepest gratitude (even if the book ultimately crashes and burns). The anonymous readers for Harvard University Press assisted indispensably in the final stage. Annamarie Why designed an amazing cover; Kate Brick and, especially, Kerry Wendt whipped the text into better shape; and Gregory Kornbluh worked to get it into the world. Daire MacFadden proofread, Brian Ostrander finalized production, and Rachel Rolnick made the index.

This book is dedicated to Joseph Nathan. His friendship, like the love of my family and especially of Alisa, Lily, and Madeleine, has always been more than I deserve. It is simultaneously more than enough and too much for me ever to express sufficient thanks for it.

Index

Index

Brandt, Willy, 144–145
Brazil, 179, 185
Brecht, Bertolt, 134
Brentano, Lujo, 30
Bretton Woods, United Nations Monetary and
  Financial Conference at (1944), 93, 107, 114
Brierly, James, 250n2
Brinkley, Alan, 235n16
British Nationality Act (1948), 43
Brown, Peter G., 163, 254n30
Brus, Włodzimierz, 207
Brzezinski, Zbigniew, 144
Buchenwald, 47
Bukharin, Nikolai, 36
Burke, Roland, 230n4

Cabet, Etienne, 26
Callaghan, James, 188
Camus, Albert, 164–165, 169, 171; *The
  Plague* (1947), 164
Cardoso, Fernando Henrique, 185
Carr, E. H., 64–66, 93–94, 104, 108;
  Nationalism and After (1945), 93
Carter, Jimmy, 121–122, 142–145, 158,
  163–164, 170, 179, 187–188
Castro, Sergio de, 178
Cauas, Jorge, 178
Center for Economic and Social Rights, 195
Charter 77, 1–2, 124
Charter on the Economic Rights and Duties of
  States (1974), 115–116
Chávez, Hugo, 186
"Chicago school" of economics, 173, 174, 178
Chichilnisky, Graciela, 247n19
Chile, 125, 173–174, 177–179, 215
China, 8, 49, 207–208, 211, 263n44;
  marketization of, 175, 216
Christian Democracy, ideology and parties,
  50–51, 70, 106–107, 178, 213
Christianity, 16, 51, 63, 106–107, 114, 134, 163
Christopher, Warren, 143
Churchill, Winston, 46, 69, 76–77, 98, 110
Clinton, Hillary, 204
Cloots, Anacharsis, 91, 156
Cocoyoc, Declaration of (1974), 131
Cold War, 66, 95, 110, 113, 123, 145,
  148–149, 180, 187–188, 190, 209, 219,
  226n19; and economic and social rights, 8–9,
  71, 121–122, 162, 166, 170, 176, 193, 196,
  201; and human rights, 2, 185–186, 194,
  200, 204; and the International Labour
  Organization, 97–98; and socialism, 2, 49, 105
Commager, Henry Steele, 156

Committee on Economic, Social, and Cultural
  Rights, 196, 200
communism, 8, 15, 45–47, 50–51, 53, 92,
  96–97, 125, 179–180, 183–185. *See also*
  Eurocommunism
Condorcet, Marquis de, 21, 24
Confédération Générale du Travail, 33
Congress of Industrial Organizations (CIO), 87
Conseil National de la Résistance, 230n7
Considérant, Victor, 26–27
Convention for the Elimination of All Forms of
  Discrimination against Women (1979), 204
Cooper, Richard N., 137, 253n17
cosmopolitanism, 6, 8, 91–92, 105, 146, 156,
  160–162, 172, 176, 216
Council of Europe, 258n17
Cranston, Maurice, 255n35
Crosland, Anthony, 188; *The Future of
  Socialism* (1957), 188
Czechoslovakia, 1, 124–125, 181–182; Civic
  Democratic Alliance of, 184

Declaration of Philadelphia (International
  Labour Organization, 1944), 95, 97
Declaration of the Rights of Man and Citizen
  (France, 1793), 21–23, 26, 51
Declaration of the Rights of Peoples
  (1976), 117
Declaration of the Rights of Persons and
  Communities (France, 1946), 47
Declaration of the Rights of Toiling and
  Exploited People (Soviet Union, 1917–
  1918), 36
dependency theory, 114, 157, 160, 251n9,
  253n19, 253n23, 254n24
development: international, 96–98, 108,
  119–145, 158–159, 164, 189–92, 206; right
  to, 141, 208–209
Dia, Mamadou, 104; *The African Nations and
  World Solidarity* (1960), 104
Dobb, Maurice, 136
Dumbarton Oaks Conference (1944), 96

East Bengal. *See* Bangladesh
Eastern Europe, 2, 45, 49, 73, 87, 90, 120,
  123–125, 145, 179, 180–181, 183–187, 189,
  196, 200–201, 207, 213, 261n33
economic rights. *See* social rights
Edelstein, Dan, 225n12
education, right to, xi, 13, 22, 30, 34, 68, 143,
  234n5
Egypt, 101, 105, 142
Emerson, Rupert, 103

Index

Index

Index

Index